KILLING IN WAR

Killing a person is in general among the most seriously wrongful forms of action, yet most of us accept that it can be permissible to kill people on a large scale in war. Does morality become more permissive in a state of war? Jeff McMahan argues that conditions in war make no difference to what morality permits and that the justifications for killing people are the same in war as they are in other contexts, such as individual self-defence. This view is radically at odds with the traditional theory of the just war and has implications that challenge common sense views. McMahan argues, for example, that it is wrong to fight in a war that is unjust because it lacks a just cause.

Jeff McMahan is Professor of Philosophy at Rutgers University.

UEHIRO SERIES IN PRACTICAL ETHICS

General Editor: Julian Savulescu, University of Oxford

Choosing Children
The Ethical Dilemmas of Genetic Intervention
Jonathan Glover

Messy Morality
The Challenge of Politics
C. A. J. Coady

Killing in War
Jeff McMahan

Killing in War

JEFF MCMAHAN

CLARENDON PRESS · OXFORD

2009

OXFORD

UNIVERSITY PRESS

Great Clarendon Street, Oxford OX2 6DP
United Kingdom

Oxford University Press is a department of the University of Oxford.
It furthers the University's objective of excellence in research, scholarship,
and education by publishing worldwide. Oxford is a registered trade mark of
Oxford University Press in the UK and in certain other countries

First published 2009
First published in paperback 2011
Reprinted 2013

British Library Cataloguing in Publication Data
Data available

Library of Congress Cataloging in Publication Data
Data available

ISBN 978-0-19-960357-2

The Uehiro Series in Practical Ethics

In 2002 the Uehiro Foundation on Ethics and Education, chaired by Mr Eiji Uehiro, established the Uehiro Chair in Practical Ethics at the University of Oxford. The following year the Oxford Uehiro Centre for Practical Ethics was created within the Philosophy Faculty. Generous support by the Uehiro Foundation enabled the establishment of an annual lecture series, The Uehiro Lectures in Practical Ethics. These three lectures, given each year in Oxford, capture the ethos of the Oxford Uehiro Centre for Practical Ethics: to bring the best scholarship in analytic philosophy to bear on the most significant problems of our time. The aim is to make progress in the analysis and resolution of these issues to the highest academic standard in a manner that is accessible to the general public. Philosophy should not only create knowledge, it should make people's lives better. Books based upon the lectures are published by Oxford University Press in the Uehiro Series in Practical Ethics.

Julian Savulescu
Uehiro Chair in Practical Ethics
Director, Oxford Uehiro Centre for Practical Ethics, University of Oxford
Editor, The Uehiro Series in Practical Ethics

This book is dedicated to my father,
Jefferson D. McMahan III, USMC

Preface and Acknowledgments

For most of us, the thought of deliberately killing another person is almost unthinkable. Even the most benign form of killing, voluntary active euthanasia, or the killing of a person at her own request when her life has become intolerable, is prohibited by most religions and in virtually all the world's legal systems. Yet as soon as conditions arise to which the word "war" can be applied, our scruples vanish and killing people no longer seems a horrifying crime but becomes instead a glorious achievement. As soon as war begins, a tidy set of rules is assumed to come into effect that tells people whom it is meritorious to kill and whom it remains murderous to kill.

The contention of this book is that common sense beliefs about the morality of killing in war are deeply mistaken. The prevailing view is that in a state of war, the practice of killing is governed by different moral principles from those that govern acts of killing in other contexts. This presupposes that it can make a difference to the moral permissibility of killing another person whether one's political leaders have declared a state of war with that person's country. According to the prevailing view, therefore, political leaders can somehow cause other people's moral rights to disappear simply by commanding their armies to attack them. When stated in this way, the received view seems obviously absurd. In explaining and elaborating this view in detail in the following chapter, I will present it in the way its proponents do, which will of course make it seem far more sensible. But it should still be evident, even when one has read the official description, that the account I have just given is accurate.

My aim in this book is to challenge the received wisdom about the morality of killing in war. Although a book in philosophy cannot be expected to have any significant effect on popular thought, I have nevertheless written this book in the hope of prompting a reconsideration of certain beliefs that have hardened into unquestioned orthodoxies yet encourage complacency about killing in war and thus make it easier for governments to lead their countries into unjust wars. Among these beliefs is the view that moral responsibility for the wrongful killing that occurs when an unjust war is fought lies solely with the political leaders whose decision it was to go to war. Political leaders are utterly powerless to kill large numbers of people without the acquiescence and complicity of all those who rationalize, pay for, and perpetrate those killings.

This book is based on three lectures that I presented at the Uehiro Centre for Practical Ethics at the University of Oxford during Hilary term in 2006. I am deeply grateful to the Director of the Centre, Julian Savulescu, for allowing me the honor of giving those lectures, and to the Uehiro Foundation for its support for the lecture series of which mine were a part. A number of people gave me written comments on my lecture notes, both before and after the lectures were delivered. For their generous help in this way, I offer my sincere thanks to Yitzhak Benbaji, Lene Bomann-Larsen, Kimberly Brownlee, Roger Crisp, Trent Dougherty, William Edmundson, David Enoch, Kimberly Kessler Ferzan, Helen Frowe, Robert Goodin, Adil Ahmad Haque, Frederik Kaufman, Whitley Kaufman, Steven Lee, Graham Long, Larry May, Lionel McPherson, Gerhard Øverland, Derek Parfit, Gregory Reichberg, Gina Rini, Julian Savulescu, Peter Singer, Walter Sinnott-Armstrong, Saul Smilansky, Uwe Steinhoff, and Peter Westen. For illuminating discussions of some of the ideas and arguments developed in the book, I am greatly indebted to Justin D'Arms, Saba Bazargan, Ruth Chang, Jules Coleman, George Fletcher, Michael Gross, Thomas Hurka, Sanford Kadish, Shelly Kagan, Frances Kamm, Christopher Kutz, David Rodin, Samuel Scheffler, Henry Shue, Daniel Statman, Larry Temkin, Evan Williams, Jonathan Winterbottom, and Noam Zohar.

I have also learned a great deal from discussions with former and present officers in the Philosophy faculty at the United States Military Academy. For both their philosophical insights and their guidance in helping me to achieve a better understanding of the soldier's perspective on the issues discussed in this book, I am very grateful to LTC Joseph Diminick, LTC Brian Imiola, MAJ William Weaver, MAJ Stephen Woodside, LTC Jeffrey Wilson, and COL Daniel Zupan (Ret.) — two of whom (Diminick and Wilson) I am proud to claim as my students.

After receiving comments on the lecture notes and discussing my ideas both with the people named above and with audiences at various other venues at which I presented ideas from the lectures, I wrote an initial draft of the book over the summer of 2008. Because of the very tight production schedule, there was no time for me to take account of more than a relatively small number of comments during the two weeks I had in which to revise the first draft before submitting the manuscript for printing. I did, however, benefit from comments by Kinch Hoekstra on the draft of Chapter 5, and I owe a special debt of gratitude to Seth Lazar, who gave me extensive and extremely valuable written comments on the drafts of Chapters 1, 3, and 4.

My editors at Oxford University Press—Peter Momtchiloff, Kate Walker, and Catherine Berry—have been exceptionally diligent and supportive, and I have found it a great pleasure to work with them. I am also pleased to be able to acknowledge financial support I received for earlier work on the ethics of war that was indispensable for the development of the ideas in this book. That support came from the National Endowment for the Humanities, the MacArthur Foundation, and the US Institute of Peace.

Finally, there are three special debts I would like to acknowledge. Gregory Kavka, late Professor of Philosophy at the University of California at Irvine, helped to shape my thinking about the morality of war and was also a source of inspiration and generous support for my early work in the area. Well before I encountered Greg's work, I was introduced to the philosophical discussion of killing in war by reading Jonathan Glover's seminal book in practical ethics, *Causing Death and Saving Lives*. Jonathan's influence has continued unabated since he supervised my early graduate work in the late 1970s. His more recent book, *Humanity: A Moral History of the Twentieth Century*, has profoundly affected my views about individual responsibility in war. Finally, all of the work I do in philosophy is inspired by the published and unpublished writings of Derek Parfit. Although in saying this I am guilty of a kind of incoherence he exposed in his work on personal identity, I cannot help thinking that if this book had been written by Derek rather than by me, it would be immeasurably better than it is.

Jeff McMahan
December 2008

Contents

1

The Morality of Participation
in an Unjust War

1.1 THE DOCTRINE OF THE MORAL EQUALITY OF COMBATANTS

Ludwig Wittgenstein is generally regarded as the greatest philosopher, and certainly the greatest philosophical iconoclast, of the twentieth century. Twice in one lifetime he revolutionized the way that philosophers conceived of their work. He was legendary for his fiery refusal to accept received assumptions uncritically.

The only book he published during his lifetime, the slender *Tractatus Logico-Philosophicus*, which ignited the first of the two philosophical revolutions for which he can be credited, was written while he was a soldier in World War I. Although he lived in England, thought that the English were "the best race in the world," and had close friends fighting on the British side, including the man he described as "my first and my only friend" and to whom he dedicated the *Tractatus*, Wittgenstein, who was Austrian by birth, enlisted in the Austrian army. Almost immediately after he arrived in Austria from Britain, he bought a copy of Tolstoy's *Gospel in Brief*, a pacifist tract, which he read over and over again. This book had the effect of converting him to Christianity, though not to pacifism, for his determination to fight seemed only to intensify.[1] Here is what two commentators say, with more than a tinge of admiration, of his participation in the war:

Wittgenstein . . . fought for Austria with conspicuous bravery as a volunteer. . . . He used his family's social connections not to avoid combat but instead to obtain a posting to the front, when an operation at seventeen for a double hernia would have allowed him to remain far from the sound of gunfire. He took on the job of artillery forward observation officer, and insisted on holding his position long beyond the requirements of duty. . . . Paul Engelmann records that "Wittgenstein considered his duty to serve in the war as an overriding obligation. When he heard that his friend Bertrand Russell was in prison as an opponent of the war, he did not withhold his respect for Russell's personal courage, but felt that this was heroism in the wrong place."[2]

According to Wittgenstein's sister, his determination to participate in the war was the result of "an intense desire to take something difficult upon himself and to do something other than purely intellectual work."[3] His biographer, Ray Monk, adds to this the comment that "Wittgenstein felt that the experience of facing death would, in some way or other, *improve* him,"[4] citing the following passage from his wartime diary: " 'Now I have the chance to be a decent human being', he wrote on the occasion of his first glimpse of the enemy, 'for I'm standing eye to eye with death.' "[5]

World War I is the paradigm of an utterly pointless war. There was, in effect, no reason for anyone to go to war. This war was a consequence of fatuous assertions of national pride together with a series of misjudgments about anticipatory mobilization, alliance commitments, and so on. Of all the participants in that futile mass slaughter, the Austrians were arguably the most culpable, having initiated the war after imposing absurdly demanding conditions on a conciliatory Serbia in the wake of the assassination of the Archduke, and then dragging Germany into the conflict against the judgment of the Kaiser, who perceived the unreasonableness of Austria's demands.

Wittgenstein had strong views about ethics and was uncompromising in living and acting as he thought he ought to, however eccentric his behavior might have seemed to others. Yet he not only had no scruples about fighting in this stupid and barbaric war, but was even determined, with characteristic intensity, to fight on the side of the aggressor and for reasons that seem to have derived primarily from his personal psychological needs and to have had little or nothing to do with the reasons that motivated the Austrian government to go to war. He believed that he was morally required to fight for Austria, while his friend and mentor, Bertrand Russell, was morally required to fight *against* Austria, or at least to support the British cause, even though these requirements were necessarily independent of which side, if either, was in the right.

This is a person who is almost universally regarded among philosophers as one of the most probing thinkers in history, a person who published only one short book during his lifetime because he hesitated to act in the absence of certainty that what he published would be correct. Yet what was at stake in his going to war was not whether he might publish under his name a mistaken argument about language; it was whether he was going to kill people of whom he had no personal knowledge. But apparently participating in the business of killing people, including the English whom he so much admired, was a small price to pay for the elevating and self-improving experience of risking death. If this is the best that a transcendently brilliant, paradigm-shattering thinker can do when his native country initiates an unjust war, what hope is there for the rest of us?

Political leaders, no matter how transparently immoral, dishonest, and intellectually bovine, have seldom had trouble finding people to fight their unjust wars. For most people, it may be more a matter of luck than anything else that they have not fought in an unjust war. Had they been ordered to by their government, most would readily have followed their country into an unjust war, as others have done throughout history. Those who are skeptical of this assertion should briefly review the unjust wars that have been fought within any given historical period and compare them with the instances during that period in which a government has sought to fight an unjust war but been prevented by the unwillingness of its citizens to fight. No nation or people is genetically immune to Nazism or to similar political and ideological movements that spawn unjust wars. We as individuals are protected from becoming Nazis by *ideas*, and by the cultural and political institutions they inspire. Those of us concerned with the problems discussed in this book are of course in no danger of becoming Nazis, but this is at least in part because our culture, or cultures, have been shaped by forces, and in particular by ideas, profoundly different from those that shaped the culture of Nazi Germany.

Our own societies are, however, perpetually in danger of fighting unjust wars. And I believe that part of the explanation for this lies in an idea that we share with the Nazis, and indeed with most people in most cultures at all times in history. This is the idea that no one does wrong, or acts impermissibly, merely by fighting in a war that turns out to be unjust. This idea lies at the core of the reigning theory of the just war and also informs the international law of war. Although the presence of this idea in the law is intended to have a restraining effect on the *conduct* of war, the widespread acceptance of this idea also makes it easier, even for independently-minded people such as Wittgenstein, to fight in war without qualms about whether the war might be unjust.

The traditional theory of the just war comprises two sets of principles, one governing the resort to war (*jus ad bellum*) and the other governing the conduct of war (*jus in bello*). The two sets of principles are generally regarded, in the words of Michael Walzer, the leading contemporary exponent of the theory of the just war, as "logically independent. It is perfectly possible," he claims, "for a just war to be fought unjustly and for an unjust war to be fought in strict accordance with the rules."[6] A parallel doctrine holds in law. According to the legal theorists George Fletcher and Jens David Ohlin, "the most basic" of the various "architectonic distinctions that structure the law of war . . . is the radical separation of jus ad bellum and jus in bello. The lawfulness of war has no bearing on the proper conduct of war."[7]

If, however, what combatants are permitted to do in war is independent of whether their war is just or unjust, or legal or illegal, their individual moral status must be independent of the moral character of their war. Combatants on all sides must have the same moral status, hence the same moral rights, immunities, and liabilities. Walzer calls this the "moral equality of soldiers," a doctrine which implies, in his words, that all combatants have "an equal right to kill."[8]

This does not, of course, imply that they have an equal right to kill just *anyone*. According to both the received theory of the just war and the law of war, the only people that combatants have a right to kill are enemy combatants. What the moral equality of soldiers does imply is that this principle permitting the killing of enemy combatants applies equally, along with other *in bello* principles, to all combatants on all sides in a war. The *in bello* principles are neutral between those who fight in a just war and those who fight in an unjust war and are held to be equally satisfiable by all.

The moral equality of soldiers is also compatible with the idea that combatants may act wrongly even when their action is in conformity with all the principles of *jus in bello*. It is, for example, compatible with the Augustinian view that it is wrong to fight with an attitude of hatred or enmity, or for the pleasure of killing. What does not affect the permissibility of killing in war, according to the moral equality of soldiers, is whether it is done in the service of a just or unjust cause. According to the moral equality of soldiers, it is not a reason to believe that a combatant acts wrongly that the war in which he fights is unjust.

It will help to pause at this point to clarify some terms. First, I will change Walzer's label to the "moral equality of combatants." This is more accurate because "soldier" tends not to be used to refer to naval and air personnel, but the doctrine of moral equality encompasses them as well as ground forces. Yet while "combatant" has wider scope than "soldier" in this respect, it is narrower in scope in another, in that it does not, for obvious reasons, tend to be used to refer to military personnel in times of peace. For this reason, I will often need to use the term "soldier" to refer to military personnel in peacetime or to refer to them generally over periods during which they are sometimes at war and sometimes not. As I will use it, "soldiers" refers to ground, naval, and air personnel.

Second, "war" is ambiguous in a way that it is important to be clear about. Most commonly it refers to the aggregate fighting of a number of belligerent parties. World War II, for example, was fought by Germany, France, Britain, and a large number of other countries. This war as a whole was not a just war, though neither was it an unjust war. War as the sum of the fighting of all the belligerents can be neither just nor unjust. Yet we can also say of each belligerent in World War II that it fought a war. Britain fought a war against Germany and Germany fought a war against Britain (among others). Each of those wars was a part of World War II. It is wars in this second sense that are just or unjust. In World War II, Britain's war was just, Germany's unjust.

To state a third and final distinction, I need to invoke a notion from the theory of the just war. That theory rightly insists that for a war to be just, it must have a "just cause." The notion of just cause is variously understood in the literature. As I understand it, a just cause is an aim that satisfies two conditions: (1) that it may permissibly be pursued by means of war, and (2) that the reason why this is so is at least in part that those against whom the war is fought have made themselves morally *liable* to military attack. With this notion as background, we can now distinguish between "just combatants," who fight in a just war, and "unjust combatants," who fight in a war that lacks a just cause. Note that these categories are not exhaustive because they leave out combatants who fight in wars that are unjust, or at least morally unjustified, despite having a just cause. Such wars include those that are unnecessary for the achievement of the just cause, those that will cause expected harm that is excessive in relation to the value or importance of achieving the just cause, and those in which an unjust aim, or a number of such aims, are pursued along with the just cause (and are unnecessary for the achievement of the just cause).

Despite the incompleteness of these categories, my concern in this initial chapter will be with the question whether the doctrine of the moral equality of combatants holds of just and unjust combatants. If just and unjust combatants, as defined, do have the same moral rights, and in particular are permitted to act in the same ways, this is sufficient to vindicate the moral equality of combatants. For if unjust combatants are permitted to fight in a war that is unjust because it lacks a just cause (which usually means that they fight *for* an *unjust* cause), there is no reason to suppose that combatants who fight for a just cause but whose war is nevertheless unjustified for some other reason would not be. This is because the most serious reason why a war might be unjustified is that it lacks any justifying aim at all. If there are reasons why it is morally permissible to fight in such a war, they will presumably also apply to participation in wars for which there is a just cause but are unjustified for other, less serious reasons.

In this chapter I will argue against the moral equality of combatants by arguing against the view that unjust combatants act permissibly when they fight within the constraints of the traditional rules of *jus in bello*. I will argue, indeed, that with a few exceptions, they cannot satisfy the constraints of *jus in bello*, even in principle, when those constraints are properly understood. The general thesis of this chapter is that it is morally wrong to fight in a war that is unjust because it lacks a just cause. This leaves open the possibility that there could be moral equality between just combatants and those combatants who fight for a just cause in a war that is unnecessary or disproportionate, or in a war in which both just and unjust causes are pursued. It is also possible that there could be moral equality between just combatants and combatants who fight in a war with a *good* cause that does not rise to the level of a *just* cause—that is, a war that pursues a good that it would be permissible to pursue by other means but not by means of war. My own view is that combatants who fight for a cause that is just or good but whose war is nevertheless unjustified do not have the same moral status as just combatants. But I will not argue for that here.

If it is correct that it is wrong to fight in a war that lacks a just cause, this has considerable practical significance. Unjust wars can occur only if enough people are willing to fight in them. To the best of my knowledge, it has been the dominant view in all cultures at all times that it is not only permissible but even good, honorable, and heroic to participate in war, even when the war is unjust. It would, of course, be absurdly utopian to expect that people would refuse to fight in unjust wars (or wars they believed were unjust) if they came to believe that participation in an unjust war is wrong. But it would also be naïve to doubt that the widespread acceptance of the moral equality of combatants has facilitated the ability of governments to fight unjust wars. Wars are now and have always been initiated in the context of the general and largely unquestioned belief that the moral equality of combatants is true. If that background assumption were to change—if people generally believed that participation in an unjust or morally unjustified war is wrong—that could make a significant practical difference to the practice of war. For most people do care about morality, and constrain their behavior in the light of their moral beliefs. Many people, including active-duty soldiers, would be more reluctant to fight in wars they believed to be unjust. Eventually there would have to be institutional accommodations to people's changed moral beliefs. At least in democratic countries, for example, legal institutions would have to offer some provisions, or protections, for conscientious refusal to fight. In that altered institutional environment, governments could expect to encounter increased risks of resistance to their efforts to initiate unjust wars. And the prospects of resistance, particularly from within the military, and the consequent risks of humiliation and failure, could deter at least some attempts to initiate unjust wars that might at present seem positively appealing and advantageous even for domestic political reasons (for example, because even initially unpopular wars ignite people's patriotic sentiments once they have begun, thereby prompting at least temporary support for the government).

That most people appear to have few scruples about setting off unquestioningly at the behest of their government to kill members of other nations is a phenomenon that has been studied by psychologists and historians, but as a moral problem it has only recently begun to attract serious attention from philosophers. Given the contribution that people's moral beliefs, as well as moral doctrines such as the moral equality of combatants, make to their readiness to fight in unjust wars, it is clearly important to determine whether these beliefs and doctrines are in fact defensible. This is a task for which moral philosophers are better qualified than anyone else, so it is rather surprising that so little careful thought has been devoted to this issue. My purpose in this chapter is to try to make some progress with this difficult, neglected, but highly important issue.

1.2 THE TRADITIONAL CRITERION OF LIABILITY TO ATTACK IN WAR

Just war theorists have offered reasons for thinking that the moral equality of combatants is true. The most familiar of these has deep roots in the just war tradition. To have a clear understanding of this familiar view, it is first necessary to understand certain terms and distinctions. Just war theorists have always distinguished morally between the innocent and the noninnocent, though they have sometimes assigned these terms different meanings. "Innocent" has three different meanings in the just war literature. In its most generic sense, "innocent" simply means "not a legitimate target of military attack." Expressed in the terms that I will employ throughout this book, the claim that a person is innocent in this generic sense is the claim that he has done nothing to make himself *morally liable to military attack*. At least part of what it means to say that a person is *liable* to attack is that he would not be *wronged* by being attacked, and would have no justified complaint about being attacked.

Liability is related to but distinct from desert, though there are different ways of distinguishing between them. One important difference between the two concepts is that people can deserve both harms and benefits, but can be liable only to harms. It is curious that we seem to lack not only a word but even a concept that is related to deserving a benefit in the way that being liable to a harm is related to deserving a harm.

I draw the distinction between liability to harm and desert of harm by reference to the further distinction between the instrumental and the noninstrumental. Desert is noninstrumental. If a person deserves to be harmed, there is a moral reason for harming him that is independent of the further consequences of harming him. Giving him what he deserves is an end in itself. Although a deserved harm is bad for the person who suffers it, it is, from an impersonal point of view, intrinsically *good*. By contrast, a person is liable to be harmed only if harming him will serve some further purpose—for example, if it will prevent him from unjustly harming someone, deter him (or perhaps others) from further wrongdoing, or compensate a victim of his prior wrongdoing. The goal is internal to the liability, in the sense that there is no liability except in relation to some goal that can be achieved by harming a person. Moreover, in further contrast with deserved harms, harms to which people are liable are bad not only for those who suffer them but also from an impersonal point of view. Although their weight is discounted in proportionality calculations, they are never of merely neutral or positive impersonal value, unless of course they are harms that the victim also *deserves* to suffer.

In war, the goal for which people may be liable to be harmed is usually defensive: to prevent the achievement of an unjust cause, and to defend people from harms that would otherwise be inflicted by unjust combatants in their efforts to achieve an unjust cause. Because people can be liable to harm only in relation to a goal of this sort, the assignment of liability is governed by a requirement of necessity. If harming a person is unnecessary for the achievement of a relevant type of goal, that person cannot be liable to be harmed. The infliction of deserved harm is, by contrast, not governed by a requirement of necessity, since the value of a person's getting what he deserves is not instrumental and hence is not necessary for anything beyond itself.

Walzer explicates the generic sense of "innocent" by reference to people's rights. "*Innocent*," he observes, is "a term of art" that we apply to people when "they have done nothing, and are doing nothing, that entails the loss of their rights."[9] The claims that I will make about liability can also be articulated in the language of rights and indeed it may be illuminating to indicate the relations between liability and rights.

Although Walzer refers to the loss of "rights," in the plural, one does not, in ceasing to be innocent in the generic sense, necessarily lose any right other than the right not to be attacked, in particular by enemy combatants. But Walzer is right to refer to the *loss* of that right. Liability corresponds to the loss of a right, not to other ways in which an attacker's action might be unconstrained by rights. Another way in which an attacker might be thus unconstrained is through the victim's *waiving* of his right not to be attacked. A right is waived when the possessor of the right consents to allow another person or persons to do what he has a right that they not do. For example, a boxer explicitly waives his right not to be hit by his opponent in a boxing match. His opponent then does not wrong him or violate his right not to be hit by hitting him during the match. But this is not because the boxer has made himself liable to be hit. Rather, the reason his right has not been violated is simply that he has consented to be hit, thereby waiving that right with respect to his opponent.

One further way in which an attacker might be unconstrained by the victim's right not to be attacked is that the right may be *overridden* by other morally significant considerations. For example, assuming that rights are not absolute, it may be permissible to attack someone who has a right not to be attacked if, for example, that is necessary to avoid violating other, stronger rights, or if it is a necessary means of preventing some terrible calamity that would involve significantly greater harm to others. In such a case, one may permissibly do to another what she has a right that one not do. When one thus permissibly acts against a right, I will say that one *infringes* that right, whereas when one impermissibly does what another has a right that one not do, one *violates* that right.[10] Even though an agent acts permissibly in infringing a right, the victim is nonetheless wronged and may thus be owed compensation.

To attack someone who is liable to be attacked is neither to violate nor to infringe that person's right, for the person's being liable to attack *just is* his having *forfeited* his right not to be attacked, in the circumstances. That last qualifying clause is essential. It is sometimes objected to theories of forfeiture that if, for example, a person forfeits his right to life, that must mean that anyone may permissibly kill him, for any reason, at any time. But the form of forfeiture that corresponds to liability to attack in war is highly specific. For a person to cease to be innocent in war, all that is necessary is the forfeiture of the right not to be attacked *for certain reasons*, by certain persons, in certain conditions. There is no loss of rights in general, nor even any loss of the right against attack, understood as a right that holds against all agents at all times. The right against attack is instead forfeited only in relation to certain persons acting for certain reasons in a particular context.

On this view, the restrictions on liability are, as I noted, "internal" to liability itself. A person cannot be liable to attack when attacking him would be wrong because it would be unnecessary or disproportionate. Rather, if attacking him is unnecessary for the prevention or correction of a wrong for which he is responsible, or if it would cause him harm that would be excessive in relation to the achievement of one of those aims, then he is simply not liable to attack. This is a corollary of the claim that a person is not wronged by the infliction of harms to which he is liable. Suppose, for example, that to attack a person in war in pursuit of some goal would be to harm him in excess of the degree of harm to which he might be liable as a means of achieving that goal. Because the excess harm would wrong him, he cannot be liable to attack.

Having now explored the conceptual relations among the generic notion of innocence, the notion of liability, and the ways in which an attacker's action might be unconstrained by the victim's rights, we can now return to the question of what people might do that would make them liable to attack in war, or entail the forfeiture of their right not to be attacked. The other two senses of the term "innocent" supply different answers to that question. They tell us, in effect, what people must do in war to retain their right not to be attacked.

One of these two senses is what we most often mean by innocent in ordinary language: morally innocent, or not guilty or culpable. But although it is more familiar, this is not the sense that has predominated within just war theory over the past two or three centuries. The primary substantive sense of "innocent" in just war theory is, however, solidly grounded in the etymology of the term. "Innocent" derives from the Latin word *nocentes*, which refers to those who are injurious or threatening. To be innocent in this sense is simply *not* to be *nocentes*. Thus, according to Elizabeth Anscombe, "'innocent'. . . is not a term referring to personal responsibility at all. It means rather 'not harming'. But the people fighting are 'harming', so they can be attacked."[11] Similarly, Thomas Nagel contends that in war "the operative notion of innocence is not moral innocence;" rather, "'innocent' means 'currently harmless,' and it is opposed not to 'guilty' but to 'doing harm.'"[12] In the reigning theory of the just war, to be innocent in the generic sense of having done nothing to lose one's rights is also to be innocent in the sense given by etymology—that is, to be unthreatening or harmless. This is why, in Nagel's words, "in warfare the role of the innocent is filled by noncombatants."[13] For a noncombatant is someone who by definition, at least in the context of warfare, does not pose a threat. But combatants do pose a threat and are thus noninnocent in both senses. It is, in effect, by posing a threat that they lose their right not to be attacked. As Walzer puts it, "our right not to be attacked . . . is lost by those who bear arms . . . because they pose a danger to other people." A combatant may "be personally attacked only because he already is a fighter. He has been made into a dangerous man."[14]

The theory of the just war represented in these quotations offers a justification for killing in war that is best understood as a justification grounded in liability. To say that a person is morally liable to be harmed in a certain way is to say that his own action has made it the case that to harm him in that way would not wrong him, or contravene his rights. He would have no justified complaint against being harmed in that way.

According to mainstream just war theory, as articulated in the quotations from Anscombe, Nagel, and Walzer, the criterion of liability to attack in war is simply posing a threat. Because all combatants pose a threat to another, they are morally liable to attack; because noncombatants do not, they are not liable—that is, they are morally immune from attack. This is the foundation of the orthodox interpretation of the central principle of *jus in bello*: the requirement of discrimination. In its most generic formulation, the requirement of discrimination states simply that combatants must confine their intentional attacks to legitimate targets. Among persons, those who are legitimate targets are those who are liable to military attack. If posing a threat is the criterion of liability to attack in war, then combatants are liable but noncombatants are not. This is the reasoning that typically underlies the almost universally accepted claim that the distinction between legitimate and illegitimate targets coincides with that between combatants and noncombatants. This claim is, indeed, so widely accepted that many just war theorists substitute the term "principle of noncombatant immunity" for "requirement of discrimination," on the assumption that they are synonymous.

This moralized notion of a combatant as anyone who poses a threat in war is different from the legal notion. In law, combatant status is accorded to persons who satisfy certain criteria, such as distinguishing themselves visibly at a distance by some conventional sign, carrying their arms openly, subordinating themselves to a hierarchy of authority and command, and obeying the laws of war. Failure to satisfy such criteria can result in the forfeiture of combatant status under the law. While combatants in this legal sense are all presumed to pose a threat, not all of those who pose a threat in war are combatants in this sense. But all those who pose a threat in war are—by definition, it seems—combatants in the moral sense: that is, in the sense of being morally legitimate targets of attack.

It is, however, a notorious problem in just war theory that there are many people who pose a threat in war who would not be considered combatants by anyone. Elderly professors of physics working for the Manhattan Project in laboratories at Los Alamos and the University of Chicago posed a far greater threat to the Japanese than any ordinary American soldier, but no one would say that they were combatants. Nor would any defender of the moralized notion of a combatant be willing to extend combatant status to a computer science professor whose research during a time of war will soon have many applications, including improvements in weapons technologies that will be used against her country's enemies.

There are also some people who in legal and conventional terms count as combatants and are considered by most just war theorists to be legitimate targets in war but who do not pose a threat to the enemy. A uniformed officer who serves as a legal adviser to the military during a war may devote all of her efforts during the war to arguing that certain methods of warfare that her country wishes to use are illegal.

She may spend the entire war actively *restraining* her country's military action, thereby *diminishing* the threat her side's combatants pose to their enemies, yet she is almost universally recognized as having combatant status.

Various writers in the just war tradition have sought to narrow the gap between the moralized notion of combatant status and the ordinary concept of a combatant by conceding that a limited class of people outside the military count as combatants, while denying that combatant status extends any further among civilians. Of the various proposals, the most widely accepted derives from Nagel, who writes that "the threat presented by an army and its members does not consist merely in the fact that they are men, but in the fact that they are armed and are using their arms in pursuit of certain objectives. Contributions to their arms and logistics are contributions to this threat; contributions to their mere existence as men are not."[15] Walzer draws much the same distinction, though he qualifies it in an interesting way, claiming that while soldiers may be attacked anywhere and at any time in war, others who are liable to attack by virtue of their contribution to the threat the soldiers pose may not be. He argues that the relevant distinction is

between those who make what soldiers need to fight and those who make what they need to live, like all the rest of us. When it is militarily necessary, workers in a tank factory can be attacked and killed, but not workers in a food processing plant. The former are assimilated to the class of soldiers—partially assimilated, I should say, because these are not armed men, ready to fight, and so they can be attacked only in their factory (not in their homes), when they are actually engaged in activities threatening and harmful to their enemies.[16]

Yet even this gloss on the moralized notion of combatant status does not solve the problem. For the work that a computer science professor is doing quietly in her campus office may well produce some medical technology that a wounded soldier needs to live, but it will also provide military hardware that other soldiers will find enormously useful in fighting. Although she is not legally a combatant, it seems that she must be a combatant in the moralized sense and thus must be a legitimate target of attack according to the reigning theory of the just war—despite the fact that few if any of that theory's proponents would accept that this is really an implication of their view.

There are even more serious objections to the idea that posing a threat to others is the criterion of liability to attack in war. The most important of these is that the idea that one makes oneself liable to defensive attack merely by posing a threat to another has no intuitive plausibility at all outside the context of war. If a murderer is in the process of killing a number of innocent people and the only way to stop him is to kill him, the police officer who takes aim to shoot him does not thereby make herself morally liable to defensive action, and if the murderer kills her in self-defense, he adds one more murder to the list of his offenses.

For many centuries there has been general agreement that, as a matter of both morality and law, "where attack is justified there can be no lawful defence." Those words were written by Pierino Belli in 1563 and were echoed a little over a century later by John Locke, who claimed that "Force is to be opposed to nothing, but to unjust and unlawful Force."[17] While there are reasons, which I will consider in Section 2.1, for thinking that the principle stated by Belli and Locke is overly broad, at least this much is true: a person can have no right of defense against a threatened harm to which he has made himself liable. In the example I just gave, the murderer has, by wrongfully threatening the lives of further innocent people, made himself liable to be killed in their defense. He therefore has no right of defense against the police, if their only effective defensive option is to kill him. It is therefore false that by posing a threat to another, one necessarily makes oneself liable to defensive action.

Thomas Hobbes disputed this in the case of lethal threats. He believed that the murderer has a natural right to kill the police officer in self-defense. But he conceded that this right is not a *moral* right; hence even his quite radical view does not support the *moral* equality of combatants. And, in any case, relatively few people today would accept his view.

That those who are liable to attack have no right of defense is true not only in relations among individuals in civil society but also in war. Those who fight solely to defend themselves and other innocent people from a wrongful threat of attack, and who threaten no one but the wrongful aggressors, do not make themselves morally liable to defensive attack. By engaging in morally justified self- and other-defense, they do nothing to forfeit their right not to be attacked or killed. This means that even though just combatants are "doing harm" and "pose a danger to other people" when they oppose the military action of unjust combatants, they do not thereby become legitimate targets of attack but retain their innocence in the generic sense. Like the police officer, they may not be attacked, even in self-defense.

Some people may grant that outside the context of war there can be no right of defense against an attack to which one is liable, yet claim that matters are somehow different in war. War, they think, is morally discontinuous with other activities and conditions. Some think that morality has no application in war—that it is wholly suspended in conditions of war. Others think that war is governed by altogether different moral principles from those that govern other areas of life.[18] Among the latter, some would argue that while merely posing a threat to another is insufficient for liability to defensive attack in all conditions other than war, it is nonetheless sufficient in the radically altered conditions of war.

Those who are tempted by such a view should consider the following possibility. Suppose that a unit of unjust combatants begins to violate the recognized principles of *jus in bello* in addition to the principles of *jus ad bellum*. They begin to attack and kill innocent, unprotected civilians. Some of these civilians, however, eventually manage to gather weapons and begin to defend themselves and the others who are under attack. Once they begin to fight back, they may not acquire combatant status in the legal sense, but they do become combatants in the moral sense if posing a threat to others is sufficient for liability to attack in conditions of war. They are now doing harm and have made themselves into dangerous men, and thus have become legitimate targets for the unjust combatants. Indeed, if the unjust combatants wanted to kill the civilians but also wanted to restrict their action so that they would attack only those who have combatant status in the moralized sense recognized by just war theory, a convenient strategy would be to supply the civilians with weapons and provoke them to fire the first shot before killing them.

1.3 CAN UNJUST COMBATANTS SATISFY THE PRINCIPLES OF *JUS IN BELLO?*

These arguments show not only that the traditional criterion of liability to attack in war—posing a threat to others—is unacceptable, but also that, except in a very restricted range of conditions, unjust combatants cannot satisfy the central principle of *jus in bello*: the requirement of discrimination. As I noted earlier in Section 1.1, both just war theory and the law of war assume that the principles of *jus in bello* are neutral between just and unjust combatants and thus that unjust combatants are at no disadvantage in their ability to obey the principles. It should be no more difficult for unjust combatants to satisfy the *in bello* requirements than it is for just combatants. But that, it turns out, is false. Recall that the requirement of discrimination holds that combatants must intentionally attack only those who are legitimate targets. It has hitherto been assumed that only noncombatants are illegitimate targets, so that even unjust combatants can satisfy the requirement of discrimination by confining their attacks to just combatants. But the foregoing arguments suggest that that assumption is unfounded. It is hard to see how just combatants could become legitimate targets simply by offering violent resistance to unjust attacks by unjust combatants. There may, of course, be a criterion of liability to attack in war, other than the indefensible criterion of posing a threat, that implies that just combatants are liable; but if there is, just war theorists have failed to identify and defend it. In Section 1.4, I will defend an alternative criterion according to which just combatants cannot be liable to attack, except in cases of the sort discussed immediately below. So for now I will assume that, in general, to attack just combatants is to attack people who are innocent in the generic sense: people who have not forfeited their right against attack, and thus are not liable to attack. They are therefore illegitimate targets. To attack them is indiscriminate.

The exception to the claim that just combatants are illegitimate targets in war is when they pursue their just cause by impermissible means. If, for example, just combatants attempt to achieve their just cause by using terrorist tactics—that is, by intentionally attacking and killing innocent people, as the Allies did when they bombed German and Japanese cities in World War II—they make themselves morally liable to defensive attack and become legitimate targets even for unjust combatants. If a Japanese pilot could have shot down the *Enola Gay* before its crew dropped the atomic bomb on Hiroshima, he would have been morally justified in doing so, despite the fact that he was an unjust combatant while the crew of the *Enola Gay* were just combatants.

This was recognized by Hugo Grotius, arguably the greatest writer in the tradition of just war theory. He wrote that "the case may arise in which there may be a just defence of subjects who engage in a war that is not merely doubtful but obviously unjust. For since an enemy, although waging a just war, does not have the true and perfect right of killing innocent subjects, who are not responsible for the war, unless either as a necessary defensive measure or as a result and apart from his purpose (for these are not liable to punishment), it follows that, if it is certain that the enemy comes with such a spirit that he absolutely refuses to spare the lives of hostile subjects when he can, these subjects may defend themselves by the law of nature, of which they are not deprived by the law of nations."[19] While Grotius here concedes that just combatants have a right to kill innocent civilians as a side effect of military action (though presumably only when the unintended killing is proportionate), he claims that when they kill innocent people intentionally or unnecessarily, the potential victims have a right of self-defense. Presumably the right to defend "innocent subjects" against an act of war that, "although done by him who in other respects has a right to make war, is unjust, and hence is justly resisted," is possessed not just by the subjects themselves but extends also to unjust combatants.[20]

That acts of war by unjust combatants can be discriminate in this limited range of cases is of negligible practical significance. For a war fought without a just cause cannot consist entirely, or even predominantly, of acts of this sort—that is, acts that prevent wrongful acts of war by just combatants. In practice only a small proportion of the acts constitutive of an unjust war could be of this sort.

One might also argue that unjust combatants can fight in a discriminate manner—that is, without attacking illegitimate targets—in wars in which both sides are in the wrong, so that all combatants on both sides are unjust combatants. In that case, it might seem that all combatants on each side would be liable to attack, so that combatants on the other side would be justified in attacking them. But this, I think, would be the wrong inference to draw. It might be true that no one on either side would be innocent in the relevant sense, but it would not follow that those on the other side would be justified in killing them. In a war in which all are in the wrong, none are justified in fighting. One need only reflect on urban gang "wars" to appreciate this.

There is much more that needs to be said about this kind of case. Here I will say only this. There are wars in which both sides fight for an unjust cause. An example might be a war in which both sides are fighting for possession and control of territory that belongs to neither and whose rightful owners are innocent victims of the war. In such a war, none of the combatants may be innocent. All might be liable to attack if a third party were to intervene to defend the territory on behalf of its rightful owners. Yet it may also be that no combatant on either of the sides fighting for an unjust cause is justified in attacking any combatant on the other. One way of describing this situation is to say that the combatants are liable to be attacked only by certain people and not by others. On this view, liability is a predicate with four variables, the fourth of which is an "agent-variable." A person cannot be liable *simpliciter*; rather, because a person *a* has acted in way *b*, he is liable to be treated in way *c* by agent or agents *d*. He is not liable to be treated in way *c* by any agents other than *d*. A person may, for example, be liable to be punished by those authorized to inflict punishment, but not be liable to be punished by anyone else. Similarly, combatants fighting in a war in which both sides are pursuing an unjust cause may be liable to be attacked by third parties but not liable to be attacked by enemy combatants. The reasons why the agent-variable is restricted in one case may be different from the reasons why it is restricted in another. The reasons why we insist that criminals are liable to punishment only at the hands of duly authorized representatives of the legal system and not to punishment by vigilantes may be largely or entirely pragmatic. But the reasons why unjust combatants on one side may not be liable to attack by unjust combatants on the other may reflect more principled considerations, such as that a person cannot be justified in attacking another person for a reason, or with an intention, that is itself wrongful. In a war in which both sides are pursuing an unjust cause, combatants on each side may take some comfort in the thought that their immediate victims are not innocent in the generic sense (as they are liable to attack by third parties), but the range of comforting thoughts they may legitimately entertain does not include the thought that they act permissibly.

Thus far I have argued that unjust combatants can seldom satisfy the *jus in bello* requirement of discrimination, since just combatants seldom make themselves liable to attack and thus are in general illegitimate targets. If just combatants were always to fight according to the moral constraints that govern their conduct in war, they would never be liable to attack and unjust combatants would never have legitimate targets at all and thus would never be able to satisfy the requirement of discrimination. What about the other main principle of *jus in bello*, the requirement of proportionality? To answer this question, we must first explore the notion of proportionality in war in some detail.

Just war theorists have traditionally distinguished two requirements of proportionality, one governing the resort to war (*ad bellum* proportionality) and one governing individual acts of war (*in bello* proportionality). The first holds that the resort to war is impermissible if the bad effects of the war would outweigh the good, while the second makes a parallel claim about individual acts of war. In both cases the relevant bad effects are generally assumed to include only unintentional harms to the innocent. Harms intentionally inflicted on the innocent are already ruled out by the requirement of discrimination, or by similar principles forbidding the intentional infliction of harms other than those caused by military attack on those who are not liable to suffer them. Harms inflicted on those who are liable to suffer them have traditionally been assumed to have no role in determining proportionality. Otherwise the resort to war might be ruled out if, for example, the number of expected killings of enemy combatants would exceed the number of people on one's own side whose lives the war could be expected to save—an implication that to my knowledge no just war theorist has been willing to embrace.

Proportionality in war is, however, far more complicated than this. It is, indeed, far more complicated than I will be able to indicate here if I am to avoid a disproportionately lengthy digression. But I will draw some basic distinctions that will be essential to the argument of the book. I will here discuss only *in bello* proportionality, though much of what I will say also applies, with relevant changes, to *ad bellum* proportionality.

Proportionality is a constraint on action that causes harm. In most cases, for an act that causes harm to be justified, it must be instrumental to the achievement of some valuable goal against which the harm can be weighed and assessed. If the assessment is favorable, the harm is proportionate; if it is unfavorable, the harm is disproportionate. For liability to be an issue, the goal sought must usually be a solution to a problem. The principal condition of a person's being liable to be harmed in the pursuit of the goal is that he or she be implicated in some way in the existence of the problem. If a person is implicated in the existence of a problem in such a way that harming him in a certain way in the course of solving the problem would not wrong him, then he is liable to that harm. This is important because liability is one of two factors that affect the demands of proportionality.

The other is intention. In different combinations, liability and intention yield four distinct proportionality requirements governing action in war. I will call the goal of an act of war a "war aim." When a person is implicated in a problem to which a certain war aim is the solution, so that he could be liable to suffer *some* degree of harm if that were necessary to achieve the war aim, we can say that he is *potentially liable* to be harmed in the pursuit of that aim.

With these bits of conceptual apparatus in place, I can now distinguish the four proportionality requirements by reference to the types of action they govern. These are: (1) acts that intentionally harm those who are potentially liable to be harmed in pursuit of some war aim, (2) acts that unintentionally but foreseeably harm those who are potentially liable, (3) acts that intentionally harm those who are *not* potentially liable, and (4) acts that unintentionally but foreseeably harm those who are not potentially liable.

It is, as I noted, the last of these that most people identify as the kind of act that raises the issue of proportionality in the conduct of war—in particular, proportionality is considered primarily a matter of weighing the harm that an act of war would cause to civilians as a side effect against the military goals the act could be expected to achieve. If the expected good would outweigh the unintended harm to civilians, the act is proportionate. By contrast, however, it is proportionality in relation to the first of these four kinds of act that is the focus of discussion in the moral and legal literature on individual self-defense. It may be helpful to consider an actual case of individual self-defense as a means of clarifying the distinction between proportionality in effects of the first kind and proportionality in effects of the fourth kind.

In 1984, Bernard Goetz shot four men on the New York subway who had crowded around him in a menacing way and demanded that he give them money.[21] His action raised two issues of proportionality. The men clearly meant to be threatening Goetz and were thus potentially liable to some sort of defensive action. But in shooting them Goetz seriously wounded all four and caused one to suffer brain damage and permanent paralysis. If he had instead given them the five dollars they demanded, they probably would have left him unharmed; and even if he had refused to give them anything, the probability was low that they would have seriously harmed him. It therefore seems that the harm caused by shooting them was excessive in relation to the harm to which they might have been liable. If Goetz had been carrying a truncheon rather than a gun and one of the men had extended his hand toward him in a gesture demanding money, it would perhaps have been proportionate for Goetz to have struck his hand with the truncheon, perhaps breaking his fingers. For the man's threatening behavior had arguably made him liable to *that* degree of harm as a means by which Goetz might defend himself and deter further threats.

Because the men were potentially liable to certain forms of harm that might have been inflicted in self-defense, but the harm Goetz actually inflicted exceeded that to which they might have been liable, his action was disproportionate in what I will call the *narrow* sense—that is, disproportionate in the harm that it inflicted on those who were potentially liable to lesser harms. Yet Goetz's action not only intentionally harmed the men who threatened him but also unintentionally endangered the other people who were in the enclosed space of the subway car in which he fired his bullets. These people were not potentially liable to any harm—that is, they were innocent in the sense relevant outside the context of war. It seems that the risks to which he exposed those people were also excessive in relation to the threat he faced from the four men. It was disproportionate in what I will call the *wide* sense—that is, disproportionate in the harm it inflicted on those who were not liable to any harm at all.

The harms that Goetz inflicted that were disproportionate in the narrow sense were inflicted intentionally, while the risks he imposed on bystanders that were disproportionate in the wide sense were imposed unintentionally. This is as one would expect, since issues of narrow proportionality usually concern harms inflicted intentionally, while issues of wide proportionality usually concern harms inflicted foreseeably but unintentionally. But it is worth mentioning two other types of proportionality—those corresponding to acts of types 2 and 3 above—for the sake of completeness.

First, there is also a proportionality restriction on harms that are foreseeably but *unintentionally* inflicted on those who are potentially liable. If such harms are within the scope of the victims' potential liability, they are narrowly proportionate; if they are beyond the scope of the victims' potential liability, they are narrowly disproportionate. If the intention with which a person acts is relevant to the moral character of her act, we should expect that the narrow proportionality restriction will be more stringent in its application to harms intentionally inflicted than in its application to harms inflicted foreseeably but unintentionally—which is in fact the common sense view. I will return to this form of proportionality in Chapter 5, as it may be of considerable significance in understanding the morality of harming civilians as a side effect of acts of war.

The third type of act listed above—the intentional harming of someone who is not potentially liable to be harmed at all—is also subject to a proportionality constraint. This may seem surprising in the context of just war theory. For consider an act of war that is of this third type: for example, an intentional attack on an innocent person as a means of achieving some war aim. Such an act violates the requirement of discrimination and is therefore ruled out. What is the point of condemning it as disproportionate as well?

In fact, however, most just war theorists, or at least those outside the Catholic Church, do not believe that the requirement of discrimination is absolute. They believe instead that if the consequences of refusing to attack an innocent person or group of innocent people would be vastly worse than those of conducting the attack, it can be permissible, and perhaps even morally required, to violate the requirement of discrimination by intentionally attacking the innocent. Michael Walzer, for example, has proposed that an exemption from the requirement of discrimination may come into effect in conditions of "supreme emergency."[22] But if the requirement of discrimination is not absolute, then when it may be overridden is essentially a matter of proportionality. Whether the requirement is overridden is a matter of how much worse the effects of obeying it would be than the effects of violating it. Again, if intention is relevant to the permissibility of action—and the requirement of discrimination itself presupposes that it is—then we should expect that the wide proportionality requirement will be more restrictive in its application to harms intentionally inflicted on those who are not even potentially liable than it is in its application to harms inflicted on such people foreseeably but unintentionally. And again, this is the common sense view.

Still, even though most people believe that it can in principle be permissible to intentionally attack innocent people in war, it is commonly assumed that only the wide proportionality requirement is relevant to the conduct of war, and that in practice it is concerned only with harms inflicted on the innocent as unintended side effects—that is, with "collateral damage." Yet as we saw in reviewing the Goetz case, the narrow proportionality requirement, particularly in its application to harms *intentionally* inflicted on those who are potentially liable, tends to be highly important in individual self-defense. Why is it not equally important in war?

One reason why the narrow requirement is more important in individual self-defense than the wide requirement is simply that acts of individual self-defense are rarely so destructive that they threaten the lives of bystanders in the way that acts of war often do. More importantly, however, both just war theory and the law of war hold that all combatants are morally and legally liable to attack by enemy combatants as long as war is in progress and they have not been rendered *hors de combat*. They are therefore liable to any harms that may be inflicted on them by military attack. And given that narrow proportionality is internal to liability, any harms to which they are liable are necessarily proportionate; therefore no attacks on enemy combatants can be disproportionate, according to the traditional view. This is why the narrow proportionality requirement is generally thought to have no application to the conduct of war, so that only the wide requirement is relevant.

Some theorists do occasionally claim that some act of war is disproportionate in its effect on enemy combatants, but in many such instances they are making a simple mistake. It is sometimes claimed, for example, that if one could eliminate the threat posed by certain enemy combatants with equal effectiveness either by killing them or by incapacitating them without killing them, it would be disproportionate to kill them. But this is to confuse the requirement of proportionality with the requirement of necessity. In these circumstances, it might indeed be wrong to kill the combatants, but not because that would be disproportionate in the narrow sense. The principle that demands that they be incapacitated rather than killed is instead the *requirement of minimal force*, which is the *in bello* version of the requirement of necessity.

Yet the requirements of minimal force and narrow proportionality do begin to blur together when considerations of probability and risk arise, as they usually do in conditions of war. If, for example, attempting to incapacitate the enemy combatants would have a slightly lower probability of success than trying to kill them, or if it would be riskier for one's own combatants, the issue arguably becomes one of narrow proportionality. And the orthodox view is that in these conditions it would be permissible to kill them—hence not disproportionate.

I believe, however, that there are cases in which the narrow proportionality requirement forbids certain acts of war. Suppose, for example, that ten innocent civilians from a country that is fighting a just war have been unjustly imprisoned in the enemy country. It is reasonable to suppose that each military guard at the prison in which they are confined is liable to be killed in the course of a military operation to free them. In other words, to kill a guard in the course of such an operation would not be disproportionate in the narrow sense, that is, in relation to his potential liability. But now suppose that all the guards are known to be reluctant conscripts and that to free the ten prisoners it would be necessary to kill five hundred guards. Even if no innocent people would be harmed as a side effect, it is intuitively plausible to suppose that an operation to free the prisoners in these conditions would be disproportionate.

Yet even if this claim seems intuitively plausible, a puzzle remains. If narrow proportionality is a matter of individual liability, and if each of the guards is potentially liable to be killed as a means or in the process of freeing the prisoners, how can the number of guards who would have to be killed affect narrow proportionality? It would seem that whether action is proportionate relative to individual liability cannot be affected by the number of individuals who would be harmed. Yet it can, at least if the contribution that each guard makes to the continued imprisonment of the ten, and thus the good that can be achieved by killing him, diminishes the more guards there are. If there were only one guard and one could free the ten prisoners by killing him, killing him might be narrowly proportionate, for all the good involved in their release would be attributable to the one killing. But if this guard is one of five hundred, killing him would make only a small contribution to the release of the prisoners. The good that would be produced by killing him alone is therefore insufficient for the harm he would thereby suffer to be narrowly proportionate—that is, proportionate in relation to his potential liability. (Notice that our intuitions may be affected by the stipulation that the guards are reluctant conscripts. I will return to the relevance of excusing conditions to narrow proportionality in Chapter 4.)

Having distinguished the narrow and wide proportionality requirements and explained how both have application to individual acts of war, I can now return to the question whether acts of war by unjust combatants can satisfy these requirements. That acts of war by unjust combatants can be proportionate has been unquestioned in the just war tradition for centuries. But I will argue that they cannot be proportionate in either the narrow or wide sense except in those rare instances in which these acts are discriminate—that is, when they have the effect of preventing just combatants from acting wrongly and causing wrongful harm.

It is a necessary truth that attacks by unjust combatants against just combatants can be proportionate in the narrow sense only if the just combatants are liable to attack. If they are not liable, the narrow proportionality requirement has no application, as the narrow requirement is internal to liability—that is, harm is proportionate in the narrow sense only if the victim is liable to suffer it, in the circumstances. I have argued that it is implausible to suppose that just combatants become liable to attack merely by defending themselves and other innocent people against wrongful attack, though I have conceded that they may be liable to attack if they pursue their just cause by impermissible means. Acts of war by unjust combatants against just combatants that are intended to prevent the latter from fighting by impermissible means, and perhaps even acts of war that merely have that effect, can thus be proportionate in the narrow sense. But in practice a war cannot be fought by unjust combatants that consists entirely of such acts. As I noted in discussing discrimination, this leaves it open that there may be other grounds on which just combatants generally are liable to attack, but in the next section I will argue for a positive account of liability in war that excludes the possibility that just combatants could be liable to attack except through the pursuit of their just cause by wrongful means.

As I noted earlier, proportionality in war is almost universally understood to be a matter of wide proportionality only. Hence for most people the question whether acts of war by unjust combatants can be proportionate is just the question whether the harms these acts unintentionally cause to civilians or noncombatants are excessive in relation to the importance of the acts' goals. As my earlier remarks have indicated, I think this is an inadequate understanding of the bad effects that are relevant to the wide proportionality requirement, and I will return to that problem shortly. But there is a further problem that we should consider first, and that is the problem of identifying the relevant good effects that can be weighed against the bad when, by hypothesis, acts of war by unjust combatants lack a just cause.

Even in the absence of a just cause for war, there are three types of good effect that acts of war by unjust combatants can have. First, and most obviously, they can have the effect of defending the unjust combatants themselves from harm. Yet it seems that this is not the kind of good effect that can count toward proportionality. For just as harms to which people are liable do not count among the bad effects in any proportionality calculation, so the prevention of harms to which people are liable does not count among the good effects. No act that would otherwise be disproportionate can become proportionate by preventing a harm to which a person is liable. Among the reasons why this is so is that, because the conditions of liability, including a condition of instrumental effectiveness, are internal, a person can be liable to be harmed only when harming him can be expected to have good effects that morally outweigh the harm. Because preventing a harm to which a person is liable would thus also prevent the good effects that would outweigh the harm, it is always worse from an impartial point of view for people to be protected from harms to which they are liable.

Of course, the claim that the good of preventing unjust combatants from being harmed by just combatants does not count in the wide proportionality calculation presupposes that unjust combatants are indeed liable to attack. Yet this is a relatively uncontroversial assumption. It is common ground between the reigning theory of the just war with its doctrine of the moral equality of combatants and the major non-pacifist alternatives that reject the moral equality of combatants. It may be, of course, that all these accounts of the morality of war are mistaken and that many or even all unjust combatants are not liable to attack. I will consider arguments for the view that many unjust combatants are not liable to attack in Chapter 4. I will, however, reject those arguments, so for the moment I will follow the just war tradition and assume that unjust combatants are liable to attack.

The second type of good effect that acts of war by unjust combatants can have, and that they often have as an *intended* effect, is the protection of innocent civilians on their own side from the harmful side effects of justified military action by just combatants. Although I will argue in Chapter 5 that some civilians on the unjust side in a war may be liable to be harmed in certain ways, I accept that few if any are liable to military attack. The prevention of harms that these innocent people would otherwise suffer as side effects of attack by just combatants must therefore count as a good effect in determining wide proportionality.

The third category of good effects that acts of war by unjust combatants can have and that may count toward wide proportionality, consists, effectively, of virtually all genuinely good effects, intended or unintended, other than the prevention of bad effects that people are liable to suffer or that they deserve to suffer. Suppose, for example, that a powerful country were to invade a smaller, poorer country in order to seize its oil fields. The unjust invasion and occupation could have as a good effect the tangible improvement of the situation of women in the country—for example, by opening access to forms of employment that had hitherto been denied to them, enabling them to vote, and so on. While it would not have been permissible intentionally to pursue these good effects by means of war—that is, while these good effects do not constitute a just cause for war—they are goods that can in principle weigh against and cancel out unintended bad effects of war in the wide proportionality calculation.[23]

I concede, therefore, that even though unjust combatants necessarily act in the absence of a just cause for war, their acts of war can nevertheless have good effects that can count toward wide proportionality.

I still think, however, that attacks by unjust combatants against just combatants who are acting with justification are in practice very unlikely ever to be proportionate in the wide sense. And I also think that even if they could be, that could seldom make acts of war by unjust combatants permissible.

Most people, including most just war theorists, interpret wide proportionality as the requirement that the harm that an act of war would foreseeably but unintentionally inflict on noncombatants not be excessive in relation to the act's expected good effects. I have conceded that such acts can have relevant good effects even in the absence of a just cause. But it is illegitimate to interpret the wide proportionality requirement so that the relevant bad effects are limited to *unintended* bad effects *on noncombatants*. The wide proportionality requirement is concerned with bad effects on those who have not made themselves liable to suffer those effects. If it is right that just combatants do not make themselves liable to be attacked simply by defending themselves and others from unjust or wrongful attack, and if there is no other basis for thinking them liable to attack, then they are innocent in the generic sense and harms inflicted on them count as bad effects in the *wide* proportionality calculation. And because these harms are inflicted intentionally, they should weigh even more heavily against the good effects than unintended bad effects. Even if intentional attacks on just combatants are already condemned as indiscriminate, that in itself is no reason to exclude them from the wide proportionality calculation.

It should now be evident why acts of war by unjust combatants are in practice very unlikely ever to be proportionate in the wide sense. We can, perhaps, imagine a war that lacks a just cause, in the sense that the people warred against have done nothing to make themselves liable to attack, but for which there might nevertheless be a lesser-evil justification. Suppose, for example, that country A is about to be unjustly invaded by a ruthless and more powerful country, B. A's best hope of successful defense is to station forces in the territory of a smaller, weaker, neighboring country, C, in order to be able to attack B's forces from prepared positions as they approach A along the border between B and C. A's government requests permission from the government of C to deploy its forces on C's territory for this purpose, but C's government, foreseeing that allowing A to use its territory in this way would result in considerable destruction, denies the request. Suppose that C is within its rights to deny A the use of its territory. Given that C is not morally required to sacrifice its territory for the sake of A, it seems that C does nothing to make itself liable to attack by A. A therefore has no just cause for war against C. Yet it is at least possible that the rights of the people of C could be overridden in such a case, and that war by A against C could be morally *justified* even though it would be *unjust*. The reason why this is so unlikely in practice, though, is that for the war to be proportionate in the wide sense, its good effects would have to be weighed against the intentional killing of just combatants in C who are innocent in the generic sense, the killing and injuring of other innocent people in C as a side effect of a war fought where they live, the destruction of property and civilian infrastructure, the infringement of the rights to self-determination of the citizens of C, and so on. Recall that in common sense morality the wide proportionality requirement is considerably more restrictive in its application to harms intentionally inflicted on those who are not liable to them than in its application to those inflicted as side effects. If common sense morality is correct that the intentional killing of innocent people can constitute the lesser evil, and thus be proportionate in the wide sense, only if it is necessary to avert a very significantly greater harm to others, it follows that for individual acts of war by A to be proportionate, the number of innocent citizens of A whose lives they would save must *greatly* exceed the number of just combatants they would kill.

The fact that an act that causes harm to the innocent satisfies the wide proportionality requirement is in most cases merely necessary, not sufficient, for that act to be permissible. Interestingly, what seems to make the difference, according to common sense intuition, is intention. It may help to clarify this point to consider an instance of individual action outside the context of war. Recall the example of the murderer who is shooting innocent people but is about to be shot defensively by a police officer. Suppose that the murderer knows that the officer has a tissue type that makes his organs suitable for transplantation into the bodies of ten people who will otherwise die. If he shoots the officer in the head in self-defense, he will not only save his own life but will also make it possible for surgeons to save the lives of ten innocent people. Most people believe that it is nevertheless impermissible for him to shoot the officer. One reason they think this is that the demands of proportionality are more stringent when harm to innocent people is intended. Because the killing of the officer would be intended, a net saving of ten lives seems insufficient to justify the killing. Yet it *would* be sufficient if the killing were an *unintended* effect of the means of saving the ten—as in the familiar "trolley case" in which a runaway trolley will kill ten people unless it is diverted onto another track where it will foreseeably kill one person.

But the *reasons* for the killing—the intentions with which the killer acts—also seem to matter. Suppose that by shooting the officer, the murderer would somehow thereby enable surgeons to save a hundred innocent people. Most people, I think, believe that the killing would still be unjustified if the murderer's intention were merely to preserve his own life. But if we substitute for the murderer an entirely innocent person who happens to find herself in a position in which her only means of saving a hundred innocent people is to kill one innocent person who is not among the hundred, many people would accept that it would be permissible for her to kill the one to save the hundred. What seems to make the difference is the agent's intention.

This means that the wide proportionality requirement is sensitive not only to whether harm caused to the innocent is intended, but also to the nature of the intention. If an act would cause harm to the innocent as a foreseeable side effect, it may nevertheless be permissible if it is intended to achieve good effects that exceed the bad by a certain margin. It may not, however, be permissible to cause the same amount of harm to the innocent as an intended means of achieving the same good effects. Yet if causing that amount of harm to the innocent could be the means of achieving much *greater* good effects, it might be permissible to cause it—though only if the agent acts with an acceptable intention, such as the intention to achieve the greater good. This is still a matter of proportionality in the relation between good and bad effects, but it seems to be affected by the agent's intentions. According to common sense intuition, intention can have a role not only in making the killing of the innocent impermissible, but also in making it permissible. I am not entirely confident that these views are defensible, but they have to be recognized and taken seriously if we are to achieve greater coherence and consistency in our moral thought.

Suppose it is right that acts of war by unjust combatants can rarely if ever satisfy either the narrow or the wide *in bello* proportionality requirement unless these acts are responsive to wrongful acts by just combatants. What have just war theorists and theorists of international law been thinking when they have claimed that the *in bello* proportionality requirement constrains just and unjust combatants equally—that is, that it imposes no greater limits on the action of unjust combatants than it does on that of just combatants? As I noted earlier, discussions of *in bello* proportionality are almost invariably concerned exclusively with the wide requirement. The question is whether the unintended harms to the innocent—the "collateral damage"—caused by an act of war are outweighed by the good effects. But in most cases, it seems that not only the side effects but also most of the intended effects of acts of war by unjust combatants are entirely bad, impartially considered. What, then, are the general types of good effect that moral and legal theorists have had in mind when they have assumed that the bad side effects of military action by unjust combatants can be outweighed, so that this action can be proportionate?

Just war theorists have generally followed the law in this matter. The first articulation of the *in bello* proportionality requirement in an international treaty, as opposed to customary international law, is in Article 51 of the 1977 Geneva Protocol I. Although the prohibited acts are described as "indiscriminate" rather than "disproportionate," the treaty prohibits attacks "that may be expected to cause incidental [i.e., unintended] loss of civilian life, injury to civilians, damage to civilian objects, or a combination thereof, which would be excessive in relation to the concrete and direct military advantage anticipated."[24] If this formula is understood in the way that proportionality has traditionally been understood—that is, as weighing unintended bad effects against the good effects of an attack—then in its application to unjust combatants, it is morally absurd. For in order for the killing of innocent civilians not to be excessive in relation to the expected military advantage of an attack, military advantage must be *good*. Yet military advantage for those who are in the wrong and are fighting for the defeat of a just cause is, except perhaps in highly anomalous conditions, *bad*, impartially considered. It makes no sense to say that the killing of a certain number of innocent people as a side effect of an act of war is *outweighed* by the contribution that the act makes to the achievement of goals that are *unjust*.

This is not, of course, what the drafters of the Protocol had in mind. They meant to separate the notion of military advantage from any evaluation, moral or legal, of the aims of the war. Their idea was instead rather simple: to prohibit the extensive harming or killing of civilians in the course of operations that could be expected to accomplish only comparatively trivial military goals. But because the items being compared—the killing of innocent people and military advantage—are of such evaluatively disparate types, and also because the second is so difficult to measure, the formula is a virtual invitation to engage in distortion and abuse. One can always claim that one's goals in war are so important, and one's situation so precarious, that what may seem like an inconsequential military advantage is in fact vital to the security of one's people.

Yet it is morally very important to get unjust combatants to exercise restraint in their military operations. They are often willing to accept guidance from legal and moral principles, and the requirement of proportionality is a familiar restraining principle that many combatants are motivated to try to respect. But because most people who are in fact unjust combatants mistakenly believe that their war is just and thus that they are actually just combatants, any requirement of proportionality that has a chance of restraining the action of unjust combatants will have to be neutral—that is, it will have to have equal application to all combatants and thus must make no reference to just cause and must indeed prescind entirely from any evaluation of the aims of the war. The formula in the Geneva Protocol satisfies these conditions but at the cost of being so vague as to have little constraining power at all. Is there a better alternative?

Here is one suggestion. The wide *in bello* proportionality requirement can be divorced altogether from the aims of the war if it takes the prevention of harm to the combatants themselves on the battlefield as the good to be weighed against the harms unintentionally caused to the innocent. On this interpretation, an act of war is proportionate only if the expected harm it will unintentionally cause to innocent civilians is not excessive in relation to the harm it will prevent to one's own forces on the battlefield. A crude illustration might be that an act of war that would prevent ten of one's own combatants from being killed but would kill one innocent civilian as a side effect would be proportionate, while an act that would kill ten civilians as a side effect but save only one combatant would not be. Because civilians are supposed to have a special protected status in war, their lives would presumably have greater weight than those of one's own combatants, even though their deaths would be unintended. So an act that would save ten of one's own combatants but would kill five enemy civilians might not be proportionate either. But whatever the comparative weightings might be, the main point of this proposal is that the *only* good effects that would weigh against harms caused as a side effect to innocent civilians would be the prevention of physical harm to one's own forces.

There are at least two advantages to this proposal. One is that the values compared are obviously commensurable: lives are weighed against lives and harms against harms. It thus offers a kind of determinacy that is lacking in the idea of comparing the deaths of innocent people with something as amorphous and manipulable as "military advantage."

The second advantage is that this proposal does not treat victory by unjust combatants as a good to be weighed against the harm they cause to the innocent. The cost of this advantage is that it requires the exclusion of victory from among the goods that count in determining the proportionality of military action by just combatants as well. Because it is impossible to determine whether the action of just combatants is *morally* proportionate without taking into account its contribution to the achievement of their just cause, this proposal for a neutral *in bello* proportionality requirement has to be understood as purely legal or conventional in character, though one might hope that unjust combatants would understand it as a binding moral constraint.

There is, however, a serious and perhaps decisive objection to this proposal, which is that it seems to rule out military operations that will harm innocent civilians but could be omitted without detriment to the security of the combatants. Among these operations are ones that would do nothing to protect or defend the combatants themselves but would greatly advance their side's cause in the war. It might be difficult to fight a war effectively without conducting operations of this sort. If so, we are back with the problem that besets us at present, which is that there is simply no satisfactory understanding of proportionality in war that can be applied independently of whether the acts that are evaluated support a just or unjust cause.

1.4 THE BASIS OF MORAL LIABILITY TO ATTACK IN WAR

I noted earlier, in Section 1.2, that in the just war literature the word "innocent" has two substantive meanings in addition to the generic meaning of "not liable to attack" or "illegitimate target." The reigning theory of the just war embraces one of these substantive meanings—namely, "not harming" or "not threatening"—and deploys it as a criterion of moral immunity from attack in war. On this view, those who pose no threat to others are immune, while those who pose a threat are morally liable to attack. The other meaning of "innocent"—"not guilty" or "not responsible for a wrong"—is usually explicitly repudiated, as it is in the earlier quotations from Anscombe and Nagel, as having any relevance to the question of which people are legitimate targets in war.

But it has not always been this way. In the early, classical just war literature, "innocent" was often used to mean "not responsible for a wrong," and it was *this* that was supposed to confer moral immunity from attack in war. Writing in the first half of the sixteenth century, for example, Francisco de Vitoria argued that a political leader "cannot have greater authority over foreigners than he has over his own subjects; but he may not draw the sword against his own subjects unless they have done some wrong; therefore he cannot do so against foreigners except in the same circumstances."[25] The implication here is straightforward: one may not attack ("draw the sword against") a person in war unless he has committed a wrong. Writing in the second half of the sixteenth century and into the early years of the seventeenth, Francisco Suárez asserts the same claim: "no one may be deprived of his life save for reason of his own guilt;" thus the innocent include all those who "have not shared in the crime nor in the *unjust* war."[26] By implication, those who have shared in the *just* war retain their innocence and may not be deprived of their lives.

This alternative understanding of innocence has also appeared, though not often, in more recent writing on the just war. The passage I quoted earlier, in which Anscombe asserts that "innocent" means "not harming," was written in 1957. When she wrote on this issue again in 1961, she said that "what is required, for the people attacked to be non innocent in the relevant sense, is that they should themselves be engaged in an objectively unjust proceeding which the attacker has the right to make his concern; or—the commonest case—should be unjustly attacking him."[27] Here "non-innocent" means neither "doing harm" nor "responsible for or guilty of a wrong," but "engaged in objectively wrongful action." This is not equivalent to being responsible for or guilty of wrongful action because the agent may lack the capacity for morally responsible action or may have a full excuse.

It is, however, not clear from this quotation, nor from the surrounding text in her essay, whether objectively unjust action is supposed to be sufficient to justify necessary and proportionate defensive action, or whether it is merely a necessary condition of justified defense. If Anscombe means only the latter, then I am with her. But it is more natural to read her as asserting the former. All commentaries of which I am aware have read the passage quoted as implying that if someone engages in an objectively unjust attack against me, that is sufficient to justify my taking necessary and proportionate defensive action against him. On this interpretation, it is irrelevant whether he is morally guilty, or even morally responsible, for the objectively unjust threat he poses. Understood in this way, Anscombe's view diverges from views, such as that stated by Suárez, that make moral guilt or moral responsibility a necessary condition of noninnocence or liability to attack. For an individual who poses a threat through objectively unjust action may nevertheless lack the capacity for morally responsible agency, or may have a full excuse that renders him entirely guiltless. Such an individual would be liable to attack on Anscombe's view but not on the view quoted from Suárez.

But however Anscombe's view is interpreted, it is clearly much closer to that found in Vitoria and Suárez than it is to the understanding that informs most contemporary writing on the just war. Along with the views of Vitoria and Suárez, it implies that just combatants who fight by permissible means are not legitimate targets of attack. So unless there can be a justification for attacking those who are not legitimate targets, Anscombe's view, like those of Vitoria and Suárez, is incompatible with the moral equality of combatants.

Although the notion of innocence as moral innocence is largely out of favor with just war theorists and has been for centuries, it is neither alien nor even unfamiliar in nonacademic discourse about war. When Franklin D. Roosevelt wrote a letter dated September 1, 1939, addressed to various European governments and warning of the menace of aerial warfare, he referred implicitly to both conceptions of innocence, presumably assuming that they would both be understood as relevant: "If resort is had to this form of inhuman barbarism during the period of the tragic conflagration with which the world is now confronted, hundreds of thousands of innocent human beings who have no responsibility for, and who are not even remotely participating in, the hostilities which have now broken out, will lose their lives."[28]

As I have explicitly rejected the view that posing a threat is the basis of liability to attack in war, it should not be surprising that I accept the view grounded in the alternative conception of innocence and noninnocence—or, rather, that I accept a *version* of that view. As I have presented it, the alternative conception of innocence is that one is innocent if one is neither morally responsible for nor guilty of a wrong. While the classical just war theorists focused on guilt, I think we should focus instead on moral responsibility. It is, I think, a mistake to suppose that noninnocence in the sense of moral guilt or culpability is necessary for liability to attack in war. Something less is sufficient: namely, moral responsibility for a wrong, particularly an objectively unjustified threat of harm. But contrary to what I think is the natural reading of Anscombe's claim, posing an objectively unjustified threat is not sufficient for liability in the absence of moral responsibility for that threat. In short, the criterion of liability to attack in war is moral responsibility for an objectively unjustified threat of harm.

I will say more in Chapter 4 about why I think that merely posing an objectively unjustified threat of harm is not sufficient for liability, why moral responsibility for the threat is necessary, and why guilt or culpability is not. For now the important point to note is that the criterion of liability to attack in war that I have proposed not only does not support the moral equality of combatants but even seems incompatible with it. The central objection that I urged against the traditional criterion is that it has no plausibility outside the context of war. In contexts other than war, the morality of conflict is almost invariably asymmetric: those who are in the right may be permitted to use force and violence but those who are in the wrong are not. For example, except perhaps in very rare conditions, whenever a potential victim is permitted to use force in self-defense, the initial attacker is not permitted to use force, even in self-defense. The doctrine of the moral equality of combatants asserts exactly the opposite. It holds that those who are in the wrong in war have the same justification for attacking and killing their adversaries as those who are in the right—namely, that their adversaries pose a threat to them and are therefore liable to attack.

This view seems to be intuitively compelling to most people, despite its apparent inconsistency with their views about the morality of conflict generally. Perhaps the explanation is that war is fundamentally different, morally, from other forms of conflict and indeed from all other types of activity. Perhaps the views about innocence and liability that are cogent and compelling in other contexts simply have no application in war. If war is morally discontinuous with other forms of conflict, the practice of war may be governed by a different criterion of liability, or perhaps the justification for attacking and killing people in war does not appeal to the notion of liability at all. If war is profoundly different in one of these ways, we need to identify what it is about the conditions of war that renders inapplicable the moral principles that govern other areas of life. In particular, we need to understand how it can become permissible to attack and kill people who have done nothing other than to defend themselves and other morally innocent people from an unjust attack. Suppose we could identify some feature, or set of features, uniquely characteristic of war that would explain why war must be governed by moral principles different from those that govern other human practices and in particular other forms of conflict. We would then have gone well beyond the simple, traditional claim that combatants make themselves liable to attack in war simply by posing a threat to others. But we might have explained why that claim seems intuitively compelling.

It is common for people to claim that war is morally different. Some—the adherents of a brand of "political realism"—claim that morality has *no* application in conditions of war. Others claim that war is governed by weaker or more permissive moral principles than those that apply outside of war. Views of these sorts are most common among those who see the source of morality in either actual or hypothetical agreements or contracts. It is, for example, often argued that conditions of war constitute a Hobbesian state of nature in which moral relations are simply not possible, or a Lockean state of nature in which the bases are present for some moral constraints but not for others. I will not consider these arguments here as I think the views about the foundations of morality that they presuppose are mistaken, but I cannot make the case against those views here. It is, however, worth making one general point that applies to all views that claim that the moral principles (if any) that govern the practice of war are different from those that govern other areas of life. This is that on these views it is essential to be able to distinguish with precision between wars and other kinds of conflict. For on all such views, if people are attacking and killing one another, whether they are acting permissibly or are guilty of murder may depend on whether their conflict counts as war. I find this extremely implausible. But there is another possibility that is perhaps more plausible, though it is less commonly articulated. This is that there are moral principles that are not restricted to war but are such that the situations to which they apply are extremely rare outside the context of war. It is possible that the intuitions about war that prompt people to say that an entirely different morality comes into operation in a state of war are actually better understood as implications of common moral principles that *seem* inconsistent with ordinary morality only because they are intuitions about extreme circumstances that are very rare outside of war.

In the following chapter, I will examine some arguments that are intended to show that it is permissible to fight in an unjust war, provided that one abides by a set of neutral constraints on the conduct of war, such as the principles of *jus in bello* as commonly formulated in the contemporary theory of the just war and the international law of war. Some of these arguments may seem to presuppose that principles different from those of ordinary morality apply in conditions of war, while others clearly extend familiar principles of ordinary morality into the realm of war. I will argue that they are all mistaken. But distinguishing these arguments from one another and carefully examining them should deepen our understanding of the morality of participation in war.

2

Arguments for the Moral Equality of Combatants

2.1 JUSTIFICATION AND LIABILITY

The doctrine of the moral equality of combatants, with its corollary that combatants on both sides in a war have, as Walzer says, an equal right to kill, is almost universally accepted among those who are not pacifists, and has been for many centuries. Although just war theorists have said surprisingly little in its defense, there are various arguments that can be advanced in its support. In this chapter I will review the best arguments I have been able to discover, stating each as persuasively as I can. In the end I will find all of them wanting, but examining them carefully should help us to achieve a fuller understanding of the morality of participation in war.

I have suggested that the criterion of liability to attack in war is moral responsibility for an objectively unjustified or wrongful threat. The notion of a wrongful threat is, however, ambiguous. In its primary sense, a wrongful threat is a threat of wrongful harm—that is, harm to which the victim is not liable—posed by action that is objectively wrong. In most instances in which unjust combatants attack just combatants, they pose a wrongful threat in this sense. Yet when just combatants attack unjust combatants within the limits of proportionality, they neither act wrongly nor wrong their victims.

In a second, broader sense, an individual poses a wrongful threat whenever his action threatens to inflict a wrongful harm. Acts that are permissible, justified, or even morally required can all inflict wrongful harms. This happens frequently in modern war. If there can be just war at all, it must be permissible in some circumstances for just combatants to engage in acts of war that they foresee will harm or kill innocent civilians as an unintended but unavoidable effect. For it is virtually impossible now to fight wars without killing significant numbers of innocent people. But when just combatants are justified in attacking a military target even though they foresee that their action will harm or kill innocent civilians as a side effect, their action, though justified, nonetheless threatens those civilians with wrongful harm. It seems, therefore, that they are responsible for a wrongful threat in this second sense, and one can argue that this brings them within the scope of the criterion of liability that I have defended.[1] When they threaten innocent civilians in this way, they seem to become legitimate targets for unjust combatants, whose military action has the effect of mitigating that wrongful threat.

One can also argue that they pose such a threat continuously while war is in progress. This is, after all, the view that just war theory and the law of war take of all combatants: that they pose a threat and are therefore legitimate targets of attack at all times during war, no matter what they may be doing at any particular time. A combatant is engaged in the ongoing activity of participating in war even while sleeping, in much the way that an individual continues to be engaged in a brawl even when he has been knocked to the ground and is thus momentarily inactive: both will soon get up and resume the fight.[2] But if it is right to regard all combatants as posing a threat to enemy combatants continuously while war is in progress, then it seems reasonable to suppose that they—just and unjust combatants alike—also pose a continuous threat to innocent civilians as well, given the frequency with which civilians are injured or killed as a side effect of attacks on military targets.

But if just combatants pose a threat of wrongful harm to innocent people at all times while war is in progress, it seems that they, like unjust combatants, must be liable to attack at all times. But to acknowledge that is tantamount to accepting the moral equality of combatants—with one qualification: that the moral equality of combatants is limited to wars that threaten innocent bystanders with physical harm. It is possible that there could be wars, such as wars fought entirely at sea or in outer space, that would pose no threat to innocent bystanders as a side effect, and in these wars only unjust combatants would be liable. But because it is unlikely that wars of this sort will ever be fought, this qualification is irrelevant in practice; thus those who are intuitively wedded to the moral equality of combatants might embrace this defense even if the rationale it offers is not the intuitive basis of their commitment to the doctrine.

It seems a mistake, however, to claim that just combatants pose a threat to innocent bystanders in war in a way that makes them liable to attack at all times. In general, those who engage in activities that *may* cause unintended harm to innocent people are not regarded as liable to defensive attack at any time at which they are engaged in such an activity. Those who drive cars, for example, are not liable to defensive action merely by virtue of driving, though they may become liable if the threat they pose to others passes a certain threshold of probability.

What, then, are the relevant differences between unjust combatants and drivers, and how do just combatants compare with both? Drivers do pose a threat of wrongful harm both to other drivers and to pedestrians, but they are not normally liable to any sort of defensive action. Given that the threat that ordinary drivers pose to others is generally negligible, it is generally true that there is no harmful defensive action that can be taken against them that would be proportionate in the narrow sense—that is, there is nothing that can be done to them that would reduce the threat they pose in a way that would be proportionate in relation to the threat they pose. In that case there is nothing that they are liable to.

One relevant difference, then, between drivers and unjust combatants is that the threat posed by a particular driver at a particular time is almost always negligible, while the threat, either to just combatants or to others, posed by a particular unjust combatant at any time during war is generally quite serious. Hence defensive action against unjust combatants can generally be proportionate in relation to the magnitude of the threat they pose, while this is not true of defensive action against ordinary drivers.

One might argue that the reason why just combatants are not liable to attack is that the threat they pose to innocent bystanders is in general more like the threat that drivers pose to innocent people than the threat posed by unjust combatants. The probability that a just combatant will kill an innocent bystander is in general considerably lower than the probability that an unjust combatant will kill a just combatant or other innocent person, in part because the action of unjust combatants is *guided* by the intention to kill just combatants, while just combatants generally strive *not* to kill innocent bystanders, just as drivers take constant care to avoid harming pedestrians and other drivers.

Yet these considerations, if plausible, might show only that just combatants are not liable to attack at all times in war, not that they are never liable. It might be that just combatants, like drivers, become liable to defensive attack whenever the probability that their action will harm innocent people passes a certain threshold, which might be quite often. For clearly, just combatants seriously threaten innocent civilians far more often than ordinary drivers seriously threaten pedestrians or other drivers. In principle, unjust combatants might also be liable only when the threat they pose passes a threshold of seriousness, so that they might not be liable to attack while asleep, or when stationed at bases remote from the fighting. If so, we would still have a version of the moral equality of combatants: one that treats just and unjust combatants as liable to attack, though only when the threat they pose to innocent people passes a certain threshold of seriousness.

I have conceded that just combatants can become liable to attack when they pose a wrongful threat to innocent civilians in the first of the two senses distinguished above—that is, when they threaten innocent civilians with wrongful harm via action that is itself objectively wrong or unjustified. They could be liable either for attacking innocent civilians intentionally in the absence of a lesser-evil justification or for inflicting unnecessary or disproportionate harm on innocent civilians as a foreseeable side effect of action intended to destroy military targets. But what about when they pose a wrongful threat to civilians only in the second sense—that is, when they threaten civilians with harm to which they are not liable but via action that is objectively *justified*?

One might suppose that even if just combatants are liable to attack when their justified action threatens innocent civilians, it is nevertheless not permissible to attack or kill them to prevent them from acting, for such defensive action would necessarily be disproportionate in the wide sense. The reason it would be disproportionate is that it is stipulated that the action of the just combatants is justified, which presupposes that their action is itself proportionate—that is, that the goal of their action outweighs the expected harm to the civilians. That being the case, and given that preventing the harm to the civilians involves preventing the success of their mission, it follows that action to defend the civilians would prevent a lesser evil at the cost of thwarting the prevention of a greater evil.

This reasoning, however, involves a subtle mistake.[3] It may help to reveal the nature of the mistake to consider a similar mistake that might be made about proportionality in individual self-defense. Consider the following example involving self-defense, which I should say explicitly is not meant to be analogous to a case in which the justified action of just combatants threatens innocent civilians, but only to illustrate a point about wide proportionality. Suppose that my life is wrongfully threatened by a malicious and culpable aggressor and that I can save myself only by killing him. Most of us believe that I would be justified in killing him in self-defense. But suppose that I know that the attacker is a surgical virtuoso who is scheduled over the next few days to perform five life-saving operations that no one else is capable of performing. Thus, if I kill him, five innocent people will die whom he would otherwise have saved. It does not seem, however, that this consideration makes my killing him in self-defense disproportionate in the wide sense and therefore impermissible. Although my killing him in self-defense will result in the deaths of five innocent people rather than only one, there are other factors at work in this case that affect the way the various deaths count in the wide proportionality calculation—for example, that I would not be killing the five but only preventing them from being saved, that I have a right not to be killed while they have no right to be saved if my being killed is a condition of their being saved, that I am not required to sacrifice my life in order that they can be saved, and so on. I will not try to identify all the relevant factors or how they operate, but it seems clear that the way in which bad effects weigh in the wide proportionality calculation is sensitive to matters of causation, agency, rights, and so on. And it seems that similar considerations are operative in the case in which just combatants threaten innocent civilians as a side effect. The civilians seem to be permitted to defend themselves against the just combatants even if that will prevent the just combatants from themselves preventing even greater harms to others (through the contribution they would otherwise have made to the success of their just cause). Even if the harm suffered by innocent people will be greater if the civilians act in self-defense, that does not seem to make their defensive action disproportionate in the wide sense.

But even if self-defense by the civilians against the just combatants could be proportionate in the wide sense, it would nevertheless be indiscriminate, in that the just combatants are not in fact liable to attack, even in self-defense by innocent people. This is because the action that makes them responsible for the threat to innocent people is morally justified.

This is an essential qualification of the claim that responsibility for a wrongful threat is the criterion of liability to defensive attack—namely, that the claim is limited to wrongful threats in the first of the two senses distinguished at the beginning of this section: threats of harm to which the victim is not liable, via action that is objectively unjustified. When action that would wrong someone or infringe someone's rights is nevertheless morally justified, the agent is exempt from liability to defensive action.

It is important to be clear about what I mean by "justified." Two points of clarification are necessary. First, I distinguish justification from permission. An act is morally permitted when, in the circumstances, it is not wrong to do it (even if it is of a *type* that is generally wrong). Justification, as I understand it, is a species of permission. A morally justified act is one that is not only permissible but that there is also positive moral reason to do. (If there is positive moral reason to do act a_1 but stronger moral reason to do a_2, a_1 may not be justified. But that will be true only if it is not permitted—that is, if the stronger reason to do a_2 makes a_2 morally required.) Not all acts that are permitted are justified, for there are indefinitely many acts that are not wrong that there is nevertheless no moral reason to do. Among justified acts, if the moral reasons to do an act are strong enough and are either unopposed by or override any countervailing moral reasons not to do it, the act may be morally required. But not all acts that are justified are required.

The second point of clarification is that justification provides exemption from liability only when it is *objective*. Both permission and justification can be either objective or subjective. An act is objectively permissible or justifiable when what explains its permissibility or justifiability are facts that are independent of the agent's beliefs. By contrast, an act is subjectively permissible or justified when two conditions are satisfied: first, the agent acts on the basis of beliefs, or perhaps reasonable or justified beliefs, that are false, and, second, the act *would* be objectively permissible or justified if those beliefs were true. So, for a person to be exempt from liability for posing a threat of wrongful harm to an innocent person, it is not sufficient that the person should believe, or even be justified in believing, that his act is justified; it is necessary that it be objectively justified. (Whether it is sufficient that the act be objectively justified is a separate question on which I will not take a stand. It is possible that a person could be objectively justified in posing a threat of wrongful harm to another while believing, perhaps even reasonably, that his act is wrong. It is arguable that his beliefs could make a difference to his liability, and in particular that his culpability in acting in a way that he believes is wrong could make him liable even though there is objective justification for his act. On this latter view, a person might be exempt from liability for posing a wrongful threat only when his act is justified both objectively and subjectively.)

This is the most important difference, where liability is concerned, between just combatants and ordinary drivers. Although the threat posed by ordinary drivers is normally so low that no defensive action against them could be proportionate, they can become liable to defensive action when the threat they pose passes a certain threshold of probability. This is because driving is normally merely permitted rather than justified—that is, driving is not normally an activity that people engage in for positive moral reasons. The threat posed by just combatants is often well beyond the threshold at which drivers may become liable, yet they may not be liable to defensive attack even when it becomes *certain* that their action will otherwise kill innocent civilians. For just combatants often act with moral justification when they threaten the lives of innocent civilians as a side effect, and that justification shields them from liability.

The idea that liability is defeasible by justification is familiar in the law. In criminal law, liability is always defeasible by a justification, and usually even by an excuse. A claim of necessity, or lesser evil, for example, can nullify criminal liability for harming the innocent. The only strict liability in criminal law is liability that is not defeasible by an excuse. In tort law, liability is never defeasible by an excuse. But the standard form of liability in torts, fault liability, is defeasible by a justification. Strict liability in tort law is liability that is defeasible neither by excuse nor by justification.[4] Strict liability in torts is, therefore, the only kind of liability in either criminal or tort law that is not defeasible by a justification, and it governs only a very limited area of the law of torts.

The notion of justification in the law is, of course, slightly different from my understanding of moral justification. And the conditions in which liability to defensive action is defeasible may be different from those in which liability to punitive action or liability to pay compensation is defeasible. But in both cases the connections are close enough to establish a presumption that what holds of justification and liability in the law should also hold of justification and liability in defense.

To say that just combatants are not liable to attack when their action is justified is not, however, to say that they are morally immune from attack. For there could be justifications for attacking them that are compatible with their not being liable to attack. One might, for example, argue that when their action threatens innocent civilians, killing them might be justified as the lesser evil. Yet this possibility is ruled out by the considerations that I earlier contended are *not* sufficient to show that self-defense by the civilians is disproportionate in the wide sense. Because the action by the just combatants is, by hypothesis, justified, it must be proportionate in the wide sense, which means its good effects outweigh the harm to the civilians. Killing the just combatants, thereby thwarting their mission, therefore cannot be the lesser evil. If, moreover, it is right that the combatants are not themselves liable to attack, any harms they would suffer from defensive action against them must count in the wide proportionality calculation, thereby making it in a sense overdetermined that defensive action against them cannot be the lesser evil. For the relevant bad effects of attacking them now include not only the failure of their just mission, which alone outweighs the saving the innocent civilians, but also all the harms they suffer. So, if their justification exempts them from liability, defensive action against them is not only indiscriminate but also disproportionate in the wide sense, so that the prohibition against attacking them on grounds of discrimination cannot be overridden by an appeal to the lesser evil.

It is perhaps worth noting that even if just combatants are not liable to attack when they act with justification, and even if there cannot be a lesser-evil justification for attacking them in the kind of case we have been discussing, there might be a lesser-evil justification for attacking them in different circumstances. Recall, for example, the type of case I mentioned in Section 1.3 in which a country A that lacks a just cause for war against country C nevertheless has a lesser-evil justification for going to war against C as a means of defending itself from aggression by B. In this case, C's combatants are just combatants who are justified in attacking A's combatants, who are unjust combatants but nevertheless act with a lesser-evil justification. Combatants on both sides act with different forms of justification in attacking one another. There is, therefore, a kind of moral equality between them. This does not, however, support the *doctrine* of the moral equality of combatants. For cases of this kind, in which just combatants are pitted against unjust combatants whose action is unjust but nevertheless morally justified, occur only rarely, if ever. But the doctrine of the moral equality of combatants is universal in scope.

The possibility of this kind of case does show, however, that it is possible to fight permissibly in the absence of a just cause, even when the just combatants against whom one is fighting have done nothing to make themselves liable to attack. Because of this, I will use the term "unjust combatant" to refer only to those who fight without a just cause and also without a lesser-evil justification. We might refer to those who fight without a just cause but with a lesser-evil justification as "justified combatants."

Return now to the case in which just combatants threaten innocent civilians as a side effect of a morally justified act of war. Even if the just combatants are not liable to attack, and even if attacking them cannot be justified as the lesser evil, it still seems that the civilians whom they will otherwise kill are morally permitted to defend themselves if that is possible. While there are cases in which an act with harmful side effects is so important morally that the innocent victims are morally required to suffer the harms rather than interfere with the action, most cases involving "collateral damage" in war do not seem to be of this sort. Intuitively, it seems that innocent civilians threatened by the action of just combatants are not morally required to submit passively to being killed but are permitted to engage in self-defense.

That innocent people seem to have a right of self-defense if they would be wronged as a foreseeable but unintended effect of morally justified action is a problem that is obscured by the claim of Locke and many others that there can be no justified defense against a justified threat. This claim focuses our attention on the cases in which it seems obviously true—namely, those in which the reason the threat is justified is that the potential victims are all liable to suffer the threatened harm. But it may not be true when the threatening action is instead justified by different considerations and will wrong or infringe the rights of at least some of the victims, such as those who will be injured or killed as a proportionate side effect of the action.

It is, however, difficult to explain how the innocent potential victims of morally justified action could be permitted to engage in harmful defensive action against agents whose moral justification both exempts them from liability and guarantees that their action is the lesser evil, impartially considered. Most contemporary theories of self-defense, both in morality and law, rule out the possibility that both parties to a conflict could act permissibly in attacking the other. The contemporary theory that is perhaps most prominent holds that self-defense is justified when one party will otherwise violate the other's right.[5] Suppose, for example, that unless he is prevented from doing so, A will violate B's right not to be killed. In these conditions, A cannot himself have a right not to be prevented, by necessary and proportionate means, from violating B's right. That is why, on this account, it is permissible for B, or indeed any third party, to take necessary and proportionate defensive action against A. But this account treats A and B quite asymmetrically. If A will otherwise violate B's right, he loses his own right not to be attacked; thus, if B attacks him in self-defense, B does not violate any right of A's; therefore B retains his right not to be attacked; therefore A is not permitted to attack B in self-defense. On this theory, if one party to a conflict is justified, the opposing party cannot be. The same is true on the other major theories of self-defense.[6]

So how is it possible that innocent civilians could be permitted to defend themselves from just combatants who do not intend to harm them but whose justified action will nevertheless harm them as a side effect? One suggestion is that just combatants are morally required to accept the costs of their own action, if possible, rather than impose them on innocent civilians. If, for example, they could deflect the harmful side effects of their mission away from the civilians, though only by directing them toward themselves, they would be required to do so. This suggests that the civilians are permitted to impose the costs of the combatants' action on them rather than being required to suffer them themselves. Yet the problem with this suggestion is that it applies only when defensive action against just combatants would not defeat their mission. Suppose that just combatants are justified in destroying a storage facility for chemical weapons, but that the destruction of the facility foreseeably creates a cloud of toxic gas that will soon engulf an area inhabited by innocent civilians. If the civilians could somehow blow the cloud of gas away, they would be permitted to do that, even if their only option was to blow it over the just combatants, who would then be killed by it. This example is, of course, contrived, and there is a reason for that, which is that in actual cases the only way civilians can protect themselves from the side effects of military action is preemptively, by killing the threatening combatants before they can act (and, of course, they can very rarely do even that). But that would prevent the combatants from achieving their justified mission, and that is *not* something the civilians are permitted to do on the basis of the reasoning given above. For it is a corollary of their mission's being justified that just combatants are not required to sacrifice *it* in order to avoid harming the civilians.[7]

Another possibility is that innocent people are permitted to defend their *rights* not only against unjustified violation but even against justified infringement.[8] Innocent civilians have a right not to be killed. Just combatants who threaten to kill innocent civilians as a side effect of military action will infringe those civilians' rights even if their action is morally justified, or even morally required. Unless what is at stake is so important that the civilians are morally required to sacrifice themselves for the sake of the just combatants' mission, they are entitled to protect their rights against infringement. They are, in other words, permitted to take necessary and proportionate defensive action against the just combatants. Because the just combatants act with objective justification, they are exempt from liability to defensive action. They do not forfeit their right not to be attacked; therefore defensive action by the civilians threatens *their* rights with infringement. Thus they are permitted to take defensive action against the civilians for the same reason that the civilians are permitted to take action against them—though they also have an additional justification for attacking the civilians preemptively if the civilians threaten to attack them, which is that they are justified in preserving their ability to carry out their mission. There is, then, on this view, a rough moral parity between the just combatants and the innocent civilians: each is morally permitted to attack the other.

There are, however, various objections to this way of understanding the conflict between just combatants acting with justification and innocent civilians threatened with harm as a side effect of that action. One is that if the just combatants are not liable to attack, it is unclear what picks them out as legitimate targets of attack when the innocent civilians are attempting to protect their rights. It is true, of course, though only contingently, that attacking them is the only, or at least the most effective, means of protection, and that certainly picks them out in a relevant way. But suppose that were not true. Suppose that for some bizarre reason attacking innocent civilians from a neutral country would be just as effective in preventing the action of the just combatants as killing the combatants themselves would be. If neither the combatants nor the neutral civilians are liable, and if both are morally innocent, why is attacking the combatants permissible while attacking the civilians is not?

There is an answer to this challenge, and it is probably adequate. The permission extends only to acts against rights-infringers, and only the just combatants will infringe the civilians' rights. Innocent bystanders, such as neutral civilians, do not threaten the civilians' rights in any way. (I will argue later, in Chapter 4, that it is also true of those who pose a threat for which they are in no way morally responsible that they threaten only their potential victims' interests and not their rights, so that there can be no rights-based justification for attacking them in self-defense.)

A further objection to the proposed explanation of the permissibility of self-defense by innocent civilians is that it supports the moral equality of combatants only if the permission that the civilians are supposed to have to engage in defensive action extends to third parties as well. For the most important issue here is not whether the civilians are permitted to defend themselves but whether unjust combatants are permitted to defend them. If it is indeed permissible for the civilians to defend themselves, it is possible that their permission is essentially agent-relative, in that it applies only to them. If neither they nor the just combatants are liable to attack and if all are equally morally innocent, so that justice is silent with respect to their conflict, it is not implausible to suppose that third parties must not intervene. For if third parties were to intervene on one side or the other, their action would involve the intentional killing of innocent people, and for that there must be a strong, positive justification. To the extent that there are impartial considerations that favor intervention, they support intervention on behalf of the just combatants rather than on behalf of the civilians. For the action of the just combatants contributes to the achievement of a just cause, whereas the action of the civilians is merely self-preservative.

Yet there are special, agent-relative reasons for intervention by unjust combatants on behalf of the civilians. First, the civilians are their fellow citizens, and citizenship in the same state is arguably a special relation that grounds special duties of rescue. Second, and more important, the unjust combatants have professional and contractual duties to protect their own civilian population. That is the ultimate aim of their profession, and the aim that best justifies (if anything does) their being in the military and training in the arts of war. Yet there is another point here that must not be overlooked, which is that in going to war in this instance, they have been worse than derelict in their duty to protect their people. Their war is, by hypothesis, unjust; it is therefore not a response to a threat of wrongful harm to their civilian population. Indeed, the likelihood is that their civilians did not face any external unjust threat at all until the war began. The threat that some of them face now is a result of the justified response by the just combatants to the earlier unjustified action of the unjust combatants. So the unjust combatants themselves bear significant responsibility for the threat their civilians face—certainly they are responsible to a greater degree than the just combatants are.

In one important respect, the unjust combatants' ultimate responsibility for the threat their civilians face strengthens the case for the permissibility of their intervening against the just combatants in defense of the civilians. For their being responsible, possibly culpably, for the threat gives them a special reason to avert it. In the absence of countervailing considerations, they would be not merely permitted but required to protect the civilians from a threat for which they bear primary responsibility. Yet there are, of course, countervailing considerations. One is that the just combatants are morally innocent, are acting with moral justification, and hence are not liable to attack. In general, it is impermissible to kill morally innocent people as a means of saving other innocent people, unless the ratio of those saved to those killed is very high. And this is very unlikely to be the case when just combatants are justified in posing a threat to innocent civilians, since it is unlikely that their action would be proportionate if the number of civilians they threatened were large.

Another countervailing consideration is, as I have repeatedly noted, that successful action in defense of the civilians would thwart the just combatants' mission and thus impede their efforts to achieve their just cause. To the extent that this action would kill just combatants and preserve the lives of unjust combatants, it would also, from an impartial point of view, adversely affect the relative strengths of the two sides, thereby diminishing the effectiveness of the just side's future efforts to achieve its just cause.

In summary, I have suggested that in situations of conflict in which neither party is liable and both are morally innocent, there are general reasons to suppose that third-party intervention on behalf of *either* side is impermissible. Yet there do seem to be reasons deriving both from special relations and from the unjust combatants' responsibility for the civilians' peril that favor intervention by unjust combatants on behalf of the civilians, as well as countervailing reasons of a more impartial nature that oppose that intervention. If there is uncertainty about how to resolve the conflict among these competing reasons, there is a final consideration that should be decisive. This is that continued military action by the unjust combatants is, at least in most cases, not their best means of ensuring the safety of the civilian population as a whole. Their best means of protecting their civilians is whatever will effectively bring an early end to the war. Acting to defend *some* innocent civilians on one occasion after another is counterproductive if the larger effect is to prolong the war indefinitely, providing continuing justification for attacks by just combatants and thereby sustaining the threat these attacks pose to members of the civilian population who have so far survived. Both moral and prudential considerations converge on one solution. The only way that unjust combatants can refrain from further killing of innocent people, and the best way that they can promote the physical security of their civilian population, is to stop their unjust war—that is, to surrender.

The problem, however, is that this is something they can accomplish only by acting collectively. No individual unjust combatant can stop the war on his own. Assuming, realistically, that other unjust combatants are going to continue to fight whatever he may do, what ought an individual unjust combatant to do? He clearly has an obligation, deriving from a variety of sources, to do whatever he permissibly can to protect innocent civilians on his side. If he could enhance their security by sacrificing himself, he might well be morally required to do that. He, after all, is not innocent. The question is whether he can permissibly sacrifice other innocent people to help save innocent civilians now, when doing so contributes to the perpetuation of a conflict that will continue to endanger other innocent civilians. I think he is more likely to serve the legitimate interests of his civilian population by refusing to continue to fight, or by sabotaging his own side's military efforts, or even by defecting to the just side. Taking into account both his obligations to his own people and the moral requirement that he not intentionally kill innocent people, what he ought to do as an individual is to work for the early defeat of his own side.

2.2 CONSENT

2.2.1 The Boxing Match Model of War

One factor that can have a role in the justification for killing a person is the consent of the person killed. Many people, for example, believe that a person's rational consent is necessary to the permissibility of euthanasia. They believe that even if it would be objectively better for a person, for her own sake, to die than to continue to live, it would nevertheless be wrong to kill that person for her own good without her free and informed consent. But they accept that if it would be better for a person if she were to die, if her death would not be so bad for others that she ought to endure her life for their sake, and if she autonomously requests or consents to be killed, then it can be morally permissible to kill her.

No one, of course, suggests that killing enemy combatants is a form of euthanasia. But it has been argued that what makes *all* combatants legitimate targets for their military adversaries, independently of whether they have a just cause, is that in one way or another they consent to be targets in exchange for the privilege of making other combatants their own targets.

There are certain conceptions of the nature of war that support the idea that the role of the combatant carries with it an implicit acceptance of the view that any combatant is a legitimate target of attack by his or her adversaries. Two such conceptions are adumbrated by Walzer when he writes that "the moral reality of war can be summed up in this way: when combatants fight freely, choosing one another as enemies and designing their own battles, their war is not a crime; when they fight without freedom, their war is not their crime. In both cases, military conduct is governed by rules; but in the first the rules rest on mutuality and consent, in the second on a shared servitude."⁹ If either of these conceptions of war is correct, it supports the moral equality of combatants in those wars that fit the description it gives. If each accurately describes certain wars and the two together are exhaustive of wars as they are actually fought, this vindicates the moral equality of combatants as a universal principle.

According to the first of Walzer's suggestions, war is analogous to a boxing match or a duel. Just as it is part of the profession of boxing to consent to be hit by one's opponents, so it is part of the profession of arms to consent to be attacked by one's adversaries. The idea that combatants consent to be attacked must not, however, be confused with the idea that they agree to accept the *risk* of being attacked. When soldiers go to war, they undoubtedly assume a certain risk. They voluntarily expose themselves to a significant risk of being attacked. But this is entirely different from consenting to be attacked. Consider this analogy. A person who voluntarily walks through a dangerous neighborhood late at night assumes or accepts a risk of being mugged; but he does not consent to be mugged in the sense of waiving his right not to be mugged, or giving people permission to mug him. Similarly, those who become police officers consent to accept a risk of being killed by criminals, but they do not give criminals their consent to kill them. But the claim about combatants is not just that they agree to accept the risk of being attacked or killed. It is that they also waive their right not to be killed, or, more precisely, that they grant enemy combatants the right to kill them.

This may initially seem an odd claim but it has been ably defended by Thomas Hurka, who argues that "by voluntarily entering military service, soldiers on both sides freely took on the status of soldiers and thereby freely accepted that they may permissibly be killed in the course of war."¹⁰ In one sense, Hurka's suggestion is that the doctrine of the moral equality of combatants is made true by our acceptance of it. He notes that "the common conception of military status has the moral equality of soldiers built in as a component."[11] So when people assume military status by joining the military, they consent to have the elements of that status, which includes being a legitimate target for enemy combatants in a time of war, since moral equality with other combatants is among the elements of military status.

Yet Hurka thinks that it is not arbitrary that the moral equality of combatants is inherent in our conception of the status of a combatant. He observes that governments demand that their soldiers commit themselves to fight in any war they may be ordered to participate in. But if in voluntarily joining the military, soldiers are agreeing to fight in any war, just or unjust, they must be accepting a neutral conception of their role, according to which they are permitted to kill their adversaries, irrespective of whether the latter are just or unjust combatants. And elementary consistency requires that they recognize that all other combatants are in the same situation and have the same privilege. They concede, in other words, that their adversaries are permitted to kill them whether they happen, on any particular occasion, to be just or unjust combatants.

It is, however, reasonable to assume that combatants consent to be attacked only if they really do accept that the moral equality of combatants is inherent in the military status they choose to adopt. This is a contingent, empirical matter. While many who enlist do understand themselves as thereby accepting the moral equality of combatants and waiving their rights against attack, not all do. Among those who do not regard enlistment as committing them to fight in any war in which they might be ordered to participate, the most important for our purposes are those who enlist only when their country has already been unjustly attacked, not intending to become professional soldiers but to fight only in this one just war. These combatants are very like a man who is suddenly compelled to defend himself against an unjust attacker. Such a man has no reason to waive his right not to be killed and there is no reason to suppose that he does so. Imagine the situation of one of the numerous young Polish men in 1939 who, on learning that the Nazis had invaded their country, rushed to enlist. It seems absurd to suppose that by enlisting they understood themselves to be waiving their right not to be killed, or to be granting the Nazis permission to kill them.

It is more realistic to suppose that most of them shared the view of Prince Andrei in *War and Peace*, expressed in a passionate and angry outburst on the eve of the battle of Borodino, as Napoleon's army advanced toward Moscow:

"One thing I would do if I had power," he began again, "I would not take prisoners. What are prisoners? It's chivalry. The French devastated my home and are on their way to devastate Moscow, and they've offended me and offend me every second. They're my enemies, they're all criminals, to my mind. And Timokhin and the whole army think the same. They must be executed!" . . . "We're told about the rules of war, about chivalry, about parleying, sparing the unfortunate, and so on. It's all nonsense. . . . They loot other people's houses, spread false banknotes, and worse of all—kill my children and my father, and then talk about the rules of war and magnanimity towards the enemy. Take no prisoners, but kill and go to your death! . . ."[12]

But suppose, on the contrary, that Prince Andrei, Timokhin and the whole Russian army, and indeed all combatants everywhere accepted the moral equality of combatants and therefore that their enemies were permitted to kill them. It would not follow that any of them gave their consent to be killed, or waived their right not to be killed. Accepting that others are permitted to kill you is not the same as granting them permission to kill you. For you might believe that they are permitted to kill you for some reason other than that you have waived your right against them.

It is conceivable, though of course not true, that all soldiers accept the moral equality of combatants simply because it is the traditional view that has been transmitted unquestioningly through the generations. That could be compatible with the doctrine's being utterly mistaken, as are so many doctrines passed from one generation to another. This process of repeated transmission and universal acceptance could occur without any soldier's even imagining that he had waived his right not to be killed by the enemy.

There is, however, a further and quite plausible reason to suppose that soldiers in fact waive their right not to be killed. Combatant status has conventional and legal dimensions, the most important of which is the requirement that combatants openly identify themselves as such, usually through the wearing of a uniform. When a soldier puts on the uniform, he is consciously identifying himself as a legitimate target. Wearing the uniform certainly makes him a conspicuous target and is therefore in an important sense highly imprudent, so he must have an important reason for doing it. One reason is, of course, to avoid being mistakenly attacked by other combatants on his own side. But the most important reason is that the uniform enables enemy combatants to discriminate between combatants and noncombatants, taking only the former as their targets. In other words, the uniform functions as a marker of a legitimate target of attack. But to identify oneself conspicuously as a legitimate target of attack just *is* to consent to be attacked.

This interpretation of the significance of uniforms conflates consenting to be attacked with upholding a convention. A Polish man who enlisted in 1939 might plausibly have reasoned in the following way. "There is a convention that combatants should attack only other combatants, who are identified as such by their uniform. It is crucial to uphold this convention because it limits the killing that occurs on both sides in war. I will therefore wear the uniform to signal that I am someone the convention identifies as a legitimate target. In doing this I am not consenting to be attacked or giving the Nazis permission to attack me; rather, I am attempting to draw their fire toward myself and away from others, in much the way a parent might attempt to draw the attention of a predatory animal toward herself and away from her child, whom she hopes thereby to enable to escape—though of course in this case the drawing of attention is mediated by convention."

One way to see that this reasoning is correct is to suppose that wearing the uniform was universally recognized as signifying the giving of consent. And suppose that the Polish patriot refuses, on principle, to consent to be attacked by the Nazis. The Nazi invasion is unjust and one cannot, he thinks, consent to any of the evil that is done in the course of it. But if wearing the uniform involves consenting to be unjustly attacked and not fighting is tantamount to capitulation, his only honorable option seems to be to fight without wearing the uniform, and hence perhaps without joining the army. If he and others were to adopt this option, it seems intuitively obvious that their private defensive action would not violate the *moral* rights of the Nazis. Their action might be morally objectionable, or morally wrong, but only because it would make it impossible for the Nazis to distinguish between combatants and noncombatants and thus provoke them to engage in indiscriminate killing and offer them a rationale for calculated reprisals against civilians. But assuming that the consent of the Polish fighters is what would justify the Nazis in attacking them, it seems that in this case the Nazis would have no moral right to kill them, even in self-defense. Hence those who fight in defense against unjust aggression could falsify the consent-based argument for the moral equality of combatants simply by refusing to wear a uniform.

This shows that wearing the uniform does not and cannot reasonably function as a signal of consent to be attacked. The uniform instead has a different function: to signal that the wearer poses a threat and is a *conventionally* legitimate target. On this interpretation, just combatants who wear uniforms are analogous to a person who volunteers to be a substitute hostage to terrorists. It has occasionally happened that people holding hostages as a means of coercing compliance with their demands have agreed to exchange particularly vulnerable hostages, such as children and people who are critically ill or injured, for others who have volunteered to take their place. A person who becomes a hostage in this way *allows* himself to be taken hostage but does not *consent* to be held hostage in the way that involves waiving his moral right not to be a hostage. If he could escape by killing his captors, he would be morally justified in doing so, and his justification would be that they had made themselves liable to be killed. They cannot claim that they have a moral right not to be killed by him because he has consented to be their hostage.

Suppose that I am wrong and that when people adopt combatant status they do, in effect, waive their right not to be killed by enemy combatants. Even if this is correct, the consent that just combatants give does not make it permissible for unjust combatants to attack or kill them, and thus does not vindicate the moral equality of combatants. Consent to be killed is not sufficient on its own to make killing permissible. In cases in which a person is not liable to be killed, and killing that person is not justified as the lesser evil, consent seems to be a necessary but not sufficient condition of the permissibility of killing. It contributes to the justification for killing but only in the presence of another good reason for killing, such as that the person's life has ceased to be worth living.

Imagine that during an era in the past when duels of honor were legal, a villain who has already wronged a man decides to try to harm him further. He thus makes various public accusations, falsely alleging that the wronged man has committed certain crimes, and then challenges the man to a duel, supposedly to vindicate his own honor. Suppose that a refusal to fight would be interpreted as an admission of guilt, so the wronged man consents to fight the duel, presents himself as a target for the villain, but, as in so many of the duels fought in novels, refuses to fire his own weapon. In this instance, however, the villain is not overcome with remorse and does not unaccountably miss, but kills the man. The man's having consented to fight the duel may make this killing in some respects relevantly different from ordinary murder, but it does not make the killing permissible, much less justified.

The form of war that is perhaps closest to a boxing match is one fought entirely by mercenaries on both sides, neither of which has a just cause. It could be argued that when war is in this way fully voluntary, when all the combatants participate for purely private reasons and could opt out at any point, and when no one on either side would be threatened by anyone on the other if they did not all go out willingly to fight, they can all be reasonably interpreted as having consented to be attacked, in the way that a boxer consents to be hit, so that none would be wronged by being killed by another. Yet intuitively it seems clear that these conditions are not sufficient to make the killings of mercenaries by other mercenaries morally permissible. They are instead like the murders of armed gang members by members of a rival gang. There may well be a kind of moral equality among mercenaries who fight without just cause, but it is not the equality of justification asserted by the doctrine of the moral equality of combatants.

Suppose that thus far in this section I have been thoroughly wrong and that it is true both that just combatants consent to be killed and that this means that unjust combatants who kill them neither wrong them nor violate their rights. It still does not follow that unjust combatants act permissibly when they kill just combatants. That acts of war by unjust combatants kill or injure just combatants is not the only reason they are morally objectionable. These acts are also instrumental to the achievement of an unjust cause and thus wrongfully threaten people other than the just combatants who are the immediate targets of attack. Furthermore, as I noted earlier, acts of war frequently kill or injure innocent civilians as a side effect, and no one claims that the victims of these harms have consented to them. Nor can these harms be justified on the ground that they are necessary for the prevention of even greater harms, as one might claim of harms inflicted as a side effect of action by just combatants. So even if we assume that all combatants consent to be killed and that their consent means that no wrong is done to them when they are killed, there is still no equality of moral status between just and unjust combatants, since the military action of unjust combatants supports an unjust cause and threatens innocent bystanders with harm that is not outweighed by good effects that their action might be expected to achieve.

2.2.2 The Gladiatorial Combat Model of War

The quotation from Walzer that I cited at the beginning of Section 2.2.1 suggests a second way in which combatants might be understood to consent to be attacked by their adversaries. The idea that war involves a "shared servitude" by combatants on both sides suggests that at least some wars are analogous to gladiatorial combat, in which the warriors on both sides are coerced to fight. In most instances of gladiatorial combat—a form of entertainment that amused the Romans for eight centuries without provoking any significant moral challenge from philosophers or others—both contestants were coerced to fight by a threat of immediate execution if they refused. But if both fought, the winner would be spared. If he subsequently achieved further victories, he might eventually win his freedom. In most cases, therefore, it was in the interest of each for both to fight. For each could see, in advance, that the prospect of one surviving would be better for each than a prospect of neither surviving. It was therefore rational ex ante for each to consent to be attacked by the other in exchange for the right of attack, and it is not implausible to suppose that both victims were often aware of this, so that there was indeed an implicit agreement between them. While one of them might have chosen to sacrifice himself for the other by allowing the other to slay him, that could not coherently have been morally required of both and thus was supererogatory. It seems, therefore, that each was permitted to try to kill the other and that the vanquished was wronged not by the victor but only by those who compelled them both to fight.

I have followed Walzer in presenting the justification for killing in cases with the structure of gladiatorial combat as based on a form of ex ante consent. But there is an alternative interpretation, which is that the justification in these cases is actually a lesser-evil justification. While it would not, of course, be the lesser evil for both gladiators to hack each other to death, it was the lesser evil for both to *try* to kill the other, given that it was likely that only one would succeed and that they would both be killed if neither tried. One might, then, construct a parallel argument for the moral equality of combatants that appeals, not to consent, but to the idea of the lesser evil. There is, of course, an obvious reason why defenders of the moral equality of combatants have hitherto not sought justification in the idea of the lesser evil. For when one thinks of war as a conflict between two "sides," one sees immediately that it cannot be that each side's war is justified as the lesser evil, impartially considered. If victory by one side would be the lesser evil, it cannot be that victory by the other side would also be the lesser evil. But when one sees war as a conflict among large numbers of individuals, then one can see how, at least in cases of "shared servitude," it could be the lesser evil for combatants on both sides to fight.

Yet war is never relevantly like gladiatorial combat. The closest that modern warfare may come to gladiatorial combat is a war in which both sides deploy brutalized child soldiers to do their fighting for them. But while a government may order the execution of individual soldiers who refuse to fight, it cannot execute or even threaten to execute its entire army. Indeed, in countries such as our own, the penalties for refusal to fight are now quite mild and are probably preferable from a purely prudential point of view to the risks involved in fighting. It is therefore never the case that it is better for all combatants on both sides to fight than for none to fight, on the ground that more will survive if they all fight than if none does.

It is perhaps worth noting another obvious failure of analogy, which is that gladiators fought only for self-preservation and their action had few bad effects beyond what they did to each other. But, as I noted in criticizing the boxing match model, the acts of unjust combatants serve an unjust cause and are therefore wrong for reasons unconnected with the harms they inflict on just combatants.

Both of the suggestions in the passage quoted from Walzer at the beginning of Section 2.2.1 presuppose unrealistic conceptions of the nature of war: (1) that war is a conflict between armies whose members all freely choose to fight rather than being driven to fight by their commanders or their adversaries, and (2) that war is a conflict between armies whose members are all irresistibly compelled to fight by their own commanders. In all wars involving just and unjust combatants, many among the just combatants are compelled to fight, though only by the moral necessity of defending themselves and others against unjust aggression, while others may fight for a variety of reasons, including coercion by their commanders. But few fight "freely," as they might if war were genuinely optional. Among unjust combatants, many may fight under varying degrees of duress but there are always many who fight for other reasons, including profit, adventure, and commitment to the unjust cause. In no actual war do all consent; in no actual war are all mere slaves.

2.2.3 Hypothetical Consent

One might argue that even though soldiers do not in fact consent to be attacked by their adversaries, it would nevertheless be rational for them all to agree, in advance, to accept principles that would permit them all to fight rather than principles that forbid fighting in an unjust war and deny those who do a right of individual self-defense. For soldiers know that when they are ordered to fight, there is a chance that their cause will be unjust but that they will not know this or will fight in spite of their suspicions, as most soldiers do. They can thus see in advance that it is more a matter of luck than anything else whether they will be on the just or the unjust side in future conflicts; but whatever side they are on, they will want to be able to defend themselves, and to be justified in doing so. Hence they would consent ex ante to be governed by rules that permit combatants on both sides to fight.[13]

One response to this appeal to hypothetical consent merely repeats what I said in response to the claims about actual consent: that consent by opposing combatants cannot render acts of war by unjust combatants permissible when these acts are also instrumental to the achievement of an unjust cause. But perhaps the appeal to hypothetical consent at least mitigates the overall wrongness of participating in an unjust war by weakening the objection that acts of war by unjust combatants wrong the just combatants who are their targets. This might be correct if it really would be rational for all combatants to agree in advance to be governed by principles that would permit all to fight irrespective of whether their cause was just. Yet it seems that this would not in fact be rational, since potential combatants would have more reason to accept a principle that would require them to attempt to determine whether their cause would be just and to fight only if they could reasonably believe that it would be. If they were to accept that principle, there would be fewer unjust wars and fewer deaths among potential combatants. Each potential combatant would be less likely to be used as an instrument of injustice and less likely to die in the service of unjust ends.

2.3 THE EPISTEMIC ARGUMENT

The claim that is perhaps most frequently made in support of the permissibility of fighting in an unjust war is that soldiers must act in conditions of extreme epistemic limitation. When they are commanded to fight, they cannot reasonably be expected to have the factual knowledge necessary to evaluate the war as just or unjust. They know neither the historical background nor all of the countless recent events that have together led to the outbreak of war. Although they cannot be sure what their political leaders' motives and intentions are, they will be aware of various assertions their government has made, all of which of course support the government's claim that the war is just. While the soldiers are aware of their own factual ignorance and lack of expertise in evaluating either the morality or legality of war, they know that their political leaders have access both to a vast body of intelligence, much of which is classified, and to expert advisers who can assist them to interpret and deliberate wisely about all the information available to them. The soldiers have little opportunity to remedy their ignorance, but even if they had access to all the information they would need for a rational evaluation of the morality of the war, they would lack not only the leisure to examine and assimilate it but also the opportunity and perhaps even the competence to deliberate about it with sufficient care to be able to form a judgment in which they could be confident. In these conditions of limitation and uncertainty, most soldiers naturally tend to accept that their war is just. But if they have doubts, it seems reasonable that, aware of how restricted their own perspective is, they ought to defer to and be guided by the judgment of the political authorities. When they do this, they are acting exactly as they ought to in the circumstances.

I earlier distinguished between permissibility and justification, as well as between subjective and objective versions of both. If an unjust combatant is epistemically justified in believing that the war in which he fights is just, or if it is epistemically reasonable for him to defer to the judgment of the political authorities in his society, then he is not merely subjectively permitted to fight but is *subjectively justified* in fighting, even though his war is objectively unjust. Various writers in the just war tradition have taken subjective rather than objective justification to be what matters. Vitoria, for example, was a subjectivist about both permissibility and justification. He was, indeed, quite a radical subjectivist, in that he held that permissibility and impermissibility were not determined by a person's *reasonable* or *justified* beliefs, but by whatever beliefs the person sincerely held. Thus he claimed that it is impermissible to act in a way that is objectively justified if one happens to believe that the act is wrong. "If their conscience tells subjects that the war is unjust," he wrote, "*they must not go to war even if their conscience is wrong*."[14] And, more importantly for our purposes, he held that unjust combatants are justified in fighting if they believe their war is just: "Where there is provable ignorance either of fact or of law, the war may be just in itself for the side which has true justice on its side, and also just for the other side, because they wage war in good faith."[15]

Assume that all unjust combatants are subjectively justified in fighting. This assumption supports the moral equality of combatants only if those who are subjectively justified in attacking and killing people have the same moral status as those who are objectively justified in doing so. If it makes a difference to a combatant's moral status whether he is subjectively or objectively justified in killing his adversaries, then the epistemic argument for the moral equality of combatants fails.

It would be curious if this distinction had no relevance to status. To act with merely subjective justification is to act in a way that is objectively wrong. According to an objective account of justification, a person who acts with subjective justification is objectively unjustified but fully excused. It seems that this difference—between being objectively justified and being objectively excused—must affect a combatant's moral status—that is, his rights and liabilities. Consider liabilities first. I argued earlier that one cannot make oneself morally liable to attack, or forfeit one's right against attack, merely by engaging in necessary and proportionate self- or other-defense against an objectively unjustified threat for which the threatening person is morally responsible. (I will elaborate on and further defend this claim in Chapter 4.) Just combatants, therefore, do not make themselves liable to attack merely by engaging in defensive action against unjust combatants. But even if unjust combatants are subjectively justified in fighting, the threats they pose are objectively unjustified and they have freely chosen to pose these threats, knowing that there is a risk that they are unjustified. That, as I will argue in greater detail in Chapter 4, is a sufficient basis for liability to defensive attack. If this is right, just and unjust combatants differ in their liability to attack.

Next consider rights. It is common to distinguish between two types of right: liberty rights and claim rights. A liberty right is merely a permission. To say that a person has a right to do *x*, when what is meant is that she has a liberty right, is just to say that it is not wrong for her to do *x*. But a claim right is not a permission but a right against intervention. To say that a person has a claim right to do *x* is to say that no one else has a liberty right to prevent her from doing *x*.

(The usual assumption is that if a person has a claim right to do *x*, it is permissible for her to do *x*. But many theorists believe that there can be claim rights to act in a way that is impermissible, meaning that it is impermissible for others to prevent them from so acting. This is what is generally meant when it is claimed that there can be a "right to do wrong.")

The claim that unjust combatants are subjectively justified in fighting against and killing just combatants is at most an assertion of a liberty right. Epistemic error may ground a permission to act, but it cannot possibly ground a right against interference. By contrast, just combatants do have a claim right to fight by permissible means in support of their just cause. This is perhaps clearest when their just cause involves the defense of their innocent fellow citizens against wrongful attack. They seem morally indistinguishable from the police officer cited earlier, who certainly has a claim right to kill a murderer who will otherwise kill a number of innocent people. How, then, could it be permissible for others to attack and kill just combatants as a means of preventing them from defending innocent people from wrongful attack? The reigning theory of the just war of course says that this *is* permissible and that the reason it is permissible is that just combatants make themselves liable by posing a threat to others. But we have seen that that account of why unjust combatants are permitted to fight cannot be sustained. The epistemic argument now offers a different explanation. It holds that unjust combatants are permitted to attack just combatants, thereby preventing them from achieving their just cause, because in the circumstances it is epistemically justified for them to believe their action is permissible, and that reasonable belief *makes* their action permissible, at least according to the subjective conception of permissibility. But if it is permissible for unjust combatants to attack just combatants to prevent them from fighting to achieve their just cause, then it follows that just combatants cannot have a claim right to fight.

This objection to the view that just combatants have a claim right to attack and kill unjust combatants in pursuit of their just cause is mistaken. Indeed, it *has* to be mistaken if there is a category of claim rights at all. If the possibility of a person's being subjectively permitted to intervene to prevent an agent from doing *x* entailed that the agent could not have a claim right to do *x*, then there could be no claim rights. For an agent can be subjectively permitted to do anything, provided that it is possible for him to be epistemically justified in believing that he is permitted to do it. So a subjective permission to prevent an agent from doing x is compatible with the agent's having a claim right to do x. What having a claim right to do x excludes is only the objective permissibility of anyone's preventing the right-holder from doing x. And the epistemic argument offers no grounds for supposing that unjust combatants are objectively permitted to attack and kill just combatants.

No one—not even proponents of the orthodox theory of the just war—believes that unjust combatants have a claim right to attack and kill just combatants. If, therefore, I am right that just combatants have a claim right to attack and kill unjust combatants, it follows that just combatants and unjust combatants have different moral rights. If that is correct, the moral equality of combatants is false.

But suppose I am wrong in claiming that just combatants have a claim right to attack and kill unjust combatants. It will seem to many people that I cannot be right, since if I am it follows that unjust combatants have no right of self-defense against just combatants. Even people who are willing to concede that unjust combatants act impermissibly if they kill people as a means of achieving an unjust cause may balk at the claim that they also act impermissibly if they kill in defense of their own lives. But even if just combatants do not have a claim right to attack and kill unjust combatants, the moral equality of combatants still cannot be adequately defended by appeal to the epistemic argument. For the moral equality of combatants is supposed to hold among *all* combatants. But it is clearly false that every unjust combatant is epistemically justified in believing that the war in which he fights is just. In every unjust war there are bound to be some combatants who are capable of recognizing, and indeed who do recognize, that their war is unjust. And, as I will argue at length in Chapter 3, there are many more who believe that their war is just but are not epistemically justified in having that belief—that is, many more whose belief is unreasonable in the circumstances. These unjust combatants are not subjectively justified in fighting, nor even subjectively permitted to fight. Their moral status is therefore quite different from that of a just combatant.

The proponent of the moral equality of combatants might be willing to settle for a more modest version of the doctrine. Suppose that *most* unjust combatants are epistemically justified in believing that their war is just, for the reasons given above. If most unjust combatants act with subjective justification, then given that just combatants cannot distinguish between those who are subjectively justified and those who are not, it seems that just combatants must act on the presumption that any unjust combatants they attack are subjectively justified, since that is, ex hypothesi, what is most likely to be true of any given unjust combatant. In that case, combatants on both sides would in practice have to act on the assumption that their adversaries were acting with moral justification, and thus had a moral status equivalent to their own. On this view, the moral equality of combatants would be, strictly speaking, false; it would be false in principle. But we would all have to act as if it were true, and that may be all that many people have in mind when they register agreement with the doctrine.

Even this epistemic argument for a modest version of the moral equality of combatants fails. For it to work, it would have to be true in *every* unjust war that it is epistemically reasonable for most combatants to believe that their war is just. Only that way would most of them be subjectively justified in fighting, thus establishing a presumption that *each* acts with subjective justification in conditions in which it is impossible to determine, of any given unjust combatant, whether his beliefs are in fact epistemically justified. But there are some wars that are so obviously unjust that it is simply not possible that the majority of those who fight in them are justified in believing that they are just. A majority may, of course, *believe* that such a war is just, but that does not mean that they have epistemic *justification* for believing it. It may be, for example, that a majority of the Nazi soldiers who invaded Poland, or Czechoslovakia, or France, or any of the various other countries they invaded, believed that their campaigns of aggression and extermination were just, but it would be absurd to suppose that in most cases those beliefs were reasonable in the context. I will say much more about this in Chapter 3. For now, the example of the Nazi soldiers seems sufficient to show that there are wars that are so evidently unjust that the reasonable presumption is that the unjust combatants who fight in them act without either objective or subjective justification. In such wars, there is no pragmatic reason for all combatants to act as if each of their adversaries was justified. And this is sufficient to refute even the modest version of the moral equality of combatants.

Despite the failure of the epistemic argument for the moral equality of combatants, at least part of what it claims is true: namely, that some unjust combatants fight with subjective justification. This ought, it seems, to affect their moral status. I will explore the implications of this fact in Chapter 3.

2.4 INSTITUTIONS AS SOURCES OF JUSTIFICATION

2.4.1 The Duty to Defer to the Epistemic Authority of the Government

One of the weaknesses of the epistemic argument is that it asserts that the epistemic constraints within which unjust combatants must decide whether to fight offer only a subjective rather than an objective justification for their subsequent acts of war. But it may be that the conditions of epistemic limitation in which soldiers must make their decisions actually provide an objective justification for their fighting in an unjust war. I noted earlier that, given their inevitable ignorance about relevant matters of fact, their comparative lack of competence in understanding the morality of war, and their lack of opportunities for careful deliberation, it may be reasonable for them simply to defer to the judgment of their government. For members of the government have access to more of the relevant facts, can consult with advisers in any area in which expertise is necessary, and together have as much opportunity for reflection and deliberation as anyone could have. Particularly if the government is democratic and thus answerable to the public for the reasons for which it goes to war, it seems in general that governmental institutions are better situated to make epistemically reliable judgments about the morality of particular wars than individual soldiers are. In the long run, therefore, individual soldiers may do better morally if they adhere to a principle requiring deference to governmental authority than if they base their decisions about participation in war on their private judgment about the morality of particular wars. While there are no doubt some soldiers whose individual judgment is consistently more reliable than that of their government, it may nevertheless be true of soldiers *as a whole* that they will collectively do better morally if they *all* submit to the judgment of their government than if they follow a principle that permits those who are confident of their individual competence in the evaluation of war to follow their own judgment. If this is right, it may be that all soldiers, including those who end up as unjust combatants, are *objectively* justified in going to war when ordered to do so.

When gravely serious disputes arise between entire societies, and the issues are complex, the number of people involved enormous, and the potential consequences almost incalculable, there has to be a division of moral labor. It makes sense to assign the task of determining whether it is justifiable to resort to war—morally, legally, and prudentially justifiable—to people who are specially qualified for that task. And these people's efforts will be facilitated if they are conducted within institutional structures designed to enable them to carry out their function effectively. It is instructive to consider the analogy with legal institutions. Among the aims of these institutions are the determination of which criminal suspects are guilty and which are innocent, and the punishment of the guilty. Within the larger system, criminal courts are assigned the task of determining who is guilty and who is not. The procedures the courts must go through are specifically designed to yield judgments of the maximum epistemic reliability. Precisely because of the institutional design, it is rational to believe that the determinations of the court are more likely to be correct than the private judgments of individuals. But for the institution to fulfill its function, all those who work within it must fulfill their assigned institutional roles. For example, the proper functioning of the institution requires that defense lawyers make every effort to ensure the acquittal of their clients, even when they reasonably believe that their client is guilty. Their working vigorously for an acquittal of course runs the risk of securing the release of a guilty and dangerous person, but overall this is thought to be the best way to balance the risks of punishing the innocent and freeing the guilty. If a defense lawyer acts on the basis of her private judgment that her client is guilty, and thus deliberately does less than she could to secure an acquittal, she subverts the proper functioning of the institution and impedes rather than facilitates the goal of producing just outcomes.

The division of moral labor is necessary not only within the working of the court but also between the court and other institutions within the criminal justice system. It is the task of the court, not of the police or the jailer, to determine whether a person is guilty or innocent. If the court has reached a verdict of guilty, it is the jailer's task to keep the convicted person in jail. The moral purposes of legal institutions would be undermined if jailers were to release convicted prisoners they believed to be innocent, or if they were to collude with the police in imprisoning people who had been acquitted but whom they personally believed to be guilty.

There is, however, an important qualification to this argument, which is that in order for soldiers to be objectively justified in deferring to the authority of their government in resorting to war, there must be good reason for them to believe that the government, or the relevant governmental institutions, are actually fulfilling the task of scrupulously evaluating potential wars as just or unjust. When this is evidently not the case, the principle requiring deference to the greater epistemic competence of the government does not apply, and there is no basis for an objective justification for participation in an unjust war. Because of this limitation in scope, this argument cannot justify the moral equality of combatants. But if the argument is otherwise valid, it supports a view that is much closer to the common sense view than that which claims that all unjust combatants act impermissibly when they fight for their side's goals in an unjust war.

David Estlund, who has recently defended a version of this argument, rightly emphasizes this restriction to its scope. He argues that when commanded to go to war, a "soldier would be wrong to substitute his own private verdict and thwart the state's will," but he is careful to state that this is true only "when the political and institutional process producing the commands is duly looking after the question whether the war is just."[16] He argues for the strong claim that when this condition is met, "even though the victim is wronged by the unjustly warring side, the soldier on that side is nevertheless morally obligated (and so morally permitted) to follow all normally binding orders—those that would be binding at least if the war were just."[17] But when the condition is not met, there is neither obligation nor even permission. Thus the fact that Nazi "soldiers were following orders is not sanitizing on [Estlund's] account. It must be combined with an epistemically adequate source of the commands, and this [was] patently absent in Nazi Germany."[18]

Estlund goes on to argue, however, that the relevant condition is, or at least tends to be, satisfied in democratic countries. He contends that "certain kinds of democratic decision-making do have epistemic value," and that "this is the reason I would offer for thinking of certain democratic political arrangements as the epistemic authoritative procedure that is the counterpart to the jury trial: it is the epistemic device that allows the authoritative order to go to war to sanitize the soldier's (otherwise impermissibly) knowingly killing innocent people."[19] This, I think, is overly sanguine about the epistemic value of democratic decision-making. There is nothing in democratic deliberation about the resort to war that corresponds to a jury trial, particularly with regard to the question whether the war would be just. Our legal institutions are an exemplary instance of the division of moral labor precisely because they are designed with procedural guarantees of maximal epistemic reliability. It is because the constrained procedures of a jury trial are in general more reliable epistemically than any individual judgment that it is rational for jailers and others to subordinate their private judgment to the judgment of the court. But even in the most democratic countries, there is no comparable procedure that is designed to yield a reliable judgment about the morality of a contemplated war. Among democratic countries, the US stands out in two respects: it has carefully designed and robust democratic institutions and also goes to war more often than any other democratic country. What procedural guarantees are there that the wars it fights will be just? The answer is: none. The only constraint on the resort to war by the executive is a requirement of Congressional authorization—a requirement that can be fudged, as it was when the Johnson administration treated the Gulf of Tonkin resolution as authorization for war in Vietnam, or can be obtained with comparative ease when the party of the President controls both houses of Congress, as was the case when Congress authorized the George W. Bush administration's war in Iraq. Congressional authorization is a political hurdle, not a moral constraint.

There are no institutional or procedural mechanisms that ensure that moral considerations are even taken into account, much less taken seriously, in decisions concerning resort to war, either by Congress or by the executive. If an administration is prudent, it will consult with its legal advisers before going to war, if only to concoct as plausible a legal rationale as the facts will allow for. But when was the last time an administration contemplating going to war called in philosophers or even theologians schooled in just war theory to get expert counsel on matters of morality? I cannot prove that it has never happened, but if it has one can be confident that the purpose was to devise some moralized window dressing, as when George H. W. Bush was inspired to christen his administration's 1989 invasion of Panama "Operation Just Cause."

Here is one further objection to Estlund's suggestion. Suppose that one is a soldier in a country whose democratically elected government has ordered a mobilization for war, yet one has reasons for suspecting that the war is unjust. Suppose further that the country that is one's intended adversary has democratic political institutions that are more advanced or better developed than those in one's own country. Suppose, for example, that the media in that country provide more extensive and less biased and distorted information to the public, that partly as a consequence of that though partly also as a cause, public debates are livelier and more sophisticated there, and that in general the citizens participate more extensively in political decision-making and hold their government to a higher standard of accountability than the citizens do in one's own country. If one's own government claims to have a just cause for war, while the government of the potential adversary denies it, which country's "democratic political arrangements" provide the "epistemic authoritative procedure" that ought to guide one's decision about whether to participate? No matter how good one's own democratic institutions may be, as long as they are inferior to those of one's potential adversary, it is hard to see how, even by the logic of Estlund's own argument, they could "sanitize" one's participation in the war if it is in fact objectively unjust.

For these reasons, I doubt that in most cases democratic political institutions offer even a presumption of epistemic reliability in decisions about the resort to war, much less a decisive reason to defer to the judgments of a democratic government. There may well be countries in which it is rational for soldiers to accept that the deliberations of their government are a more trustworthy guide to the morality of war than their own private convictions. But in cases in which this is true, if indeed there are any, the reason for the government's moral authority will have more to do with the country's traditions and culture and with the known moral character of its political leaders than with their having been democratically elected or with their democratic accountability to the citizens.

There may eventually be countries in which the political institutions charged with making decisions about the resort to war will be structured to yield judgments that are presumptively more reliable morally than the private judgments of virtually all normally situated individuals. In such a country, it would be rational and perhaps morally required for soldiers to subordinate their own moral judgment to that of the government, and in effect to abdicate their autonomy in matters concerning the resort to war. But there are no countries of this sort now.

2.4.2 The Duty to Sustain the Efficient Functioning of Just Institutions

There are different reasons why it might be rational or morally required for a soldier to subordinate his private moral judgment about the justifiability of going to war to that of his government. We have explored one possible reason: that the moral judgments of the government are more likely to be correct than the private judgments of individuals.

Another, more compelling reason has to do with the necessity of sustaining the efficient functioning of institutions that enable people to act together in coordinated ways in the service of morally important ends. One such institution is the military. Even though in some countries the primary function of the military is the repression and control of the domestic population, military organizations in all countries have at least the potential functions of deterring external threats and defending the country if deterrence fails. These are morally important functions. But for the military to be able to carry them out effectively, individuals within the military must fulfill their assigned roles in a consistent and predictable manner rather than following their own judgment about the orders they receive on a case-by-case basis. The same is true, of course, of all complex organizations in which the activities of different individuals and groups are carefully coordinated in the effort to achieve collective goals. But the efficient regulation and coordination of individual action is of significantly greater moral importance in the military than in virtually all other types of organization. Military institutions have to be able to react quickly and efficiently in moments of crisis. Because of this, they are organized hierarchically with a rigid chain of command. Success or failure, which can make the difference between life and death for a great many people, may depend on whether those lower in the chain immediately and unhesitatingly obey the orders they receive from above. The exigencies of war may afford no time for those lower down to engage in careful reflection, and the necessity of classifying information may in any case deprive them of resources necessary for informed deliberation. Military institutions may thus be better able to achieve their morally vital aims if those who occupy the various positions in the chain of command surrender their autonomy and defer entirely to the authority of those above them. Morality itself seems to require soldiers not to exercise their moral judgment in matters of war, but to abdicate their moral autonomy, converting themselves into the instruments of others. For if they do not, they may thwart the achievement of goals of overriding moral importance, such as the preservation of their society. This, it can be argued, is what makes it objectively morally justifiable for combatants to fight in any war in which they are commanded to fight, even when the war turns out to be unjust.

This is an important argument. In its most general form, the argument is that there are duties that accompany certain roles within complex institutions and that these role-based duties can sometimes conflict with and override other duties, thereby making it permissible to do what it would be impermissible to do if one were not the occupant of a certain institutional role. Because the failure to fulfill the duties of one's institutional role can impair the functioning of the institution of which one is a part, and because it is often highly important morally to sustain the efficient functioning of an institution, this form of argument has wide application and in many of its applications it is obviously right. Yet there are two reasons why it cannot justify the doctrine of the moral equality of combatants.

The first is that in conflicts between duties that derive from institutional roles and duties that have other sources, there can be no a priori guarantee that the institutional duties will be overriding. In some cases they will, but in other cases they will themselves be overridden. The relevant question here is whether a soldier's role-based duty to obey an order to fight in a war that is objectively unjust overrides the duties that his participation in the war would require him to violate. The answer, of course, depends on the strength or seriousness of those other duties. But the conflicting duties include such basic negative duties as not to intentionally kill or gravely injure innocent people, not to kill or injure other innocent people as a side effect of morally unjustified action, not to collaborate in depriving innocent people of their freedom and political independence, and so on. The violation of these duties generally lies well beyond what can be justified by the duty to maintain the functioning of a morally important institution by fulfilling the demands of one's role within it.

Consider the analogy with role-based duties within the institutions of the criminal justice system. I conceded earlier that the division of labor in the criminal justice system requires that jailers respect the verdicts of the courts rather than using their own judgment to determine whom they should keep imprisoned. The reason I gave is that the courts are designed to deliver verdicts that are epistemically more reliable than the private judgments of individuals. But there are obviously exceptions. Suppose the jailer *knows*, with certainty, that a particular prisoner is innocent. And suppose an opportunity arises for him to enable that prisoner to escape. Once he had escaped, the prisoner would soon be able to prove his innocence. But the jailer has to weigh his duty to help this innocent person against the duties that go with his institutional role, and against the possible effects of the precedent he would set in violating those duties. Rather than freeing the prisoner on his own, he probably ought to present his evidence for the prisoner's innocence to the legal authorities and to work to have the prior conviction reviewed and overturned. But suppose now that it is not the jailer but instead the executioner who knows, with certainty, that a particular prisoner is innocent, and suppose that prisoner is scheduled for execution without the possibility of appeal. If the executioner has an opportunity to enable that prisoner to escape, he must do so. His duty not to execute an innocent person outweighs and overrides his institutional duty to perform the execution.[20] (If it were the jailer who knew of the innocence of the inmate scheduled for execution, he would have a duty to prevent the execution, if he could. The duty to prevent the execution of an innocent person is weaker than the duty not to execute an innocent person, but it is still sufficient to override the duties of his institutional role. So even the jailer would be justified in facilitating this prisoner's escape.) These examples show that what I have claimed about role-based duties in the military is also true of other role-based duties—namely, that while it may be a person's duty, all things considered, to fulfill his institutional role, even when he thereby wrongs an innocent victim of the malfunctioning of the institution, there are nevertheless other instances in which his duty not to wrong the victim overrides his duty to uphold the functioning of the institution. It is simply a matter of the relative importance of the conflicting duties.

The second reason why a soldier's duty to maintain the efficient functioning of the military cannot vindicate the moral equality of combatants is that this duty is generated only within military institutions that are just, so that preserving their ability to function is of great value and importance. There can be no moral requirement to fulfill the functions of an institutional role in order to maintain the efficient functioning of the institution, when the functions of the role require the violation of other significant duties, and the institution itself does not serve moral purposes, and especially if it positively serves immoral purposes. The Nazi military, for example, was incapable of imposing moral duties on those who occupied roles within it. On occasion the orders that a member of the Nazi military received coincided with what that person was morally required to do, but the source of the requirement was never a duty to maintain the functioning of the Nazi military. The same is true of all other military institutions, such as the now defunct Republican Guard in Iraq, that are designed and structured for external aggression and internal repression, torture, and murder. So even if most soldiers have duties to fulfill the functions of their role even when they are commanded to fight in an unjust war, not all do. While the role-based duties of those who serve in fundamentally just military institutions may be overridden when they are called to fight in an unjust war, those who serve in unjust or illegitimate military institutions have no duties to be overridden.

I have conceded that role-based duties within morally important institutions can, in some instances, make it permissible, or even morally required, to violate other duties with which they conflict. But I have also expressed two grounds for skepticism about whether a soldier's role-based duties can actually provide an objective justification for participation in an unjust war, particularly in a war that is unjust because it lacks a just cause. I have argued that there are cases in which soldiers have no role-based duties at all, and other cases in which, while they do have such duties, these duties are overridden by conflicting negative duties not to harm innocent people. But are there cases in which the role-based duties are not overridden—that is, are there cases in which a soldier's role-based duties, which are themselves anchored in the importance of preserving the functioning of the military institution in which he serves, ground an objective justification for fighting in an unjust war? Suppose, for example, that the unjust war in which he has been commanded to fight is an aberration in the history of his country and its military. Suppose that the military organization of which he is a member is overall a just institution that has for decades served only morally defensible goals and is likely to be necessary for other morally important purposes in the future. It is, all things considered, an institution that it is morally important to preserve. Might the importance of preserving the integrity of the institution objectively justify the soldiers who are a part of it in fighting in this one unjust war?

It is doubtful that it can. When the malfunctioning of political or military institutions that are fundamentally just results in unjust war, some people will have to suffer the costs of that malfunctioning. Who, as a matter of justice, ought they to be: those who are being unjustly warred against, or those whose institutions have gone off the rails? It seems that when an institution malfunctions in a harmful way, those who designed, direct, participate in, and normally benefit from it are liable to pay the costs. They are responsible for the functioning of the institution by virtue of having established and administered it as a means of furthering their purposes. It would be unjust if they were to impose the costs of its malfunctioning on others.

The situation may be different if the victims of the malfunctioning of an institution are among those whom the institution is designed to serve. Particularly if they have in some way consented to accept the risks in exchange for the benefits of having the institution, or if they have actually benefited from it, the injustice they suffer if they become victims of its aberrant malfunctioning is less than it would be otherwise. Thus, a person who occupies a role in an institution that is just overall may have a strong moral reason to continue to adhere to the requirements of her role even when she believes that the institution is functioning unjustly, provided that the victims are members of the group the institution is designed to serve. But if the victims are not members of the group by and for whom the institution has been constructed, as is true when a normally just military fights an unjust war, the reason a participant has to fulfill the requirements of her role must generally yield to the demands of justice. Certainly it must yield when the conflicting demand is that she not kill the innocent.

Thus far in this discussion of role-based duties I have taken for granted the assumption that no military institution can function cohesively and efficiently unless those at the top of the chain of command can confidently expect immediate and unquestioning obedience by all soldiers to an order to go to war. It is obvious, of course, that a large-scale mutiny within the military would impair, probably fatally, a country's ability to prosecute the particular war in which the mutiny occurred. But that is not what is at issue. The relevant question is whether a military institution in which a soldier's role-based duty to fight was regarded as nonabsolute would necessarily be less cohesive and efficient than one in which this duty was treated as absolute. It may seem obvious that the answer is "yes," but this is largely an empirical question and to my knowledge there is little evidence available, partly because military institutions have virtually always demanded unconditional obedience to an order to fight. The idea that soldiers may have a right to refuse to participate in an unjust war has rarely been "field tested."

There is, however, a little evidence from the recent history of the Israeli Defense Force (IDF). In 1982, when Israel invaded southern Lebanon, a group of soldiers refused to serve in the war, or in certain campaigns in the war. The group later took the name "Yesh Gvul" ("there is a limit"). Twenty years later, a second group of IDF officers and soldiers, "Courage to Refuse," declared their refusal to serve in missions in the Occupied Territories. Members of both groups continue to refuse to participate in military operations in the Territories, and many have suffered penalties, though generally quite mild. Neither group has caused any detectable impairment of the IDF's ability to fight just wars of defense and it is arguable—and has been argued—that the

debates, both within the military and among the general public, that
have been stimulated by the groups' activities have had healthy effects on
military, political, and in particular democratic institutions in Israel.[21]

It is also worth noting that unjust wars can themselves be highly
damaging to military institutions by which they are waged. It took
many years for military institutions in the US to recover from the
damage done to their reputation, and thus to their ability to recruit
qualified officers and enlisted personnel, and to attract public support
for Congressional funding, in the aftermath of the war in Vietnam. At
present, as the war in Iraq continues after more than five years, the US
Army is experiencing severe problems in recruiting enlisted personnel
and has been forced to lower its recruitment standards generally and to
grant a sharply increased number of "moral waivers" to persons with
criminal records in order to meet its recruitment goals.[22] The retention
rate for young officers is also alarmingly low. More than a third of the
West Point class of 2000 retired from active duty at the earliest possible
point, in 2005.[23] While the explanation for these problems is complex,
it is uncontroversial that one of the factors is a reluctance to participate
in the war in Iraq, which is widely perceived to be unjust.

Given that unjust wars tend to have destructive effects on military
institutions, particularly in democratic societies, and assuming that
treating role-based duties of participation as absolute tends to facilitate
the ability of governments to fight unjust wars, it is arguable that
increased tolerance of resistance within the military to participation
in unjust wars could, all things considered, be less disruptive of the
integrity, cohesion, and efficiency of military institutions than continued
adherence to the idea that role-based duties are absolute. I will return to
the issue of the effects of tolerating disobedience within the military at
the end of this chapter.

2.4.3 Fairness to Fellow Participants

There is one further, related argument that is worth considering. I
argued in Section 2.4.1 that democratic decision-making procedures
do not offer even a presumption that the *morality* of a democratic
government's decision to resort to war has been subjected to any kind
of epistemically reliable deliberation or scrutiny whatsoever. Although
I did not mention this earlier, part of the reason why this is so is
that the decision-making procedures that govern the resort to war in
contemporary democracies are designed for representative rather than

direct democracies. And there is little evidence for, and considerable evidence against, the assumption that political representatives, taken singly or collectively, are more reliable in their moral judgments about the resort to war than the average person.

One might argue, however, that because of this deficiency in representative democracy, decisions of great moral significance, such as whether to go to war, ought to be taken by plebiscite. Yet this alone would do nothing to enhance the moral reliability of decisions concerning the resort to war; thus an intelligent and morally conscientious soldier would have no reason of an epistemic nature to defer to judgments reached in this way. Yet the possibility of making decisions about the resort to war by plebiscite does offer an argument for a possible objective justification for participation in an unjust war that merits a brief examination.

Suppose that we as a society conduct a referendum on the resort to war. You are a member of the military but suffrage is universal and you are entitled to vote. You judge, correctly, that the war would be unjust and therefore vote against it. But the vote goes against you; the majority vote in favor of going to war. By voting, you have committed yourself to the other participants in the referendum to abide by the results. You therefore have a moral reason to fight—namely, that by participating in the vote you conditionally pledged yourself to your fellow voters to do so. If you vote but then refuse to abide by the results, you will have acted in bad faith and betrayed the trust of the other voters, who have reason to vote only on the assumption that all are willing to be bound by the outcome.

Even if this argument is right, it has no application in a representative democracy. When, for example, a person in the US votes in a presidential election, she does not thereby bind herself to supporting or participating in any war to which the winner of the election might commit the country. She binds herself merely to accepting that the winner of the election will occupy the relevant office and exercise the powers that are appointed to it.

Even in the context of a plebiscitary democracy, the argument is insufficient to establish an objective justification for participation in an unjust war. The reason why this is so is the same as one of the reasons I offered against the claim that the moral equality of combatants can be defended by appealing to soldiers' role-based duties. If you participate in a referendum on whether to go to war, that does give you a duty that you owe to the other participants to abide by the outcome of the vote.

But that duty is not absolute. It can be overridden if fulfilling it would require you to violate other, even stronger duties. And it is clear that your duty not to engage in the intentional killing of innocent people outweighs your duty to abide by the results of a referendum in which you have freely participated. Those you would wrong if you were to fulfill the duty derived from participation in the referendum would be wronged to a far greater degree than those you would wrong if you were to default on that duty.

The possibility of deciding by plebiscite whether to go to war raises further important issues. Suppose again that you are a soldier in a society that is contemplating going to war. Some of the citizens believe that going to war would be morally wrong, while others believe that it is morally obligatory. The government decides, perhaps reasonably, that the fairest way to resolve the dispute is by plebiscite. You are among those who believe, correctly, that the war would be unjust. You have three options. You can (1) vote against the war and participate in it if you lose the vote, (2) vote against the war but refuse to abide by the outcome if the vote goes against you, or (3) abstain from voting. What ought you to do? I claim that the first is not a morally acceptable option. You cannot make it permissible for you to kill innocent people simply by voting, and especially not by voting *against* the war. The second option—to vote but with no intention of abiding by the result if you lose—would be an act of deception and manipulation that would exploit the willingness of others to cooperate in good faith. This leaves the option of abstention. But there are powerful objections to that as well. The vote offers you and other like-minded people the opportunity to prevent an unjust war. You may owe it to the potential victims of that war to do what you can to prevent it. Suppose that those who are opposed to the war constitute a majority but that this cannot be known in advance of the vote. If these people ought not to vote on the ground that they would wrong the voters on the other side by voting in bad faith—that is, with no intention of accepting the result if they lose—then the consequence of their doing what they ought to do will be that an unjust war will be fought that would have been prevented if they had acted in bad faith by voting against it. Surely it is more important that they should prevent the unjust war than that they should not betray the trust of those who would vote in favor of the war. Perhaps in this case voting in bad faith does not wrong those who vote for war because they have no right against being manipulated when they will otherwise start an unjust war. And perhaps voting in bad faith can also be understood as a permissible instance of paternalism, an effort to protect your fellow citizens from making a serious moral mistake.

2.5 THE COLLECTIVIST APPROACH TO THE MORALITY OF WAR[24]

Earlier I mentioned that it is common to believe that the practice of war is governed by different principles from those that govern the acts of individuals outside the context of war. Among the most influential reasons why many people have held this belief is that they think that war is only derivatively a matter of individual action at all. Instead, war is essentially a relation between or among collectives, and in particular *states*. The canonical statement of this view was given by Rousseau in 1762 in *The Social Contract*. There he wrote that "war . . . is something that occurs not between man and man, but between States. The individuals who become involved in it are enemies only by accident . . . A State can have as its enemies only other States, not men at all."[25] On a view such as this, it is not surprising that the morality of individual conduct in war is not governed by familiar principles of liability as they apply in relations among persons, for the moral principles that govern the activity of war apply primarily to the acts of states and only derivatively and thus indirectly to the acts of persons.

Perhaps the commonest way of thinking about war in collectivist terms is to think of states themselves as sovereign individuals whose relations with one another are governed morally by principles that are *analogues* of the principles governing relations among persons. Walzer refers to this way of understanding moral relations among states as the "domestic analogy."[26] According to this view, the principle that individuals have a right not to be unjustly attacked, and have a right of self-defense if they are, applies at two different levels: to persons and to states. As Walzer says, states "possess rights more or less as individuals do."[27] When a state defends itself, it is of course through the acts of persons, but what is at issue morally is not individual self-defense by persons, and what individual persons are morally permitted or required to do is determined in part by their relation to the state and the manner of their involvement in its action.

Those who accept a collectivist approach to the morality of war are also almost invariably partisans of the doctrine of the moral equality of combatants, and most assume that the collectivist approach is essential to the defense of the doctrine. Rousseau, for example, assumed that his view that war is a relation that obtains only between states supported not only the moral equality of combatants—the idea that all combatants are legitimate targets yet have "an equal right to kill"—but also the corresponding doctrine of noncombatant immunity. Thus he claimed that, "the object of war being the destruction of the enemy State, a commander has a perfect right to kill its defenders so long as their arms are in their hands: but once they have laid them down and have submitted, they cease to be enemies, or instruments employed by an enemy, and revert to the condition of men, pure and simple, over whose lives no one can any longer exercise a rightful claim."[28]

Yet at least initially it seems that the collectivist approach to war is actually incompatible with the moral equality of combatants. Rousseau seems not to have considered what might be the source of a commander's "perfect right" to kill the defenders of a state when the reason that they have become its defenders is that it and its inhabitants have been unjustly attacked by the commander and others like him. If his right derives from his being not a man, pure and simple, but only an instrument employed by his state, the question is then how it can be permissible for his state to seek "the destruction of the enemy State" when that enemy state has offered it no provocation. If we combine the domestic analogy with the uncontentious claim that it is wrong to seek to kill an innocent person for reasons of self-interest, the implication is that an aggressor state does *not* act permissibly in seeking the destruction of another state that has done no wrong. But if the state acts wrongly, it seems that the wrongness of the collective act must be transmitted to the individual acts of persons by which the collective act is constituted.

This seems to be the view implicit in Noam Zohar's argument for a synthesis of individualist and collectivist approaches to war.[29] Zohar argues that the reigning theory of the just war cannot be defended on purely individualist grounds but requires both individualist and collectivist assumptions for its coherence. What is interesting is that he does not call upon collectivist assumptions to defend the moral equality of combatants (a central element of the overall view to which he claims allegiance) but instead to explain how it can be permissible for just combatants to attack and kill unjust combatants in cases in which the latter are entirely morally innocent. For Zohar believes that it cannot be permissible to kill a person who is morally innocent (that is, nonculpable), even in self-defense. His explanation of how it can nevertheless be permissible to kill a morally innocent unjust combatant appeals to the idea that he presents himself in war not in his individual but in his collective identity. It is in his capacity as an agent of the guilty collective that he becomes a legitimate target. But by this same logic, it seems that the just combatant, both as an individual and as an agent of the collective, retains his immunity to attack and thus is not a legitimate target.

The collectivist approach has, however, been developed in ways that have been thought to block the transmission of wrongness from the collective action of fighting an unjust war to individual acts of war by unjust combatants. For example, Christopher Kutz, in the most careful development of the collectivist approach of which I am aware, argues that "the fact that my nation is at war, not me, does not absolve me of responsibility towards my enemy, but it does create a normatively distinct relation between us, one structured through a set of rules specific to our interrelationship as individual members of warring nations."[30] In the context of war, violence that would otherwise be morally impermissible can become permissible in a special way by virtue of its collective, political character. "When individuals' wills are linked together in politics," Kutz claims, "this affects the normative valence of what they do individually as part of that politics, even to the point of rendering impunible what would otherwise be criminal."[31] In order to explain how this can be, he distinguishes between individual moral permissions and collective political permissions. "The privilege to kill as part of a collective is not," he writes, "a moral permission attaching to the individual soldier. A soldier who kills as part of an unjust war morally wrongs those he kills." But this is compatible with there being "an essentially *political* permission to do violence [in war], because when I do violence, I do it as a member of one group towards another."[32]

There are serious questions about the logic of these different types of permission—in particular about how they combine or interact. Suppose that, as an agent of a collective, an unjust combatant has a political permission to kill just combatants. Kutz denies that this permission is a moral permission and concedes that the unjust combatant wrongs any just combatants he kills. That strongly suggests that the absence of a moral permission here entails moral *impermissibility*. So one and the same act is morally impermissible and politically permissible. What is the unjust combatant to make of this? If he is looking for guidance, should he look to morality or to politics?

There are other problems as well. Kutz concedes that mere membership in a group is not a sufficient basis for a special political permission to do violence to members of another group. Collective violence in the context of domestic society that is unauthorized by the state is normally subject to the law of complicity, whereby individuals may become liable to punishment for crimes of violence through certain forms of collective association, *even* in the absence of any personal engagement in acts of violence. So what, on this collectivist view, distinguishes collective violence in war from collective violence in domestic society, rendering the one permissible at the level of individual action while the other remains criminal?

Kutz's answer is that the privilege of engaging in violence even for unjust ends can be claimed only by members of "political groups [pursuing] political goals, in the sense of aiming at creating (or restoring) a new collective ordering."[33] A group is political in the relevant sense, rather than criminal, only if it is internally ordered or regulated, has political aims, and has a reasonable prospect of achieving those aims.[34] The suggestion, then, is that by organizing themselves politically, with internal norms of authority and obedience, individuals can somehow authorize each other to use violence for political reasons, thereby making it permissible for each to do what none would otherwise be permitted to do.

This, however, presupposes a form of moral alchemy that is difficult to accept. How can certain people's establishment of political relations *among themselves* confer on them a right to harm or kill *others*, when the harming or killing would be impermissible in the absence of the relevant relations? How could it be that merely by acting collectively for political goals, people can shed the moral constraints that bind them when they act merely as individuals, so that it then becomes permissible for them to kill innocent people as a means of achieving their political goals?

Even if there could be such an alchemical moral action, Kutz has not identified all the elements necessary for its occurrence. For no one supposes that the members of organized domestic political collectives, such as political parties, have special political permissions to attack and kill the members of rival domestic collectives in their efforts to establish a different "collective ordering." The political permissions seem highly restricted in their application. They do not apply to members of all political groups but mainly just to individuals acting as agents of states, and indeed not to all members of states, but only to soldiers, and only in the context of war.

There is a further restriction that must also be explained. The moral equality of combatants implies that ordinary combatants are absolved of any responsibility for wrongs that follow simply from a war's being unjust, as opposed to those that result from violations of the principles of *jus in bello*. Combatants are held to be accountable only for matters of *jus in bello* and not for matters of *jus ad bellum*. The collectivist approach purports to explain this. It holds that their role as agents of the state somehow licenses them to kill people even in pursuit of aims that are unjust. Yet virtually all collectivists who accept the moral equality of combatants also accept that, in contrast to ordinary combatants, political leaders *are* constrained by the principles of *jus ad bellum*. While unjust combatants are permitted to pursue unjust aims by violent means, political leaders are not, and it is considered acceptable to hold political leaders morally responsible for wrongs committed in the course of unjust wars, and even to punish them for the crime of aggression. Yet political leaders are agents of the state just as combatants are. If acting as an agent of a political collective releases combatants from responsibility for their contribution to the fighting of an unjust war, it seems that it should also release political leaders from responsibility for their role in the fighting of that war. I do not, however, know of any collectivist theorist of the morality of war who has offered to explain why this is not so.

That a collective is organized specifically for the pursuit of political goals is held to be one of the necessary ingredients in the alchemical brew that is supposed to generate political permissions to kill people during the prosecution of an unjust war. Yet it seems irrelevant morally whether the goals a group seeks by violence are political in character. Goals that are paradigmatically political may also be paradigmatically evil—for example, the goal of eliminating a people in order to create an ethnically "pure" society. It is morally impossible that the collective pursuit of such goals could somehow generate political permissions that immunize individual agents from the possibility of just punishment. What matters in the justification of violence is not whether a goal is *political* but whether it is *just*.

If this is right, there is no reason to suppose that states, or any other kinds of political collective, are fundamentally different morally from collectives that are not political in nature. It therefore seems that the same account of the morality of collective action should apply to both political and nonpolitical collectives. The principles governing collective violence in war should be the same as those governing collective action in domestic contexts. If so, we face a dilemma. We can hold individual action in war to the same standards to which we hold individual action on behalf of collectives in domestic contexts, insisting on the logic of complicity, or we can treat collective violence in domestic contexts the way it is conventionally treated in war, claiming that even in domestic society individuals acting together as a collective acquire special permissions and exemptions from liability. No one, so far as I know, accepts the latter view; nor is anyone likely to. Unless the various objections I have pressed against the collectivist view can be satisfactorily answered, it seems that that view cannot offer a credible foundation for the moral equality of combatants.

2.6 TRANSFERRED RESPONSIBILITY

One intuition that helps to explain the appeal of collectivism about war is that moral responsibility for acts of war done by soldiers acting under the authority of the state lies with the state itself, or perhaps with its political leaders. Members of the government are legitimately authorized by the terms of the political association to make decisions about war on behalf of the state. Because the authority to make decisions about the resort to war lies with them, so too does the responsibility for the decisions they make about matters of *jus ad bellum*. Soldiers are merely the instruments the leaders use to implement those decisions.

This idea has a venerable history. A version of it appears in *The City of God* by Augustine of Hippo, the earliest writer of significance in the just war tradition. According to Augustine,

there are some exceptions made by the divine authority to its own law, that men may not be put to death. These exceptions are of two kinds, being justified either by a general law, or by a special commission granted for a time to some individual. And in this latter case, he to whom authority is delegated, and who is but the sword in the hand of him who uses it, is not himself responsible for the death he deals. And, accordingly, they who have waged war in obedience to the divine command . . . have by no means violated the commandment, "Thou shalt not kill."[35]

Here, of course, the relevant authority is God, not the political leadership. But Augustine and others had to assume that God exerts his authority to wage war through the delegated authority of kings.

By the time that Shakespeare wrote, 1,200 years later, the authority who bears responsibility for acts of war done in obedience to his commands had taken a more explicitly secular form. In a well-known scene in *Henry V*, the King, disguised as an ordinary soldier, is conversing with some of his men on the eve of the battle of Agincourt. Hoping to find or to inspire support among them, he remarks: "Methinks I could not die anywhere so contented as in the King's company, his cause being just and his quarrel honorable." One soldier replies: "That's more than we know," whereupon a second says: "Ay, or more than we should seek after; for we know enough if we know we are the King's subjects: if his cause be wrong, our obedience to the King wipes the crime of it out of us."[36] Here it becomes explicit that moral responsibility is transferred to the political leader even when a soldier's acts of war are done in pursuit of an unjust cause.

A philosophical defense of this view was offered by Hobbes, writing a few decades later. In *De Cive*, published in 1642, Hobbes wrote that

what I beleeve to be another mans sin, I may sometimes doe that without any sin of mine. For if I be commanded to doe that which is a sin in him who commands me, if I doe it, and he that commands me be by Right, Lord over me, I sinne not; for if I wage warre at the Commandement of my Prince, conceiving the warre to be unjustly undertaken, I doe not therefore doe unjustly, but rather if I refuse to doe it, arrogating to my selfe the knowledge of what is just and unjust, which pertains onely to my Prince.[37]

While the passages from Augustine and Shakespeare appeal to the idea that responsibility is transferred from an agent to a commander simply by virtue of the latter's authority to issue commands, Hobbes adds a further layer of explanation and justification when he suggests that those who command by right have a presumptive *epistemic* authority in determining what is just and what is unjust. Indeed, this authority may be more than merely epistemic, on Hobbes's view. For in the immediately preceding paragraph, he states his signature doctrine that "Legitimate Kings . . . make the things they command, just, by commanding them, and those which they forbid, unjust, by forbidding them."[38]

Samuel Pufendorf, citing Hobbes with qualified approval, insists that three conditions must be met for responsibility for a commanded act to transfer from the agent to the commander.

A man may undertake the mere execution of an act enjoined upon him by a sovereign, which is imputed for sin upon him who commands it, not upon him who carries it out. Yet for this to obtain, we hold it necessary, first, that the mere execution alone be commanded him, that is, that he lend only his body and its strength to the act, and in general that he give no occasion or pretext, or furnish the least excuse for it, but only carry it out as though it were another's act and not his own. And second, that so far as he can, he avoid and beg to be excused from such a task. . . . And lastly, that because of his reluctance a threat of death or some other serious evil, which neither justice nor love requires him to undergo for the sake of another, be laid upon him by the sovereign, who is strong enough to carry it out.[39]

In addition to imposing these three rather exacting conditions on the avoidance of sin or responsibility, Pufendorf's view is more restrictive than Hobbes's in another respect. For Pufendorf claims that even when the conditions are satisfied, obedience is merely permitted, not required: "whoever refuses to obey such commands is free from all crimes."[40] But for Hobbes obedience is always required.

The view that one finds either explicitly or implicitly in these passages—that when an agent obeys a command to act in a way that would otherwise be wrong, responsibility for his act sometimes remains entirely with the person who gave the command, which renders the agent's action permissible—has an impressive historical pedigree. It also has very considerable psychological power. In the early 1960s, psychologist Stanley Milgram performed a well-known series of experiments in which people who believed that they were merely assisting an experimenter were themselves the actual experimental subjects. They were told they were assisting in a learning experiment and that when a person they believed to be an experimental subject—in reality an actor—gave the wrong answer to a question, they were to press a switch that they believed would give him an electric shock. There were thirty switches with designated intensity levels ranging from 15 to 450 volts. The four switches for voltage levels from 425 to 440 were marked "Danger: Severe Shock," while the switches for 445 and 450 volts bore the sinister legend "XXX." As the real subjects pressed switches marked with higher and higher voltage levels, the actor would produce simulations of increasingly intense agony and demand that the experiment stop, but after 330 volts would remain ominously silent. Milgram observed that "the abrogation of personal responsibility . . . is the major psychological consequence of yielding to authority. As strain arises, some subjects seek further assurance that they are not accountable for their actions and they may actively solicit it as a means of reducing tension." He cites this

exchange between the experimenter and a subject (the "teacher") who
had already gone up to what he believed was 375 volts.

TEACHER: . . . Something's happened to that man in there. You better check
in on him, sir. He won't answer or nothing.

EXPERIMENTER: Continue. Please go on.

TEACHER: You accept all responsibility?

EXPERIMENTER: The responsibility is mine. Correct. Please go on. (*Teacher
returns to his list . . .* [and] *works through to 450 volts.*)

TEACHER: That's that.

Milgram comments: "Once the experimenter has reassured the subject
that he is not responsible for his actions, there is a perceptible reduction
in strain."[41]

The subject in the experiment seems to have assumed both that the
experimenter had the power to relieve him of responsibility for his own
action by somehow taking that responsibility on himself, and that the
relocation of the responsibility somehow affected the permissibility of
his action—that is, that it became permissible for him to proceed with
the experiment once it was clear that the responsibility would lie with
someone else. A less charitable interpretation is of course that the subject
simply wanted assurance about the legal consequences of his action.
But that was not Milgram's interpretation and in any case the subject
probably believed, as most people do, that criminal responsibility and
moral responsibility coincide.

There are, however, reasons for skepticism about both of these
assumptions. It is obvious that in the Milgram experiment the subject
bears full responsibility for his action, since the experimenter has
no real power or authority over him at all. His commitments to the
experimenter are minimal and his duty not to harm the putative research
subject clearly override any duty he might have to fulfill his role in the
experiment. If the subject had actually been doing what he believed
he was doing, the experimenter would have shared responsibility for
the harm done to the victim, but that would not have diminished the
subject's responsibility by even the slightest degree. It is a commonplace
that moral responsibility is not a zero-sum matter.

Conditions are of course relevantly different in war. Commanders
have legitimate authority to issue orders and soldiers have moral reasons
to obey orders that are independent of any other reasons they might

have to do whatever they have been ordered to do. But unless the reasons that support obedience are absolute, so that there could be no reason to disobey that could outweigh the reason to obey, soldiers have a moral choice to make when they receive an order and there is a possibility of their making the wrong choice. If they make the wrong choice, they cannot plausibly deny their responsibility, claiming that responsibility lies solely with their commander.

There is also a reason based on consistency to accept that unjust combatants bear at least some responsibility for the bad effects of acts that they are legitimately commanded to do. If responsibility for the bad effects of acts that combatants are commanded to do remains entirely with the commanders, it seems that the same must be true of responsibility for any good effects of the combatants' acts. So if responsibility for the bad effects of acts of war done by unjust combatants under orders lies entirely with the political leaders who are the ultimate source of the commands, it seems that all responsibility for the good effects of acts of war done by just combatants under orders must also rest with their political leaders. Only if they exceed their orders—if then—can just combatants claim any responsibility or credit for the achievement of their just cause. Yet no one believes this. Either there is an asymmetry between responsibility for bad effects and responsibility for good effects, which seems unlikely, or else the idea that all responsibility for wrongs committed by unjust combatants in obedience to lawful commands lies with their political leaders is false.

Suppose that this is mistaken and that in fact unjust combatants bear no moral responsibility for the bad effects, such as the killing of just combatants and the achievement of an unjust cause, of acts that they are lawfully commanded to do. Does it follow that such acts are permissible? Is Hobbes right that they "doe not . . . doe unjustly," even though the war is "unjustly undertaken?"

Suppose that you have been commanded by a person with legitimate authority to issue commands to you to act in a way that you know would be wrong in the absence of the command. You are deliberating about whether to obey. You should obviously consider the reasons you have to obey lawful commands and weigh them against whatever the reasons are that explain why the commanded act would be wrong without the command. You might, for example, consider whether the person with authority is in an epistemically privileged position, or whether disobedience would weaken or undermine chains of authorization necessary for collective action by an institution whose continued functioning is of the utmost moral importance. But would it be sensible, in deciding whether it is morally permissible to obey, to consider who will have responsibility if you do? The question of where responsibility for your action would lie may be relevant to issues of liability, punishment, and so on, but how could it be relevant to what you ought to do? Does it really makes sense to think "I ought to do it only if they will be responsible, not me"? Can it really be a moral reason not to do the act, a reason that is entirely independent of other reasons, that the responsibility for it would be yours rather than theirs? These are not rhetorical questions. There may well be reasons why an affirmative answer is correct. But the questions suggest the oddness in the idea that the location of responsibility for an act can affect the act's permissibility.

There is a further reason for skepticism about this idea. Normally, if an agent's act would be wrong were it not for some condition that absolves him of all responsibility for it, the effect of that condition is not to render the act justified but rather to provide the agent an excuse. A more general way of making this point is to note that when an act has bad effects for which the agent is not morally responsible, the reason why the agent is not responsible may be that the act is permissible, or it may be that the act is wrong but that the agent is nonetheless excused. Both possibilities are compatible with the absence of responsibility on the part of the agent.

Which of these possibilities is most plausible in the case of unjust combatants? Suppose that acts of war by unjust combatants would be both wrong and culpable were they not done under orders from a legitimate authority. But suppose further that all responsibility for these acts lies, not with the unjust combatants who do them, but with the authorities who have commanded that they be done. Does the location of the responsibility with the authorities provide a moral justification for these otherwise wrongful acts, or does it merely excuse the unjust combatants for doing them? If the acts would be wrong in the absence of the command, and in particular if the political authorities act wrongly when they issue the command, and are responsible for doing so, it is hard to see how their having the responsibility for the acts they command could make those acts permissible for those who do them. It seems more plausible to suppose that those who do such acts while under the command of legitimate authorities are simply excused of any wrongdoing if it turns out that moral responsibility for the acts lies not with them but with the authorities. The permissibility of an act does not depend on who is responsible for it. If an act that would otherwise be unjustified is commanded by a legitimate authority, the location of the responsibility for it with the commander rather than with the perpetrator simply indicates who is to blame and who is not.

Before concluding this section, it is worth noting that Frances Kamm has offered some examples in which it may seem intuitively plausible to suppose an otherwise impermissible act becomes permissible when the person who does it acts as the agent of a principal and all responsibility for the act lies with the principal rather than with the agent. One such example is a lawyer's evicting a poor tenant on behalf of a client who owns the building. Another is a person who acts at the request of a paralyzed person to break a beautiful vase that the paralyzed person owns. Kamm claims that in these cases, "responsibility gets shifted," so that the agent "is not morally responsible for the bad effects of his act."[42] And in these and other cases, the shifting of the responsibility affects the permissibility of the act. Thus, of a different example, Kamm says this: "That [X] will alone be morally responsible and accountable for the negative consequences is part of what makes it permissible for [Y] to kill [Z]."[43]

Kamm notes that one interesting feature of these examples is that what it is permissible for the agent to do, provided that responsibility remains with the principal, is something that it would be wrong even for the principal himself to do—that is, it is a presupposition of the examples that it is wrong for the landlord to evict the poor tenant and wrong for the paralyzed person to break the vase merely on a whim. If the position of unjust combatants in war is relevantly analogous to that of the agents in Kamm's examples, this suggests that they might act permissibly in fighting even when it is wrong for their commanders to order them to fight and even when no one could permissibly do what they do except in their role as agents of the state.

There is, however, a crucial difference between the situation of the agents in Kamm's examples and that of unjust combatants in war. This is that in both of Kamm's examples, the principal has a *right* to do what he gets the agent to do on his behalf. Even though it is wrong for the landlord to evict the tenant, he has a right to do it because he owns the building. And even though the paralyzed person ought not to break the vase, he has a right to do it because it is his. These are examples of the kind of case I mentioned earlier in which an agent has a right to do wrong. Such a right obviously cannot be a liberty right—a permission—but is instead a claim right without a permission. All that such a right entails is the absence of a permission for others to prevent the exercise of the right.

It seems that what happens in Kamm's examples is that the principal transfers the claim right to the agent, who has a duty that is owed to the principal. In the case of the lawyer, the duty is contractual. In my view, if the lawyer were not already employed by the landlord, it would be wrong for her to take the commission to evict the poor tenant. But if the lawyer were already under contract to the landlord, her contractual duty combined with her authorization to enforce the landlord's right by proxy make it permissible for her to evict the tenant. In the second case, there could be a duty to help paralyzed people do what they cannot do for themselves. In both cases, the duty and the transferred right together override the reason that the agent has not to do the act (evict the tenant, break the vase). But because the landlord has the right but not the duty, it is wrong for him to evict the tenant himself and to have the lawyer do it on his behalf. A similar claim applies to the paralyzed person, if he could somehow arrange to break the vase himself.

It is clear why the situation of unjust combatants in war is not analogous to that of the agents in Kamm's examples. What unjust combatants are commanded to do as agents of the state—fight in an unjust war—is not something that their state, or its leaders, have a claim right to do, or to delegate to others. Since the right to do wrong is a necessary condition of the permissibility of the agents' proxy action in Kamm's examples, these examples seem to have no relevance to the morality of participation in an unjust war. Kamm actually does have a further example in which it seems permissible for a person, acting as the agent of another, to do something that the other has neither a permission nor a claim right to do. But this example is highly complex and has no parallels or analogues in war and is therefore better omitted here.

The upshot of the discussion in this section is that unjust combatants cannot reasonably claim that all responsibility for their participation in an unjust war lies with the authorities who have commanded them to fight; but even if they could, the most that would follow is that they are excused for their acts of war, not that they act permissibly or with justification. Since just combatants, by contrast, do act with justification, claims about the assignment of responsibility for the acts of unjust combatants are incapable of vindicating the doctrine of the moral equality of combatants.

2.7 SYMMETRICAL DISOBEDIENCE

It is worth considering one final argument for the permissibility of obeying a command from a legitimate authority to fight in a war that is objectively unjust. This argument appeals to considerations of consistency. Assume for the sake of argument that it is in fact impermissible to fight in a war that is unjust because it lacks a just cause. It follows that if a war in which a soldier is commanded to fight is objectively unjust and the soldier knows this, he must not obey the command. He must disobey what is at present a lawful order if what obedience to that order requires is participation in an unjust war. But if that is true, it seems that it should be at least permissible for him also to disobey a lawful order *not* to participate in a war if the war is objectively just. It seems that there ought to be a certain symmetry here. The permissibility of disobeying a command to fight in an unjust war suggests the permissibility of disobeying a command not to fight in a just war. Yet we reject the idea that it can be permissible for soldiers to fight in the absence of proper political authorization, even if the war is otherwise a just war. The subordination of the military to civilian control is a political principle that is vitally important to the stability of civilized societies.[44]

It might be thought that there is necessarily an asymmetry here because, while a soldier can refuse to fight in an unjust war entirely on his own, he cannot fight a just war on his own, for war is a collective activity. But there is nothing in this point. A soldier can fight in a just war without being commanded to, or even in disobedience to an order not to, provided that there is a just war in progress, or in the making. The same condition applies to refusal to obey an order to participate in an unjust war: there has to be an unjust war either in progress or in prospect, which necessarily involves the participation of others.

The worry is not that an individual soldier will fight a just war on his own but that a group of soldiers will fight a just war in the absence of legitimate authorization, or in defiance of a command not to. I agree that in general it is morally impermissible for soldiers to fight a just war in opposition to lawful orders or even just in the absence of proper authorization. Hence the challenge is to explain why soldiers are in general morally required to obey an order not to fight in a just war when they are *not* required to obey an order to fight in an unjust war and are indeed morally required to disobey. I think the explanation has two parts, one political and to some extent pragmatic, the other a matter of basic moral principle.

The political reason is that war has such serious consequences, both for those warred against and for those who are led into it, that it must be subject to institutional constraints designed to ensure that it is not undertaken without moral justification. The military must not have the discretion to go to war on its own initiative. Quite apart from institutional pressures within the military to find wars to fight so that its own *raison d'être* remains secure, military decision-makers are neither chosen by the people nor representative of them. They have no claim to act on behalf of the nation they serve without authorization from an appropriate political source. Yet if the military were to go to war without authorization, those attacked and others as well would understand it to be acting as the agent of the state and its citizens. Its action would expose the state to all the dangers of war, commit the resources of the taxpayers to war without their consent, and establish a precedent for doing the same thing again in the future.

For these and other reasons, soldiers must not go to war except when authorized to do so through the procedures that their society has established for committing itself to war. Yet suppose that soldiers believe that they have a just cause for war, that fighting for that just cause is better from an impartial point of view, and that they in fact have a duty to fight. Their government is unwilling to authorize them to fight and even explicitly commands them not to; but in fact they are right and their government is wrong; it ought to authorize them to fight. Is their duty to fight overridden by their duty of obedience? It might not be. One cannot exclude the possibility of a case relevantly analogous to a spontaneous *levée en masse*—for example, a case in which their government decides not to fight in defense against foreign aggression in exchange for a commitment from the aggressor to allow senior government officials to remain in power as a puppet regime. In such a case, it might be permissible, all things considered, for the soldiers to fight, assuming that among the things considered is the effect of their disobedience on future respect for the principle of military subordination to political control. Nevertheless the correct moral principle may well be that soldiers must not fight, even in a just war, without appropriate political authorization. The example in which it is permissible for them to fight without such authorization merely indicates that the principle is, like other such moral principles at this level, not absolute.

This principle is of a particular kind: namely, principles that govern the distribution of rights of decision-making—in this case the right to make decisions about the resort to war. The right to make this kind of decision cannot, for the reasons given earlier, lie with soldiers, or with the military as an institution.

Nothing I have said thus far implies that it is impermissible for individuals to fight in war without authorization from their state. I have argued only that individuals may not fight without authorization in their role as soldiers—that is, as individuals who act officially as agents of the state in its military conflicts. If there is a war in which a soldier believes that he is morally required to fight and his government refuses to authorize the state's military to fight, then he must somehow extricate himself from his role as a soldier. Once he ceases to be a soldier, it is permissible for him to join a war to fight for a just cause, as members of the International Brigades did in fighting against the Fascists in the Spanish Civil War.

In addition to these political considerations, there are also matters of basic moral principle that underlie the moral asymmetry between fighting in an unjust war and not fighting in a just war. The most significant of these is the distinction between doing and allowing, and in particular between killing and letting die. It is a fundamental component of common sense morality that the negative duty not to kill an innocent person is in general stronger, or less easily overridden, than the positive duty to prevent an innocent person from being killed. The objection to fighting in an unjust war is that it involves intentionally killing people who are innocent as a means of achieving aims that are unjust. To obey an order to fight in an unjust war is to violate the stringent negative duty not to kill innocent people. By contrast, the objection to not fighting in a just war is that it involves a failure to promote a just cause, which includes a failure to prevent innocent people from being killed. To obey an order not to fight in a just war is to violate the weaker positive duty to prevent innocent people from being killed.

A soldier may have good moral reasons to participate in an unauthorized just war, but they seldom rise to the level of a moral requirement. If those reasons are not strong enough to outweigh whatever reasons he has to remain in the military, they will almost certainly not be strong enough to outweigh his reasons for obedience. If they *are* strong enough to outweigh his reasons to remain in the military, he ought to resign or desert from the military in order to fight in the just war. But if he cannot release himself from his role as an agent of the state, his reasons to fight in an unauthorized just war are almost invariably overridden by his duty not to involve his state and its citizens in a war that for them is optional and that they have not chosen to enter.

The moral asymmetry between doing harm and failing to prevent harm helps to explain why the reasons a soldier has not to participate in an authorized unjust war are generally significantly stronger than the reasons he has to participate in an unauthorized just war. This fact about the relative strengths of his basic moral reasons combines with the political considerations cited above to explain why one cannot infer from the permissibility of disobeying a command to fight in an unjust war that it is also permissible to disobey a command not to fight in a just war.

2.8 CONSCIENTIOUS REFUSAL

I have tried to show that the arguments for the moral equality of combatants, and for the permissibility of fighting in a war that is unjust because it lacks a just cause, all fail. While they all point to considerations that are of moral significance, none of these considerations is sufficiently weighty to justify the intentional killing of people who have done no wrong and thus are not liable to attack. This means that we must stop reassuring soldiers that they act permissibly when they fight in an unjust war, provided that they conduct themselves honorably on the battlefield by fighting in accordance with the rules of engagement. We must cease to regard them as mere instruments or automata and recognize that they are morally autonomous and therefore morally responsible agents. And we must insist that they too recognize their own moral autonomy and abandon the comforting fiction that all responsibility for acts they do in obedience to commands lies with those who command them, so that it is only when they disobey, or when they breach the norms governing their professional action as warriors, that they become responsible for wrongdoing.

Ironically, we must unlearn one of the lessons we learned from the Vietnam war. During that war, soldiers were often greeted with insults when they returned to the United States. A Vietnam veteran whose son was killed in Afghanistan in 2005 was recently quoted as saying that "this time people are not taking it out on returning soldiers. They have been able to draw the distinction: honor the warrior no matter what your attitude to the war."[45] Within limits, this principle is right. It is not only possible but indeed it happens very frequently that unusually noble and admirable people fight in a war that is unjust and deserve to be honored for the sacrifices they make. But, as I will argue at length in the next chapter, we must distinguish our evaluation of the person from the evaluation of his action. That a person acts with conspicuous courage or generosity toward his comrades cannot make what he does entirely admirable if it is done ultimately in the service of an unjust cause. Even if an unjust war is the occasion for numerous acts of heroism and sacrifice, it is seldom that those who deserve praise for those acts are wholly without blame for the contribution they make to the achievement of an unjust cause, and the harms they inflict on innocent people. There are many considerations, which I will discuss at length in the next chapter, that mitigate whatever blame unjust combatants may deserve for their participation in an unjust war, but it is rare for unjust combatants to deserve no blame at all.

Yet who among their fellow citizens has a right to cast the first stone? The civilian members of the society that sent them to war are in no position to abuse them for doing what the society demanded of them. Many of these civilians have been actively complicit in the waging of the war, and most of them share some responsibility for it. They have, moreover, failed in their responsibility to the soldiers themselves, who are usually young and vulnerable, to prevent them from being commanded to fight in an unjust war. As members of the society the soldiers serve and protect, the civilians owe it to them to reduce their burden in complying with the demands of morality. While the civilians may have fulfilled their responsibility to ensure that the soldiers are trained in the means of fighting, they have failed in their responsibility to ensure that the soldiers are also trained for the exercise of moral and political judgment.

Soldiers are more likely than most other people to be used as instruments of wrongdoing and injustice, so they have a strong reason to acquire the moral and political knowledge that is relevant to the evaluation of their action as soldiers. Their vocation is of the utmost moral importance. It is notoriously risky physically, but it is also morally perilous. The activities of soldiers have a profound impact on the lives and well-being of a great many people. Very few of us ever have the ability and the opportunity to do so much good as a soldier has; yet few of us also have the capacity to do so much harm in our professional activities. It makes an enormous difference whether soldiers exercise their skills as warriors for just purposes or for unjust purposes. It is therefore imperative that they seek to understand the moral constraints by which their professional action is governed, and it is equally imperative that those for whose benefit they act do what is necessary to provide them with the tools for the judicious exercise of moral and political judgment. (Of course, for a society to transmit moral knowledge about war to its soldiers, it must first possess that knowledge. To provide it is a task for philosophers, one that we have hitherto not performed very well, in my view.)

Suppose that philosophers were to achieve a greatly enhanced understanding of the morality of war, that our society had devised ways of making that understanding available to its soldiers, and that it had also urged and encouraged those soldiers to take responsibility for their own action in matters of *jus ad bellum* as well as in matters of *jus in bello*. Yet suppose the government then commands them to fight in a war that many correctly believe to be unjust. They are now burdened with a terrible dilemma. If they obey the command to fight, they will be guilty of serious wrongdoing. If they conscientiously refuse to fight, the society that has trained and encouraged them to exercise their moral autonomy will punish them for disobedience. Either way, the government and the society unfairly impose on them the costs of the government's wrongdoing.

Some injustice of this sort seems unavoidable. But it can be mitigated through institutional provisions for conscientious refusal to fight. During the last period in which there was conscription in the US, pacifists whose convictions were religiously based could be granted an exemption from military service, though they were often required to perform some other form of public service instead. Even now, active-duty soldiers who become pacifists for religious reasons can receive a similar exemption. During the days of the draft, good arguments, both moral and legal, were advanced in favor of permitting *selective* conscientious objection—that is, refusal to serve in particular wars rather than indiscriminate refusal to serve in all wars—and on secular moral grounds as well as religious grounds.[46] Often these arguments focused on resistance to conscription, but the thrust of the argument in this chapter is that provisions for nonreligious, selective conscientious objection should be extended to active-duty soldiers as well.

The typical reaction to this suggestion is that it is plainly crazy. To permit soldiers to opt out of fighting particular wars on moral grounds would wholly undermine the ability of military organizations to perform their functions of deterrence and defense with even minimal effectiveness. It would require us to invest in training soldiers and paying their salaries only to find that when their services are most needed, they could decide to take a moral holiday.

These fears are reasonable. But I think they are usually exaggerated. People living a hundred years ago, had they been able to conceive of it as a possibility at all, would have said the same about the possibility of conscientious disobedience to orders concerning the conduct of war in the midst of combat. The suggestion that soldiers could be granted the right to disobey orders from a superior officer if they believed those orders to be unlawful would have been dismissed as utterly incompatible with the maintenance of discipline and thus of organized and coordinated action on the battlefield. Yet today a soldier is legally *required* to disobey a manifestly unlawful order—provided, that is, that the law the order would violate is an *in bello* rather than an *ad bellum* law—and military organizations function no less efficiently as a result. Why should we suppose that permitting disobedience to a command that is manifestly unlawful in *ad bellum* terms would have a radically different result?

In one respect at least, provisions for conscientious disobedience to unlawful *ad bellum* orders are *less* likely to be disruptive than permitting conscientious disobedience to unlawful *in bello* orders. This is because a soldier's capacity for rational deliberation is greatly diminished in conditions of combat. Grant him any latitude for disobedience to orders in these conditions and the consequences are wholly unpredictable—or so one might reasonably have supposed, in advance of our actual experience of the requirement of *in bello* disobedience. By contrast, soldiers deliberating about whether to fight at all in a war they suspect may be unjust have at least some opportunity for reflection in conditions in which their lives are not in immediate danger.

One might argue that it is safer to allow soldiers some discretion in obedience to *in bello* commands than it would be to allow them a similar discretion in obedience to *ad bellum* commands on the ground that the law of *jus in bello* is more determinate, so that there cannot be as much uncertainty and dispute about what counts as a legitimate act of war than there is about which wars are just and which unjust. But this is not obviously true. What, for example, ought a soldier to do when ordered to fire upon a group of children whom his commander claims are child soldiers with concealed weapons? Or if it is in fact true that there is greater indeterminacy about matters of *jus ad bellum*, the proper response may not be to accept that that excludes the possibility of options for conscientious objection but instead to endeavor to make our understanding of *jus ad bellum* more precise, and to codify it in legal rules that are more plausible and more determinately applicable than the present broad generalizations of international law about aggression and defense.

If there were legal provisions for soldiers to refuse to fight in a war that they could plausibly argue was unjust, this could indeed impair the ability of their government to fight an unjust war. But this is hardly an objection, since from an impartial point of view that would be an overall good effect. The concern is instead that such a provision would impede the ability of the government to mobilize sufficient forces, with sufficient discipline and cohesion, to be able to fight a *just* war as efficiently as it could if it were to prohibit conscientious objection. I cannot pretend to have the expertise in history, psychology, and other areas that would be required to offer a credible opinion on this matter. But I will offer a couple of observations. First, there have been a great many instances of unjust wars throughout human history, which suggests how comparatively easy it is for governments to assemble the soldiers they need to fight their wars, whether just or unjust. Yet there are relatively few recorded instances of a government being unable to fight a just war because of its inability to motivate people to fight. Mass insubordination or mutiny has been comparatively rare, especially in wars that were just. In particular, when people have been threatened by unjust aggression by a foreign power, they have almost always been willing to fight, even when the prospect of successful defense has seemed remote. It is illuminating to recall that the contemporary military organization that has the most conspicuous record both of instances of conscientious refusal to serve in certain campaigns or operations and of toleration of this sort of conscientious action is Israel's IDF, which operates on the basis of universal conscription and extensive reserves. Yet no one doubts that everyone in the IDF would fight with the utmost cohesion and determination in a just war of national defense.

If we ask what has been the greater problem historically, conscientious refusal to fight in just wars or unreflective obedience to commands to fight in unjust wars, the answer is obvious. Considered impartially, therefore, greater toleration of selective conscientious objection, even by active-duty soldiers, would almost certainly have good effects overall. Yet perhaps it is also true that for any particular country, the threat that tolerance of conscientious objection would pose to military preparedness for just wars might seem to outweigh the effect it could have in hindering the fighting of unjust wars. But I very much doubt it. If most just wars are wars of defense against unjust threats, and if people are generally willing to fight to defend themselves and their community from unjust threats, there seems to be little reason to suppose that increased tolerance of selective conscientious objection would compromise a country's ability to fight the just wars that would be most important to it.

There is, moreover, a tendency to underestimate just how bad unjust wars are, not only for those against whom they are fought but also for those who fight them. While fighting an unjust war is often highly beneficial to certain elites, it is usually disastrous for the population as a whole, quite apart from the moral costs. The continuing US war in Iraq, which was advertised to those who have fought it and to those who have paid for it financially on the basis of a variety of lies and distortions, has resulted in remarkably few casualties among US forces, at least in comparison with other major wars, such as those in Vietnam and Korea. But the financial costs have been very great, necessarily diminishing the resources available for the pursuit of other goals. According to Senator Charles Schumer, the war is currently costing the US about $430 million per *day*, though that could be a significant underestimate once long-term health care costs for veterans are factored in.[47] To put that figure into perspective, consider that the US government spent only $227 million during the entire *year* of 2007 on research for lung cancer, a disease that kills an estimated 161,840 Americans each year.[48]

I have suggested that professional soldiers would not be tempted to try to exploit a provision for selective conscientious objection as a means of evading service in a just war of national defense. And I have suggested that most just wars are of this sort. But there is another, increasingly important type of just war: humanitarian intervention. A war of humanitarian intervention is a war fought by one state, or a set of allied states, to defend the members of a group within another state from serious violations of their human rights by a different group within that same state, usually the government and its supporters. In general, when a soldier fights in a just war of humanitarian intervention, he risks his life for the sake of people who are not only strangers but not even compatriots. It would not be surprising if some soldiers sought to exempt themselves from fighting in such a war by spuriously claiming to be opposed to it on moral grounds.

This is only one of many problems with humanitarian intervention that might be solved through the creation of a special force under international control whose only purpose would be to carry out humanitarian military operations. This would have to be a volunteer force composed of individuals who would not be members of any national military force. They would have to be imbued with a warrior ethos distinctively suited to humanitarian intervention. They would have to see themselves as entrusted with the special mission of protecting the weak and vulnerable, regardless of their group identity, wherever such people might be threatened by their own government. The members of such a force would have to regard it as dishonorable to seek to evade the risks necessary for the fulfillment of their mission.[49]

There is of course no such force, nor is there likely to be anytime soon. Until there is, the possibility that soldiers commanded to fight in a war of humanitarian intervention will attempt to escape the risks by pretending to have moral scruples will remain a serious objection to offering options for selective conscientious objection to active-duty soldiers. One possible response to this problem, which is admittedly only a partial solution, is to impose significant penalties on active-duty conscientious objectors. Soldiers granted selective conscientious objector status after receiving wages, training, and so on from the military would have to submit to these penalties as a means of demonstrating their sincerity. Penalties could range from forfeiture of the benefits of military service, such as educational assistance and retirement funds, through compulsory public service, to imprisonment. Although the action of conscientious objectors need not be an instance of civil disobedience, in that it need not be intended to make a public statement, genuine objectors might be compelled, like those who engage in civil disobedience, to make themselves martyrs to morality.

The idea that obedience to authority is among the supreme virtues, and consequently that disobedience is never to be tolerated, has nowhere been more evident than in the culture of Nazism. The central thesis of Hannah Arendt's celebrated and notorious book on the trial of Adolf Eichmann is that he, along with many other senior Nazi officials responsible for directing the invasions and occupations of various European countries, and organizing the extermination of the Jews, saw himself simply as a conscientious bureaucrat punctiliously fulfilling the duties of his role and office. The typical Nazi administrator was, in Stanley Milgram's words, "a functionary who has been given a job to do and who strives to create an impression of competence in his work."[50] Despite the extensive analyses and evaluations of his action during his trial, Eichmann never saw beyond the platitudes of the cult of obedience. Arendt summarizes his final statement to the court as follows:

The court did not understand him: he had never been a Jew-hater, and he had never willed the murder of human beings. His guilt came from his obedience, and obedience is praised as a virtue. His virtue had been abused by the Nazi leaders. But he was not one of the ruling clique, he was a victim, and only the leaders deserved punishment.[51]

But at least one other senior Nazi official who also survived in exile well beyond the trials of other Nazi war criminals in Nuremberg did finally achieve some understanding. Franz Stangl, the Commandant of Treblinka and the only commandant of an extermination camp ever to be brought to trial, was extensively interviewed by Gitta Sereny shortly after he began to serve his sentence of life imprisonment in 1970. On one occasion he offered to explain why a book written by a Polish pediatrician who had been killed at Treblinka was not selling well in Germany:

"I know why they don't want to buy it. Now listen to this . . ." and he read aloud from the fairy tale in the book. " . . . 'When a soldier gets an order, he must obey it. He must not ask questions, he must not hesitate, and must not think: he must obey.'" He closed the book. "Of course parents here don't want their children to read this. . . . I don't want my little grandson to read this either. That is exactly the sort of thing they must not read, ever again."[52]

During Eichmann's trial, a former member of the Jewish underground in Poland, Abba Kovner, told the story of a sergeant in the German army, Anton Schmidt, who had covertly aided the anti-Nazi partisans by providing them with forged papers and military trucks. Within a few months his activities were discovered and he was executed. We would all do well to pause and exercise our moral imaginations in reflecting on Arendt's comment:

During the few minutes it took Kovner to tell of the help that had come from a German sergeant, a hush settled over the courtroom; it was as though the crowd had spontaneously decided to observe the usual two minutes silence in honor of the man named Anton Schmidt. And in those two minutes, which were like a sudden burst of light in the midst of impenetrable, unfathomable darkness, a single thought stood out clearly, irrefutably, beyond question—how utterly different everything would be today in this courtroom, in Israel, in Germany, in all of Europe, and perhaps in all countries of the world, if only more such stories could have been told.[53]

Why did not more soldiers sabotage the Nazi effort from within, as Schmidt did? Why did not more desert? Why did not more refuse to serve at all? Why did not more declare, as a character in Vasily Grossman's *Life and Fate* does: "It's wrong to make out that only the people in power are guilty, that you yourself are only an innocent slave. . . . I'm free. I can say 'No!' What power can stop me if I have the strength not to be afraid of extinction? I will say 'No!' "[54] I will address these questions in the next chapter.

3

Excuses

3.1 SOURCES OF ALLEGIANCE TO THE MORAL EQUALITY OF COMBATANTS

3.1.1 The Conflation of Morality and Law

We can ask an even broader question than those posed at the end of the last chapter. Why do most of us, even now, think that only the high officials, such as Eichmann and Stangl, deserve punishment for the unprecedented slaughter of innocent people perpetrated by the Nazis in World War II? Why do we so readily accept that rank-and-file Nazi soldiers who killed other soldiers from all over Europe as a means of conquering their countries were merely doing their duty as soldiers, provided they refrained from deliberately attacking civilians? More generally still, why have most people in virtually all cultures at all times believed that a person does not act wrongly by fighting in an unjust war, provided that he obeys the principles governing the conduct of war? It is not surprising that people do not tend to think of their own fellow citizens who fight in unjust wars as guilty of wrongdoing—for example, that even those Americans who believe that the Vietnam War was unjust in general reject the idea that veterans who fought by the rules did wrong merely by fighting. What is more surprising is that most Americans probably also accept that Nazi soldiers did not do wrong either, provided they participated only in the invasions of other countries and not in the exterminations of civilian populations.

Surely there have been and continue to be some people whose allegiance to the moral equality of combatants derives from their acceptance of one or more of the arguments discussed in Chapter 2. But most people who accept the moral equality of combatants have never encountered any of those arguments and are unlikely to produce subtle philosophical arguments on their own. The explanation of why people accept the moral equality of combatants is not that they have been persuaded by philosophical argument. Nor is it that the doctrine is just immediately intuitively compelling. Granted, most people believe it, but unreflectively accepting a dogma that everyone else accepts is not the same as finding that dogma intuitively plausible. If one were to pose the question in terms that make it clear what is really at issue—that is, is it permissible to kill people who have done nothing wrong in the course of a war whose goals are unjust?—I doubt that most people would really find the moral equality of combatants intuitive. So why do most people accept it? There are no doubt many layers to the full explanation, but two explanatory claims stand out as most important. One derives from the ubiquitous tendency to conflate the morality of war with the law of war.

The law of war does not assert the *moral* equality of combatants but it does assert the *legal* equality of combatants. That is, it makes the *legal* status of combatants entirely independent of whether the war in which they are fighting is just or unjust, or legal or illegal. The legal rights, liabilities, and immunities of combatants are unaffected by the *ad bellum* status of the war in which they fight. They are not legally liable for anything they do in war provided that they obey the laws governing the conduct of war. Those laws, which are stated in neutral terms and thus recognize no distinction between just and unjust combatants, are equally satisfiable by all who fight. Unjust combatants are at no disadvantage in their ability to conform their behavior to the requirements of the law of *jus in bello*. I will refer to this equality of legal status among both just and unjust combatants as the "legal equality of combatants."

There are various reasons why it is natural and understandable for people to fail to distinguish between the legal equality of combatants and the moral equality of combatants—that is, for people to think that the moral equality of combatants is either equivalent to, presupposed by, or entailed by the legal equality of combatants. Like domestic criminal law, the law of war serves moral purposes, and is designed to do so. Domestic criminal law, with which most people are better acquainted than they are with the law of war, tracks the prohibitions of morality quite closely. The most fundamental criterion of criminalization is moral impermissibility. While not all morally wrongful acts are legally criminal (primarily, though not exclusively, because many morally impermissible acts are insufficiently serious to merit criminal punishment), and while some criminally unlawful acts are morally permissible, most of the gravest forms of wrongdoing are nevertheless also illegal, and the ideal in criminal law is never to hold a person criminally liable for an act that is morally permissible, or morally required. It is natural for people to assume that the same is true of the international law of war. And if it were indeed the case that the law of war is as closely congruent with the morality of war as the domestic criminal law is with the morality of interpersonal relations within a society, then it would be reasonable to infer from the legal equality of combatants that something quite close to the moral equality of combatants must be true.

There are also historical reasons why people tend to conflate the morality and law of war. The moral theory of the just war antedated any serious legal regulation of war. When juridical thinkers began to develop accounts of the "law of nations," the framework within which they formulated their theories and proposals was inevitably provided by the prevailing understanding of natural law found in classical versions of just war theory. Legal principles were thus couched in just war idioms. Partly for this reason, the morality of war and the law of war share a common vocabulary, which obviously exacerbates the difficulty of keeping them distinct.

As the legal regulation of war became more effective, particularly in the eighteenth and nineteenth centuries, the practical significance of just war theory was gradually eclipsed by that of the evolving law of war. For the first three-quarters of the twentieth century, virtually nothing of interest or significance was written on the just war, or indeed on the morality of war generally. All the important work was instead done by legal theorists. Perhaps the main reason for this is that moral philosophers were seduced, beginning early in the century, by a succession of philosophical dogmas that convinced them that they, *as philosophers*, could have nothing more authoritative to say about matters of practical morality than anyone else. Some of the most influential of these dogmas were derived, directly or indirectly, from the pronouncements of Wittgenstein, whose personal convictions about the morality of war were cited in the opening passages of this book. But during the course of the Vietnam War, philosophers generally at last began to liberate themselves from the stultifying effects of these dogmas, and moral philosophers were thus enabled to take a professional interest in matters of practical morality, the most urgent of which at the time was, of course, war. Just war theory was revived, mainly in the United States, but the new generation of just war theorists naturally looked for inspiration to the recent and remarkable achievements of the legal theorists who had been involved in debating and formulating legal doctrine during both the Nuremberg Tribunals and the drafting of the

UN Charter and the various Geneva Conventions and their subsequent Protocols. Late twentieth-century just war doctrine was thus modeled quite closely on the international law of war in the form that the latter took at that time.

For at least the last sixty years, the law of war has had two principal goals: to prevent wars from occurring and to limit and contain the violence and destruction when they do occur. This almost exclusive concern with consequences is characteristic of certain moral theories, which perhaps have maximal plausibility in their application to conditions of war, in which the enormity of the possible consequences may seem to overshadow all other considerations. Of course, all moral theories with a modicum of plausibility recognize that consequences are important to the evaluation of action. But most hold that consequences are not all that matters. In common sense morality, what it is permissible to do to a person is not determined solely by what the consequences of one's action will be for all those affected. It depends also on what rights the person has and whether he or she has done anything to waive or forfeit them. Domestic criminal law and the law of torts have inherited this concern with rights and liability. Thus, very few people suppose that criminal law should be designed simply to minimize harm overall, assigning the same weight to harms suffered by criminal aggressors and those suffered by their innocent victims. Although the weighing of harms does have a role in law in judgments of proportionality, the criminal law in general gives priority to the defense of rights over calculations of consequences.

This is precisely what the law of war—particularly the law of *jus in bello*—does *not* do. Unlike the domestic criminal law, the law of war is designed not to protect moral rights but to prevent harm. This is why it diverges so radically from the morality of war, which requires both respect for rights and attention to consequences. I argued in Chapter 1 that people neither waive nor forfeit their right not to be wrongfully attacked simply by defending themselves and other innocent people against a wrongful attack. This is true in war just as it is true in other contexts. What this means is that when unjust combatants attack just combatants, they are violating the latter's moral rights not to be wrongfully attacked and are thus acting impermissibly. Yet they are acting within their legal rights.

It is imperative that we work to bring the law of war into closer conformity with the morality of war, as we have succeeded, to a considerable degree, in bringing criminal law into conformity with the morality of interpersonal relations in domestic society. For it is uncontroversially a defect in the law to exempt an entire class of people—combatants—from criminal liability for the intentional killing of innocent people. Achieving in the area of war the kind of congruence between law and morality that we find in criminal law will thus require the rejection of the legal equality of combatants. Yet at present that cannot be done without making the situation worse in moral terms.

The current law of *jus ad bellum* is crude and simplistic, and we lack a sophisticated understanding of the morality of the resort to war that could guide us in reforming *ad bellum* law. More importantly, even if we could formulate a better set of *ad bellum* legal rules, we would still lack an authoritative judicial body that could judge the *ad bellum* status of wars while they were in progress. Because of this, we do not and at present cannot provide combatants with authoritative guidance about whether the war in which they are fighting is just or unjust, or lawful or unlawful. Combatants tend, therefore, to defer to the judgment of their own government, which they naturally take to be legally authoritative in its application to them. As a result, most combatants believe that the war in which they are fighting is just and lawful. In these conditions, rejection of the legal equality of combatants is pointless, for if the law of *jus in bello* were to impose highly stringent restrictions only on unjust combatants—if, at the limit, it were to deny them the right to fight at all—unjust combatants would not recognize those restrictions as applying to themselves. They would instead claim the legal prerogatives accorded to just combatants and the law would lack the resources to controvert them.

So far this shows only that an asymmetric, nonneutral law of *jus in bello* would not be better; I have not shown that it would be worse. What I claim would be worse is an *in bello* law that would be *as asymmetric* as *in bello* morality. I believe that there could *in principle* be circumstances in which it would be morally permissible for people with a just cause to act in ways now prohibited by law. It could, for example, be permissible for just combatants intentionally to harm certain civilians or prisoners of war; it could be permissible for them to disguise themselves as civilians to facilitate an attack on unjust combatants; and it could be permissible for civilians themselves to attack combatants participating in an unjust occupation. I concede that such acts could rarely be permissible in practice, if only because they would provoke reprisals against the innocent; but what could make them permissible in principle is that those who would be their intended targets would have made themselves liable to attack by virtue of responsibility for a wrong that could be prevented or corrected only by attacking them in a proportionate manner.

The law of war denies the permission to act in these ways to just combatants, and at present it is right to do so. As I noted, in current conditions whatever is legally permitted to the just will be done by the unjust. And it is more important to try to restrain unjust combatants from acting in these ways than it is to grant just combatants legal permission to do such things in the rare conditions in which it would be morally permissible for them to do so. A neutral law that permitted all combatants to attack civilians in certain specified conditions, or to harm or kill prisoners, or to disguise themselves as civilians, would be exploited by the unjust and inevitably abused by the just, leading to greater violence, and in particular to more and worse violations of the rights of the innocent, than a law that prohibits these forms of action to all.

At present, in other words, when all who fight claim to be just combatants, and most also sincerely believe what they claim, and when their belief cannot be authoritatively controverted, we must deny them all permission to act in certain ways that on occasion might be morally permitted to actual just combatants, or even morally required of them. We must do this because it would be intolerable to offer unjust combatants any legal rationale or protection for acting in these ways. The law must of course permit just combatants to kill enemy combatants. Just wars cannot be fought in any other way. And it would be wholly inefficacious to forbid unjust combatants to do the same; therefore the law must at present permit all combatants to kill their enemy counterparts. But just combatants can generally fight effectively without intentionally killing civilians, and it would be intolerable to offer unjust combatants any legal pretext for intentionally killing civilians on the just side; therefore the law must at present include an exceptionless prohibition of deliberate attacks on civilians.

There are other reasons why the law cannot presently abandon the legal equality of combatants. One concerns the ways in which the abandonment of that doctrine would make it easier for an unjust but victorious side in a war to inflict punishment on just combatants whom it had defeated. I will return to this in Section 4.4. The crucial point here is that while there is a widespread tendency to assume that the morality of war is closely reflected in the law of war, that assumption is in fact false. The legal equality of combatants is a fixture of the law and must remain so until we are able to alter the conditions that make it necessary. But there is no corresponding moral equality of combatants. The common view that the law of war is like the criminal law in being modeled directly on morality, and must therefore, at least for the most part, merely *restate* the permissions and requirements of the morality of war, is wholly unfounded. It is a mistake to suppose that one can draw inferences about the morality of war by examining the current state of the law of war. That this mistake is ubiquitous is one of the two most important explanations of the widespread acceptance of the moral equality of combatants.

It applies, however, only to people who have been influenced in their thinking by the modern law of war. It cannot explain why something very like the moral equality of combatants was widely held even before the development of the law of nations. To explain that, one must consider people's failure to recognize a distinction more subtle than that between morality and law.

3.1.2 The Conflation of Permission and Excuse

In law, there is a familiar, though disputed, distinction between justification and excuse. The distinction I will discuss is similar, though not exactly the same. Recall that in Chapter 1, I distinguished between justification and permission, stipulating that as I will use the term, an act is justified if and only if it is permissible in the circumstances *and* there is positive moral reason to do it. Some acts that are justified are optional, others are required. Acts that are permitted or justified have in common that they are not wrong. When an act is wrong but the agent who does it is not blameworthy, he or she is excused. (Note that an agent who acts in a way that is permitted, justified, or even required may nonetheless be blameworthy if he or she acts with a bad motive, or for a discreditable reason.)

The moral equality of combatants might be a claim about permissibility or it might be a claim about justification. The weaker interpretation is that because just combatants are permitted to fight provided they do not violate the principles of *jus in bello*, unjust combatants are also permitted to fight on the same condition. The stronger interpretation is that because just combatants are justified in fighting, unjust combatants are as well. That leaves a further possibility that is not strictly a claim of moral equality: namely, that while just combatants are justified in fighting, unjust combatants are merely permitted to fight. To my knowledge, no one has ever explicitly considered, much less defended, this latter possibility, though it may actually capture what many people believe more accurately than any other version of the moral equality of combatants.

Some people who accept the moral equality of combatants seem to do so because they confuse permission with excuse. The confusion of these two notions is common. It appears explicitly in Vitoria, in a passage in which he defends a limited doctrine of moral equality. Vitoria does not accept the familiar, universal version of the doctrine, for he holds that a combatant does wrong if he fights when "the war seems patently unjust" to him, even when ordered by a legitimate authority to do so, for "one may not lawfully kill an innocent man on any authority, and in the case we are speaking of [when the soldier is confident that the war is unjust] the enemy must be innocent."[1] But Vitoria does claim that there are certain cases in which those who fight for a just cause and those who fight against them for an unjust cause are moral equals. He writes that

where there is provable ignorance either of fact or of law, *the war may be just in itself for the side which has true justice on its side, and also just for the other side, because they wage war in good faith and are hence excused from sin.* Invincible error is a valid excuse in every case. This is often the position of subjects: even if the prince who wages war knows that his cause is unjust, his subjects may nevertheless obey him in good faith . . . In such situations, the subjects on both sides are justified in fighting, as is well known.[2]

It is possible to interpret this passage in such a way that it does not confuse permission and excuse. Because Vitoria elsewhere seems to embrace a subjective understanding of permissibility, it is possible that what he means here is that subjects who are not certain that their sovereign's cause is unjust are entitled to presume, and thus to believe, that it is just. In that case, because they are acting on the basis of a reasonable belief that, if true, would objectively justify their action, their action is subjectively permissible. In that case, soldiers on both sides would be acting permissibly: those with a just cause would be acting both subjectively and objectively permissibly, while those whose cause was unjust would nevertheless be acting subjectively permissibly. Yet Vitoria's reference to "true justice" suggests that he implicitly recognizes a distinction between subjective permissibility and objective permissibility. So even if in this passage he takes the "excuse" of "invincible error" to be a subjective permission rather than an excuse in the contemporary sense, he need not, and ought not, to take a merely subjective permission to be substantively equivalent—that is, equivalent in its substantive implications—to an objective permission, much less to an objective justification.

Another writer whose defense of the moral equality of combatants seems to involve a conflation of permission and excuse is Michael Walzer, the doctrine's most prominent contemporary advocate. In various passages in *Just and Unjust Wars*, Walzer associates the doctrine of the moral equality of combatants with the idea that unjust combatants are not *criminals*. He cites the sense that combatants often have "that the enemy soldier, though his war may well be criminal, is nevertheless as blameless as oneself." If I am a just combatant, I may see my enemies as " 'poor sods, just like me.' . . . I find in them my moral equals." Walzer interprets this perception of unjust combatants as "precisely the recognition of men who are not criminals."[3] And it is the absence of criminality in the action of the unjust combatant that grounds the moral equality of combatants. "Soldiers fighting for an aggressor state are not themselves criminals: hence their war rights are the same as those of their opponents."[4]

In various places Walzer also identifies the absence of criminality with the absence of blameworthiness. "It would be very odd," he claims, "to praise Rommel for not killing prisoners unless we simultaneously refused to blame him for Hitler's aggressive wars. For otherwise he is simply a criminal, and all the fighting he does is murder or attempted murder."[5] In short, Walzer claims that if an unjust combatant is blameless, he is not a criminal, that if he is not a criminal, he is the moral equal of a just combatant, and that he is therefore permitted to fight if the just combatant is.

The mistake here is to ignore the possibility that blamelessness implies nothing more than that the unjust combatant is excused. That a person is blameless does not entail that he or she has acted permissibly; for both those who act permissibly and those who act wrongly but with a full excuse are blameless.

The same is true of the absence of criminality. It may be that a person is not a criminal simply because he has not committed a crime; but it is also possible that he is not a criminal because, although he has done a criminal act, he is nevertheless excused. In law, the commission of a criminal act is not sufficient for a person to be a criminal. That person must also be culpable for the criminal act in order to be a criminal, a fit subject for criminal punishment.

That Walzer regards unjust combatants in a way that is best understood as merely excused is suggested by the reasons he gives when claiming that they are blameless. He argues, for example, that choice on the basis of reasons of their own

effectively disappears as soon as fighting becomes a legal obligation and a patriotic duty. Then "the waste of life of the combatants is one which," as the philosopher T.H. Green has written, "the power of the state compels. This is equally true whether the army is raised by voluntary enlistment or by conscription." For the state decrees that an army of a certain size be raised, and it sets out to find the necessary men, using all the techniques of coercion and persuasion at its disposal. And the men it finds, precisely because they go to war under constraint or as a matter of conscience, . . . are political instruments, they obey orders, and the practice of war is shaped at a higher level.[6]

The appeal here is primarily to duress: combatants are compelled to fight; they have no choice. But duress is not a justification; nor does it ground a permission—not even a subjective permission. It is, instead, an excusing condition.[7]

Consider an extreme case: someone puts a gun to your head and credibly threatens to kill you unless you kill an innocent third party. You are no more permitted to kill this innocent person as a means of saving yourself than you would be to kill him by taking one of his vital organs in order to save yourself from organ failure. The full explanation of why it is wrong to kill an innocent person as a means of self-preservation is no doubt quite complex, but two salient considerations are worth mentioning, in part because we will return to them later. First, to accede to the demand of the person who threatens you would involve *killing*, whereas to refuse would involve allowing someone—yourself—to be killed. And it is, and always has been, widely accepted that the moral presumption against killing is in general stronger than the presumption against allowing someone to be killed (that is, failing to prevent someone from being killed). Second, killing the innocent third party would involve *intending* a harmful death, while refusing to kill him would not. And it is, and always has been, widely accepted that the moral presumption against bringing about a harmful death as an intended effect is in general stronger than the presumption against bringing about a harmful death as a foreseen but unintended effect.

Some philosophers have advanced serious arguments that challenge the moral significance of the distinctions between killing and letting die and between bringing about a death intentionally and bringing it about foreseeably but unintentionally. If they are right, many of the most fundamental intuitions about harming and killing that most people have shared throughout human history must be abandoned. Until we are prepared to act consistently on the basis of a morality from which these distinctions have been systematically purged—and I know of no philosophers who have been willing to do that not just in their writings but in their lives—we should probably continue to assume that the distinctions and their significance are more firmly grounded than the challenges to them. This is a reactionary position at a time when most practitioners of experimental philosophy are doing their best to discredit the epistemic and normative authority of moral intuition. Even so, it is the position I will adopt in this book.

If it is true that it would be wrong to kill an innocent bystander even if that were the only means of preventing oneself from being killed, then duress is merely an excusing condition, not a source of permission or justification. One may be misled to believe otherwise by cases in which it *is* permissible under duress to harm an innocent person as an intended means of averting a harm to oneself. Suppose, for example, that a person puts a gun to your head and credibly threatens to kill you unless you give an innocent third party a vicious pinch. In this case you are morally justified in pinching an innocent person as viciously as you can. But the justification is not that you are acting under duress. It is instead a lesser-evil justification: you are justified in wronging an innocent person in a minor way in order to avert a vastly greater evil to yourself (or indeed to another third party, for nothing here hinges on whether the gun is at your head or the head of a stranger).

Note the insistence that the harm averted be *substantially* greater than the harm caused. At least part of the explanation of that requirement derives from the moral differences between doing harm and allowing harm and between intending harm and bringing about harm foreseeably but unintentionally. These distinctions together establish a strong moral presumption against doing harm intentionally. When choosing the lesser evil requires *intentionally causing* that evil, the presumption against the intentional infliction of harm must be overridden. It is because of the strength of that presumption that the harm averted must be substantially greater than the harm caused. Otherwise the presumption could not be overridden. So the greater the moral significance of these distinctions is, the greater the difference must be between the harm inflicted and the harm averted in order for the intentional infliction of harm to be justified as the lesser evil.

The conclusion we should draw from this discussion is that even if the considerations Walzer and others cite were to show that unjust combatants are blameless for participating in an unjust war, and are therefore not criminals, it would not follow that their participation in an unjust war is permissible; and therefore it would not follow that they have the same moral status as just combatants, assuming that just combatants act permissibly when they fight within the limits imposed by the principles of *jus in bello*. It may be that just and unjust combatants are equally undeserving of blame, but it does not follow that they are moral equals in all respects, or have the same moral status. For it may be that just combatants are blameless because they act with justification, while unjust combatants are blameless because, although they act wrongly, the conditions in which they act are such as to excuse them for their wrongdoing. Or even if Vitoria is right that in some wars unjust combatants are subjectively justified in fighting, it does not follow that their moral status is identical to that of just combatants, whose action is objectively justified. I will return to this in Chapter 4.

If Walzer, writing at a time when the distinction between justification and excuse was discussed and deployed pervasively in the legal literature, could have failed to recognize that the denial that unjust combatants are criminals, or blameworthy for wrongdoing, is compatible with the claim that they act wrongly, it should be entirely unsurprising that people in the more distant past, including many of his predecessors in the just war tradition, made the same mistake—or that most people today, who are considerably less sophisticated than Walzer in their thinking about war, should continue to do so.

Together with the tendency people have to assume that the morality and law of war coincide, the tendency to assume that those who are blameless cannot have done wrong provides what I think must be the major part of the explanation why most people believe that unjust combatants do not do wrong merely by fighting in a war that is unjust.

3.2 EXCUSING CONDITIONS FOR UNJUST COMBATANTS

3.2.1 Duress

Most of the claims that are offered in defense of unjust combatants, whether they are intended to justify their action or to excuse it, are familiar. But it will be helpful to try to assemble them here to examine them in detail, consider how much force they have as excusing conditions, and determine what they may imply about the moral status of unjust combatants.

The common practice is to distinguish three broad categories of excuse: duress, epistemic limitation, and diminished responsibility. The Model Penal Code (§2.09(1)) holds that a person has acted under duress if he has been "coerced . . . by the use of, or a threat to use, unlawful force against his person or the person of another, which a person of reasonable firmness in his situation would have been unable to resist." This defines duress as a full excuse in the law. But not all excuses are full excuses. An excuse may be partial; it may only mitigate a person's culpability rather than exclude culpability altogether. I will take duress to include threats to an agent that exert varying degrees of pressure against his will to resist. If one acts as another demands because one has been threatened with harm in the event of noncompliance, one acts under duress even if a person of reasonable firmness could have resisted the threat. If the act is wrong, one may not be fully excused, but one's guilt or culpability may be mitigated because of the threat.

The Model Penal Code, and the law generally, limits duress to threats intentionally imposed by agents. I propose to broaden the scope of the term in my use of it here so that it also includes threats to a person that may arise unintentionally from natural or social conditions if the person fails to act in a certain way.

Like duress, epistemic limitation is also a matter of degree, and is so in several respects. A person's knowledge of relevant matters may be limited or defective to varying degrees, he may be responsible for his epistemic deficiencies to a greater or lesser degree, and so on. As I have indicated, epistemic constraints may provide more than just an excuse. When they are, as Vitoria puts it, "invincible," they can provide a subjective permission or justification. But when they provide only an excuse, that excuse may be full or partial, and if only partial, it may have variable force in mitigating the agent's culpability.

Finally, diminution of the capacity for responsible action is also a matter of degree rather than all-or-nothing. This capacity arises gradually, by degrees, in all who have it, and can be possessed by an individual at a given time to any of those degrees. The greater the diminution of the capacity, the stronger the excuse. At the limit, there are some human beings who altogether lack any capacity for morally responsible agency. The absence of that capacity may be temporary or permanent. If it is permanent, that may be contingent or it may be that it is in principle impossible for the capacity to arise or, if it was previously present, to be restored. In cases in which the capacity is entirely absent, an individual's behavior ceases to be excused because it ceases to be subject to moral evaluation. Like a natural event or the behavior of a lower animal, it is neither permissible nor impermissible.

There are excusing conditions in each of these categories that commonly apply to unjust combatants. Under the heading of duress, for example, it is commonly noted that a significant proportion of those who have fought in unjust wars have been conscripted. The penalties for refusing conscription have varied in different times and places, ranging from a fine to imprisonment to execution.

Even those who are not conscripted, but instead enlist, often do so under a kind of compulsion deriving from the grinding exigencies of their economic or social circumstances. In the world's poorest countries, where vast numbers of people have lived in conditions of appalling poverty and despair, dictators have been able to maintain power indefinitely by offering young men abundant food, salaries sufficient to support their entire families, and various other inducements in exchange for service in the military. When these men would otherwise face a prospect of gradual wasting from malnutrition and disease, the privileges and powers they receive through military service are virtually irresistible. They are, indeed, usually sufficient to ensure the men's loyalty even up to and beyond a willingness to slaughter their own compatriots in whatever numbers their benefactors might require. In these conditions, the prospects that people who have the option of enlisting may face from failing to do so may be much worse than the penalties that people in other countries may suffer for resisting conscription. In other words, the level of duress under which some people enlist, and in a clear sense voluntarily, may exceed the duress under which others submit to conscription. (Recall that I am using "duress" broadly to include any threat of harm arising from a failure to act, even if the threat is not the product of intentional agency.)

Even in affluent countries such as the United States, economic pressures appear to be the principal motivation for enlistment.[8] In times of war, however, social pressures may become even more coercive than economic ones. The fictional but surely autobiographical narrator in Tim O'Brien's novel, *The Things They Carried*, observes that American soldiers fought in Vietnam under pressure of their

> greatest fear, which was the fear of blushing. Men killed, and died, because they were embarrassed not to. It was what had brought them to the war in

the first place, nothing positive, no dreams of glory or honor, just to avoid the blush of dishonor. They died so as not to die of embarrassment. They crawled into tunnels and walked point and advanced under fire. . . . It was not courage exactly; the object was not valor. Rather, they were too frightened to be cowards.[9]

Later in the novel, the narrator recounts the reflections that finally got him to acquiesce in going to war.

All those eyes on me—the town, the whole universe—and I couldn't risk the embarrassment. It was as if there were an audience to my life . . . and in my head I could hear people screaming at me. Traitor! they yelled. Turncoat! Pussy! I felt myself blush. I couldn't tolerate it. I couldn't endure the mockery, or the disgrace, or the patriotic ridicule. Even in my imagination, . . . I couldn't make myself be brave. It had nothing to do with morality. Embarrassment, that's all it was.
   And right then I submitted.
   I would go to the war—I would kill and maybe die—because I was embarrassed not to.[10]

These pressures are often deliberately employed to shame men into fighting. In London during World War I, women would hand white feathers, symbols of cowardice, to men of military age whom they saw on the streets. Few were invulnerable to this sort of humiliation. (Lytton Strachey was. When a woman challenged him to explain why he was not fighting to save civilization, he is reputed to have replied, "I am, Madam, the civilization for which they are fighting." It was not that Strachey had what O'Brien's narrator lacked: the courage to be a coward. He had, rather, the moral and physical courage to be a selective conscientious objector.[11])
   I have thus far been discussing the pressures to join the military. But of course many people join the military not under pressure but for idealistic and admirable reasons, such as to be prepared to defend their country should it come under unjust attack. It often happens, however, that people who join for morally good reasons later find themselves ordered to fight in a war that they believe, usually correctly, is unjust. (I say "usually correctly" because the natural tendency of combatants to believe that the war in which they are fighting is just is generally so strong that it takes a compelling countervailing force to overcome it. And there is more likely to be such a force to operate against the combatant's complacency when the war is in fact unjust than when it is just.) But once people have joined and become active-duty military personnel, the penalties they face for conscientious disobedience or desertion tend to be far harsher than those for refusing conscription.

3.2.2 Epistemic Limitation

Although duress of the broad sort I have discussed is an important excusing condition for unjust combatants, the epistemic conditions in which they act constitute an arguably even stronger ground for denying that they are culpable, or at least for recognizing that their culpability is significantly mitigated. Combatants usually act in ignorance of a great many factual matters that are relevant to the determination of whether the war in which they have been commanded to fight is just. These include the historical background to the war, what each side has done to produce the war, what the motives and intentions of their leaders are, what options there might be other than war for the achievement of their country's aims, and so on. They may realize that some of the information that allegedly supports their government's case for war is classified. They may be subject to the suppression of information in other ways, such as government control of the media, or they may be victims of positive deception by their government, as American soldiers were in 2003 when they were assured by the Bush administration that Iraq possessed weapons of mass destruction. If, moreover, the war erupts suddenly, they may simply have no opportunity for gathering relevant information and engaging in careful moral deliberation.

In most military organizations, the ability of soldiers to engage in autonomous reflection and deliberation about the content of their orders is also deliberately and systematically sabotaged. They are subjected to intensive conditioning and indoctrination, to endless drills, and to processes intended to efface their individuality and subvert their autonomy. The suppression of individual identity is achieved in part through shaving of the heads of males and making all soldiers wear the same uniform. They are all to look and act in exactly the same ways. Their wills are broken through intimidation, bullying, and humiliation by their instructors, through demands for repeated public displays of deference and submissiveness, and so on. The aim is to convert them into largely unreflective instruments of the wills of their superiors.

Soldiers also tend to lack all but the most rudimentary understanding of the morality of war—though in recent years this has begun to change in the case of the officer corps, who in the US tend to receive instruction in the elements of just war theory in the service academies. Enlisted personnel, however, tend to be schooled only in the conventional rules of engagement, and told they must disobey a manifestly unlawful order, though the demand for disobedience is restricted to unlawful orders concerning the conduct of war rather than orders concerning the resort to war—that is, to matters of *jus in bello* rather than *jus ad bellum*. Otherwise soldiers are discouraged from thinking about the morality of war, and especially about whether wars are just or unjust. On that issue they are expected to defer to the judgment of their government.

This they readily do. Most are aware of the limitations of their own knowledge and assume their government must have both superior knowledge and superior judgment. They also assume that it has normative authority to which they ought to defer. It is the government that punishes them if they do wrong in domestic life; thus they tend to assume, if only subconsciously, that if the government would also punish them for refusing to fight, it must be their duty to fight. Tendencies to patriotism and loyalty further dispose them to trust what their government tells them.

There is an extensive literature on the psychology of our tendency to obey perceived authority. In the experiment discussed earlier in Section 2.6, Stanley Milgram induced a high proportion of experimental subjects to deliver what they thought might be lethal electric shocks to innocent people when told to do so by people in presumed positions of authority, indicated by their wearing white coats. The subjects who were willing to risk seriously harming or even killing an innocent person at the behest of a minor authority figure believed that they were merely participating in an experiment about learning. How much more powerful, then, must the impulse to obedience be when the command comes, not from an anonymous figure in a white coat engaged only in a psychology experiment, but from an officer authorized by the state to issue commands, and during a time of apparent national emergency when the security of the society may be imperiled.[12]

Even if soldiers were less willing to defer to the authority of their government, it would still be difficult for them to deliberate competently about whether a war in which they have been commanded to fight is just or unjust. Even the acknowledged experts—the theorists of the just war—disagree among themselves about the justice of virtually every war. There is a widely-accepted theory to which they can appeal—namely, the theory of the just war in its received form. Yet it is one of the themes of this book that that theory is not a reliable source of guidance. And even if it were, there would remain ample scope for dispute about its application. Even now, when people tend to agree on the main outlines of the theory, they disagree about its implications for particular wars. Moreover, even if the theory were reliable and the experts were able to apply it consistently to reach agreement about the justice of particular wars, their judgments would presumably be no more accessible to soldiers than the arguments and conclusions of just war theorists are now. For neither the military nor the society as a whole makes any effort to make either the principles or the conclusions of just war theory available to ordinary soldiers. Soldiers are instead actively discouraged from questioning whether wars in which they are ordered to fight are just.

Those soldiers who do reflect on whether it is morally permissible to participate in a particular war, and who do so in a comparatively sophisticated way, are nevertheless likely to be biased toward finding a justification for participation, as most would prefer the risks of combat to the odium, obloquy, and penalties for public disobedience, as O'Brien observes. They may thus rationalize their participation by reference to one or more of the arguments I discussed in Chapter 2. They are likely to believe, for example, that they have a duty to serve the society that they have pledged to defend, and in particular that they are under a contractual obligation to fight. For the state that has trained and paid them now calls upon them to repay the investment, and loyalty demands that they comply.

The ones who are morally conscientious in this way may also reflect that their presence could exercise a restraining influence, at least on the conduct of the unjust war, and that if they were to refuse to fight, they would simply be replaced by someone who would probably be less scrupulous than they are. They are also likely to be reassured by the regnant theory of the just war, which tells them that they do no wrong if they fight, by international law, which says that they also do nothing illegal, and by the civilian population, who perhaps silence their own consciences by noisily trumpeting their support for the troops. Further reassurance is provided by the observation that others are doing exactly as they are. There may not be a single soldier in the whole of their military who is overtly refusing to fight on the ground that the war is unjust. Even if a soldier is initially assailed by doubts, they are likely to be assuaged when his government, his superior officers, his fellow soldiers, and his fellow citizens all seem confident that the war is just.

3.2.3 Diminished Responsibility

Diminished responsibility is a common excusing condition in the criminal law: most of us, for example, are familiar with notorious cases in which the insanity defense has been invoked. Diminished responsibility is not, however, among the excuses commonly available to unjust combatants. There are very few cases in which a soldier is wholly lacking in the capacity for morally responsible deliberation and agency. There are, of course, some cases in which a soldier's capacity for responsible agency is diminished to some degree or other, though for obvious reasons the military tries to exclude such people through screening procedures. Some soldiers do of course incur psychological disabilities while serving, sometimes during the course of an unjust war, and they may be fully or partially excused for wrongs they commit thereafter. Tragically, soldiers in World War I who were incapacitated for further combat by post-traumatic stress disorder—then called shell shock—were often not recognized as mentally disabled but were simply shot as deserters. But such cases are comparatively rare and contain no general lessons concerning the moral status of unjust combatants.

It should perhaps be conceded that to a minor though not altogether negligible extent, many soldiers are actually responsible to a diminished degree. Many are in their late teens and early twenties, when their prefrontal cortexes have not fully developed. This area of the brain is involved in producing the capacity for judgment; hence moral judgment in those in whom it has not matured may be correspondingly immature. There are, of course, some 18-year-olds who have better moral judgment than most adults, just as there are some adults whose moral judgment is inferior to that of most 18-year-olds. Yet there are clearly biological reasons why males in the primary age range for military service are more prone to engage in violence and crime, drive more recklessly, and so on, than people of other ages, and the underdevelopment of the prefrontal cortex appears to be among these reasons. These biological factors suggest that soldiers have, on average, a slightly lesser capacity for responsible agency than others. Yet this is not recognized in law as even a partial excusing condition for criminal action, and I will follow the law in assuming that it is also not sufficiently significant to count as an excusing condition for unjust combatants in the relevant age range.

3.3 SKEPTICISM ABOUT EXCUSING UNJUST COMBATANTS

3.3.1 Consistency

As I noted earlier, people have often assumed that the various factors I have cited actually *justify* participation in an unjust war, at least in the weak sense of showing that participation is *not wrong*. But, with one possible exception to which I will return, these considerations function at most as excuses. But even considered only as excuses, to what extent do they mitigate the culpability of unjust combatants to whom they apply?

This is an issue of considerable significance. A number of moral and legal theorists have argued that culpability is a necessary condition of liability to defensive attack and thus that if unjust combatants are morally innocent, they cannot, as individuals, be legitimate targets of attack in war. Noam Zohar, for example, has argued that "in situations of confrontation and tragic choice, the balance between two lives cannot be tipped except by appeal to an aggressor's moral culpability."[13] Yet he claims that many unjust combatants are not culpable: "Enemy soldiers are not all murderous aggressors; judged as individual persons, only some of them can [permissibly] be killed: the machinating leaders and generals, and those officers and soldiers who knowingly participate in their country's criminal aggression."[14] Other unjust combatants who are not in these categories may not, as individual persons, be killed. (The clause "as individual persons" is, for Zohar, critical, since he argues that they can be legitimate targets *qua* agents of the collective.) Others have argued that although it can be permissible to fight against unjust combatants when they are morally innocent, their innocence does impose constraints on the way in which just combatants are permitted to fight. Thus Gerhard Øverland contends that "the typical innocent aggressor acts on reasonable grounds, and should therefore not be held morally responsible for the aggression," and argues on this basis that "if we are engaged in a just defensive war, . . . we must accept a higher level of risk and more harm if we can assume that the aggressors are innocent rather than morally responsible for their harmful or threatening behavior."[15] (I will return to this suggestion in Section 4.5.)

So if we find that the excusing conditions that apply to the action of unjust combatants are sufficient to render most such combatants morally innocent, this will make it difficult, on some views, to vindicate the possibility of just warfare. If most unjust combatants are morally innocent because they are excused, and if it is wrong intentionally to kill morally innocent people, then a contingent form of pacifism may be inescapable.[16] It is therefore important to consider whether most unjust combatants really can be considered morally innocent and if so whether this exempts them from liability to defensive attack.

I think there are decisive reasons to reject both of these assumptions. There are, to begin with, reasons of consistency for doubting that the excusing conditions that often apply to the action of unjust combatants actually have the high degree of mitigating force that many of us readily assume they do. Consider an impoverished, barely-educated 18-year-old in Gaza who has repeatedly been assured by the political and theological authorities in his society, and by his parents and friends, that the best and noblest act he can perform is to detonate a bomb strapped to his body in the midst of a randomly chosen group of Israeli civilians. He has a passionate hatred for Israelis, whose air force killed his younger sister just a month ago while striking what they alleged was a military target, and whom he believes are *all* guilty of violating the human and political rights of his people. He has been told by those he regards as authoritative that if he fulfills his sacred duty to attack the enemy, his act will gladden the heart of the deity and earn him a special place of honor in heaven, he will be forever celebrated as a martyr and hero by his people, and his family members will never again suffer the poverty in which they have languished for as long as he can remember. He has felt such despair and hopelessness over his own prospects that death seems to him to involve little sacrifice, little loss. In such circumstances, how could he hold his head up in public were he *not* to carry out the bombing mission? In the end, with pride and very little fear other than fear of failure, he does it, killing many and maiming even more.

Many of the excusing conditions I have discussed apply in this case. Although the Gazan is not subject to duress in the sense defined by the Model Penal Code, he is nevertheless subject to a variety of pressures. He has various grounds for believing that killing Israelis is what both morality and religion require of him and, in part because he is credulous and immature, he *does* believe it—indeed, the nature of his act reveals that he believes it with far greater conviction than most unjust combatants have in the justness of their cause. Yet we do not excuse him, at least not in the way or to the extent that we do those who fight in unjust wars. If he were to kill ordinary people in a marketplace without killing himself simultaneously and were captured afterward, it would be hard to believe that he would be fully excused and ought therefore to go unpunished, even if it would be permissible to detain him as long as he would continue to pose a threat, as a carrier of a lethal infectious disease might be quarantined. It is revealing that we think these considerations barely function as *excuses* at all in the case of a terrorist, when most of us readily accept that they can *justify* the action of unjust combatants.

There are, of course, excuses that are often available to unjust combatants that are seldom available to terrorists. One is duress: unjust combatants have often been conscripted, or have enlisted for what seemed to be acceptable or even admirable reasons, only to find themselves later faced with a threat of severe punishment if they refuse to fight in what they believe or suspect may be an unjust war. Most terrorists, by contrast, appear to be fervent volunteers. One might argue that this latter fact simply highlights the benighted epistemic condition in which most terrorists act; yet there are in general significant epistemic differences between unjust combatants and terrorists as well. One of these is that while mere participation in an unjust war is not illegal in either domestic or international law, terrorism is. Terrorism is explicitly illegal under international law and it is scarcely conceivable that it could be permissible in any domestic jurisdiction. This alerts all potential terrorists that they cannot simply take it for granted that what they propose to do is morally permissible.

The most significant epistemic difference between unjust combatants and terrorists is that while participation in an unjust war has been regarded by most people in virtually all cultures as not just excusable but even permissible, the intentional killing of innocent bystanders as a means of achieving one's aims has been recognized as wrong by almost everyone in virtually all cultures in all times. That this is so is probably the main reason that there have always been far more unjust combatants than terrorists. It is not that terrorists have a sophisticated ethical theory that challenges the ubiquitous and historically pervasive conviction that it is wrong to attack innocent bystanders as a means of coercing others. On the contrary, when terrorists express their bitter grievances against the group whose members they attack, they often accuse those people of harming and killing the innocent as a means of attaining their ends—that is, of action that sounds rather like terrorism. The Gazan terrorist I have imagined seems to have no alternative but to accept that the only morally significant difference between himself and

Baruch Goldstein, an Israeli who slaughtered twenty-nine Muslims at prayer in 1994, is that he supposedly has a just cause while Goldstein did not. He has to accept that if Palestinians had been doing to Israelis what Israelis have done to Palestinians, Goldstein's act would have been justified. Yet I doubt that any actual Gazan terrorist would accept that.

So perhaps the main reason for denying that moral ignorance can provide a compelling excuse for the action of terrorists is that in most cases their ignorance could be overcome simply by testing their moral beliefs for internal consistency. One can hardly be excused for wrongfully killing people when one has not bothered to do even that. Still, this general difference between the epistemic excuses of terrorists and those of unjust combatants does not hold in all cases—since there are many cases, such as the various Nazi invasions, in which it is luminously obvious that a war is unjust—and in any case the difference is only a matter of degree, not kind.

A second doubt about the consistency of our beliefs is whether the view that unjust combatants are excused for participation in an unjust war is compatible with the view that neither they nor just combatants are in general excused for violations of the rules governing the conduct of war. The common view is, in Walzer's words, that when a combatant "violates the rules of war, superior orders are no defence. The atrocities that he commits are his own; the war is not."[17] Although we do not regard unjust combatants as culpable and do not hold them legally liable for participation in an unjust and illegal war, we do hold them morally accountable, as well as individually liable under international criminal law, for the commission of war crimes. Yet the conditions that most people think excuse or even justify participation in an unjust or criminal war are often present to an equal or even greater degree when combatants commit war crimes by violating the rules of war. How can these conditions fail to excuse violations of *jus in bello* when they do excuse the violation of *jus ad bellum* that is involved in participation in an unjust and criminal war?[18]

As I noted, most people consider that duress, in both the narrow and broad senses—that is, both explicitly coercive threats as well as social, psychological, and other pressures—can readily and fully excuse participation in an unjust war. Yet the forms of duress that may force a person to join the military, or a soldier to go to war, are often no greater, and are sometimes less severe, than those that may pressure a soldier in combat to commit a war crime. When war criminals describe their motives, the descriptions sometimes echo those given by people explaining why they fought in an unjust war. In a recent case in Iraq, for example, eight US marines, frustrated by the release from detention of a person they believed to be a terrorist, murdered a randomly chosen Iraqi civilian as a surrogate for the person they believed ought to have been punished. One of the conspirators said at his trial: "I knew what we were doing was wrong . . . I tried to say something and then I decided to look away . . . I wanted to be a part of the team. I wanted to be loyal."[19] This is a little different, but not too distant, from the fear of ostracism, rejection, and scorn that O'Brien describes as the principal motivation for participation in the Vietnam War.

War crimes are often committed, not on the initiative of the perpetrator, but in response to orders. Although combatants are now required to disobey a manifestly unlawful order, it requires considerable courage and composure to do this when a doubtful order is accompanied by an implicit or explicit threat of sanction for noncompliance. The battlefield is governed only tenuously by the rule of law. In the past, combatants with a principled reluctance to obey an order were often simply killed on the spot for insubordination, and doubtless this practice continues, though not unabated. This kind of threat from superiors may combine with fear of the enemy to overwhelm a combatant's will. Indeed, the stresses of battlefield conditions are frequently so severe as to impair a combatant's capacity for rationality, creating a state of genuinely diminished responsibility.

Just as there is often considerable uncertainty about whether a war is just, so there can also be uncertainty about whether an individual act of war is permissible. Even if the legal rules are clear and explicit, they may not coincide with the principles governing the morality of conduct in war. They may, on occasion, permit what it would be morally wrong to do, or prohibit what morality requires. So there can be considerable uncertainty about what morality demands even when the order a combatant has received is clearly legal—for example, when a combatant has been ordered to bomb a large concentration of enemy combatants in a prepared position whom he knows to be unwilling conscripts who would be very likely to surrender if given the opportunity.

Even if we assume that *in bello* morality coincides with *in bello* law, and even if the legal rules are clear and explicit, there can also be uncertainty about their application in particular circumstances.[20] A combatant might receive an order to fire on children whom his commander has identified as child soldiers; or he may be ordered to destroy a house in a civilian area in which his commander claims that enemy combatants are sheltering; or he may be ordered to fire on enemy combatants who appear to be trying to surrender, though his commander insists that their signals are only a ruse intended to lure his forces into a trap. Are such orders unlawful? The answer may depend on whether the commander's factual claims are true, which is a matter about which the combatant may have good reason to disagree with the commander.

So it seems that the same conditions that are commonly thought to excuse participation in an unjust war are also present in at least some instances in which combatants commit war crimes. This leaves us with several options. We can argue that there are differences between the *ad bellum* and *in bello* contexts that in general give duress and uncertainty a greater excusing effect in the former than in the latter. Or we can deny that these excuses have much force in either context and thus accept that unjust combatants are generally blamable, even when they scrupulously adhere to the laws of warfare. Or we can accept that duress and uncertainty have considerable mitigating force in both cases, thereby abandoning the idea that combatants are generally culpable for the commission of war crimes.

I think that reality is sufficiently varied and complex that all these views contain an element of the truth. In some cases, combatants who commit war crimes are indeed excused to one degree or another by the same kinds of consideration that often excuse unjust combatants for participation in an unjust war. In other cases, unjust combatants who fight within the limits of the laws governing the conduct of war are nevertheless highly culpable just for fighting at all. But in general unjust combatants who fight according to the rules are less likely to be culpable, and less likely to be highly culpable, than combatants who commit war crimes or participate in atrocities. If this is right, the simple account according to which unjust combatants who fight within the rules are excused while war criminals are not is too simple to be sustainable.

It is revealing about our attitudes in general that we sometimes do take combatants who have committed war crimes to be fully excused, or even justified, and not just in cases involving extreme duress, invincible ignorance, or insanity. Perhaps the most notorious case of this sort is that of General Paul Tibbets, who was the commander and pilot of the *Enola Gay*, the plane, named for his mother, from which the atomic bomb was dropped on the Japanese city of Hiroshima in August of 1945. According to the US Department of Energy, approximately

70,000 people were killed immediately, while more than 30,000 more died over the next few months from injuries and exposure to radiation. The DOE estimates that "the five-year death total may have reached or even exceeded 200,000, as cancer and other long-term effects took hold."[21] This figure does not include those survivors who continued to live, though burned, maimed, or otherwise disabled, for many years after the bombing. This single act by Tibbets, with contributions by the other members of his small crew, had as an immediate physical effect the killing of more people, the vast majority of whom were civilians, than any other single act ever done. The law of war prohibits—and prohibited at the time of Tibbets's action—the intentional killing of civilians for the purpose of coercing their government to surrender.[22] And all plausible moral theories, including even the most radical forms of consequentialism, prohibit the intentional killing of *that many* innocent people in virtually all practically possible circumstances. Tibbets's act is therefore the most egregious war crime, and the most destructive single terrorist act, ever committed, even though it was committed in the course of a just war. Yet he was congratulated for it by President Truman, who had given the order that he do it, and was awarded various medals and promoted from colonel to brigadier general. When Tibbets died in 2007 at the age of 92, the obituary in the *New York Times* carried a caption in bold type that read "A war hero who never wavered in defending his mission," and ten days later the same newspaper printed a further celebratory op-ed piece with this caption: "Paul Tibbets, the hero we wanted to forget."[23]

Tibbets naturally embraced the common view that the bombing was necessary to secure the surrender of the Japanese without a land invasion in which far more Japanese, as well as tens or hundreds of thousands of Americans, would have been killed. "I was anxious to do it," he subsequently said, meaning that he was eager to do it. "I wanted to do everything I could to subdue Japan. I wanted to kill the bastards . . . I have been convinced that we saved more lives than we took . . . It would have been morally wrong if we'd have had that weapon and not used it and let a million more people die." These are the words of a man who has successfully subdued not only the Japanese but also his own conscience, though without troubling overmuch to determine in either case whether the means used were acceptable—or even, in the silencing of his conscience, consistent: for he added to his consequentialist moral justification the fatuous and self-serving claim that "there is no morality in war."[24] No doubt he believed at the time

that he would save more people than he would kill, and that is certainly
an important mitigating consideration, but he seems thereafter never to
have been disturbed by the arguments of historians and philosophers
that combine to demonstrate that the bombing was in fact unnecessary
to end the war. The key points are

- that the explosion of an atomic bomb on an uninhabited Japanese
  island could have served to show the Japanese leadership what they
  might face if the war continued;
- that the decisive factor in forcing Japan's unconditional surrender
  was the entry of the Soviet Union into the Pacific war on the day
  before the second atomic bomb was dropped on Nagasaki;
- that the achievement of an unconditional surrender can never be
  a justification for the continuation of war, since there are always
  conditions that a vanquished adversary, no matter how evil, can be
  justified in demanding;
- that the US knew from intercepted cables that the Japanese were
  seeking to persuade the Russians to intercede to help them secure
  a conditional surrender that would have allowed them to keep the
  Emperor; and, therefore,
- that with the entry of the Soviet Union into the war and perhaps
  the detonation of an atomic bomb on an uninhabited island, the
  US could almost certainly have secured a *conditional* surrender
  without either the annihilation of cities or a land invasion.

Yet for all that Tibbets remains to us a hero: not just excused, not even
merely justified, but a *hero*. Why? I think that at least part of the answer
is that patriotic Americans would find it intolerable to acknowledge
that their country won the war in the Pacific theater through a series
of terrorist acts—that is, by the intentional slaughter of the civilian
populations of Tokyo, Hiroshima, and Nagasaki as a means of coercing
the Japanese government to surrender unconditionally—especially in
the knowledge that it could have won by other means. It was natural
to believe at the time that these bombings brought Japan to its knees.
People were told that the only alternative for ending the war was a land
invasion of the Japanese islands, and the fanatical intransigence of the
Japanese supported the credibility of that claim. If it is too painful even
for Americans born after the event to abandon this consoling claim
in light of the evidence that has subsequently emerged, how much
more painful would it have been for Tibbets himself. He therefore told
himself, and most Americans have agreed, that he did nothing more

than what was necessary to bring the monstrous evil of Japanese imperial aggression and conquest to an end.

When the Palestinians finally get the state to which they have been entitled for decades, they too will delude themselves by claiming, with regret, that they did no more than was necessary to secure their rights. Unlike Americans, who have crafted definitions that make it an essential feature of terrorism that it be done without legitimate political authorization, or by "sub-state actors," the Palestinians will be unable to deny that the word "terrorism" applies to what they did.

One explanation, then, of why we honor war criminals such as Tibbets by calling them heroes, though with ambivalence and our collective face averted, is that this is a way of expiating our country's own guilt. We try in this way to repay them for having dirtied their hands and stained their souls in doing, for our ostensible benefit, the terrible things we made them do. In general people do this only for their own war criminals (though it would be interesting to know whether Tibbets is also generally regarded as a hero in countries, such as China and Korea, whose people were the immediate victims of Japanese aggression and atrocities), and they generally canonize only those whose action seems to have brought great benefit to the nation. In contrast to the destruction of Hiroshima, the My Lai massacre in Vietnam served no purpose but to disgrace the United States; so, although Lt. Calley, who instigated and directed the slaughter of innocent villagers, was legally pardoned after being subject for several years to house arrest, he was never widely regarded as morally excused, though—amazingly—even he was defended and celebrated as a martyr and hero by some.

3.3.2 Are Unjust Combatants Excused by Duress?

In addition to being doubtfully consistent with our general tendency to deny that terrorists and war criminals are excused on grounds of duress or moral uncertainty, the view that unjust combatants are fully excused for participating in unjust wars is also vulnerable to challenges to both the factual and normative assumptions on which it is based. Consider first the claim that unjust combatants are excused on grounds of duress, taking duress in the broad sense stipulated earlier, according to which duress includes not only intentionally coercive threats but also pressures from natural, social, or psychological sources.

I noted earlier that in some cases duress provides not an excuse but a justification of lesser evil. That is true, for example, in the example I gave of the person who is credibly threatened with death unless he gives an innocent bystander a nasty pinch. There are few, if any, realistic equivalents of this case in war. Participation in an unjust war involves attacking and perhaps killing people who have done nothing to make themselves liable to be attacked or killed. It is hard to think of realistic cases in which the threatened harm for an individual's failure to participate in an unjust war would be so great that his killing one or more just combatants would constitute the lesser evil, taking into account the significance of the distinctions between killing and letting die and between innocence and noninnocence. It is, perhaps, possible that a person who has been credibly threatened with the torture and murder of his entire family if he refuses to fight would be morally justified in fighting, even if fighting would involve killing innocent people. But this kind of extreme case is sufficiently rare that even if it is an example in which duress provides a lesser-evil justification for fighting in an unjust war, it remains true that *in general* duress provides unjust combatants with at most an excuse.

It is incontestable that in many cases unjust combatants have an excuse of duress. But excuses can be full or partial and, if partial, may vary in degree from nearly fully excusing to barely mitigating. So the relevant question is not whether some unjust combatants are excused by duress but rather what proportion are excused and to what degree. Again, the reality is complex. Some are fully excused, others are partially excused to varying degrees, and some are not excused at all. But are there any defensible generalizations? The common view, of course, is that unjust combatants do not act wrongly merely by fighting, so that there is nothing to excuse them for. I have argued that that view cannot be sustained. The best one can do for the common view is to argue that the great majority of unjust combatants are either fully excused or excused to a high degree. The question here is whether one can make that case by appealing to duress.

The extent to which duress can excuse wrongdoing is a function of the expected harm from a threat (which is itself a function of the magnitude of the threatened harm and the probability of the threat's being fulfilled) and the moral gravity of the wrong that is demanded. The wrong that is involved in fighting in an unjust war is very serious: it is the wrong of intentionally killing people who are doing nothing more than defending themselves and other innocent people from threats of wrongful harm. In many areas of the world—in particular, those areas in which this book might be sold and read—the penalties either for refusal of conscription or for conscientious refusal by soldiers tend, at present, to be sentences of imprisonment that may be severe but are seldom intolerable. When those who fight in unjust wars would otherwise be imprisoned, that may greatly mitigate their culpability, but it cannot excuse them altogether. A threat of temporary imprisonment is by itself insufficiently terrible to overmaster a person's will when the alternative he must resist involves killing innocent people.

There are, however, still areas in the world where the penalty for conscientious refusal to fight may be as draconian as execution. When it is true that if a person does not obey a command to go to war he will simply be shot, it is hard to deny that he is fully excused if he obeys—*not* justified, but fully excused. Reverting to the language of the Model Penal Code, this is a threat that "a person of reasonable firmness . . . would have been unable to resist."

Although a credible threat of death is a formidable excusing condition, it is worth asking what exactly it can excuse when the demand is that a person fight in an unjust war. Consider again the hypothetical example I cited in Section 3.1.2 in which a person puts a gun to your head and credibly threatens to kill you unless you kill an innocent third party. Suppose that circumstances are such that if you do everything in your power to kill the third party, you will have only a 90% probability of being able to kill him, and suppose that the person who threatens you knows that. In these conditions, you might be able to satisfy the threatener if you compellingly *appear* to be trying to kill the third party. If, for example, you are supposed to shoot the third party but he is attempting to flee, you could try to fire very close to him without actually hitting him. If there was a good chance that you could save both the third party and yourself in this way, this is probably what you ought to do, even though it would involve some risk of failure and thus of death.

Deception of this sort is much easier to achieve in war. One can "go to war" without ever harming anyone. Unless perhaps one is a member of a team that collectively operates a weapon, one can refrain from harming anyone even in conditions of combat: one can fire one's weapon into the ground, or one can refrain from firing it at all. General S. L. A. Marshall, the official US historian of operations in the European theater during World War II, famously reported that in any given combat engagement, only about 15–20% of combatants had fired their weapons at all.[25] Marshall's findings have subsequently been challenged but the challenges leave the points that are relevant here unaffected. These are, first, that even if a higher proportion of combatants fire their weapons than Marshall's figures indicate, the proportion who do not is still surprisingly high; and, second, that these matters have to be determined after the fact, since no one has the opportunity to monitor the firing of weapons while an engagement is in progress. What this means is that it is usually possible to "go to war," even when the war is unjust, without actual wrongdoing, provided one's active participation is feigned rather than genuine. Thus, when one is threatened with death if one refuses to participate in an unjust war, it may even be *permissible* to go, provided that one is privately resolved not to advance the war's unjust aims or to kill innocent people on the other side. (One might even be able to do positive good if one could exploit one's position to impede the achievement of one's own side's unjust aims.) But the threatened penalty for refusal cannot provide even a partial excuse for killing just combatants if, by merely appearing to fight, one could avoid the threatened sanction without actually killing anyone.

It is worth noting that when a government threatens draconian penalties for refusal to fight in the wars it wages, this itself suggests that there are good reasons not to comply with its demands, and in particular not to kill people on the other side. For a government that threatens to kill its own citizens as a means of coercing them to fight its wars thereby offers evidence of its own illegitimacy and may not be worth serving. And wars that cannot be effectively fought without threats to kill those who refuse to participate are very likely unjust. As I have noted, history shows that people are usually extremely pliant in their willingness to go to war and there is usually no shortage of volunteers for wars that are clearly just, particularly wars of national self-defense. When a significant proportion of potential combatants are so unwilling to fight that they have to be threatened with death to get them to go to war, that is evidence that the war is unjust.

I have suggested that one permissible response to threats intended to coerce one to participate in an unjust war is to acquiesce but with a private resolve not to kill people on the other side. But once one is in the midst of war, one's private reservations will be no more apparent to the enemy than they have been to those who have coerced one's presence on the battlefield. Just combatants will perceive one to be a threat and will respond accordingly with what they take to be defensive force. What should a person who knows his side is in the wrong do in such a situation?

The person who is posing the threat is a just combatant who has done nothing to lose his right not to be killed. The apparent unjust combatant did not, we are supposing, actually pose a threat to the just combatant, but the just combatant could not know that and the unjust combatant is responsible to a greater degree for the predicament in which they both find themselves than the just combatant is. Thus, if anyone is liable, it is the apparent unjust combatant, who also lacks a lesser-evil justification, since his life is presumably worth no more than that of the just combatant, whose death may be worse instrumentally because his action serves a just cause. There seem to be no grounds on which the apparent unjust combatant can claim a justification, or a permission, to kill in self-defense. But his situation is clearly one of extreme duress—not duress in the sense of the Model Penal Code, but in the broader sense stipulated earlier. His position is one in which even "a person of reasonable firmness" would be unable to resist the impulse to kill in self-defense. If he kills the just combatant, he does wrong but is nevertheless blameless. In this case, duress provides a full excuse.

Recall that it is a feature of this example that the apparent unjust combatant was coerced by his government to go to war (though not actually to kill anyone), where he was then subjected to further, irresistible duress from the enemy. If this person had not been coerced to go to war—if he had gone to war neither permissibly nor excusably—then whatever his intentions might have been on the battlefield, he would not be fully excused for killing in self-defense. He would not be fully excused because he earlier had a tolerable option that would not have placed him in a situation in which he would be forced to choose between killing a just combatant and allowing himself to be killed.

Even if a person has been effectively coerced to be among forces fighting an unjust war, and even if he then finds himself at grave risk of being killed by just combatants, he may still have options other than killing in self-defense or allowing himself to be killed. One such option is surrender. To surrender individually, without an order from a superior and without being compelled to do so by the enemy, could count as desertion. Yet if the war is objectively unjust, this may be what morality requires. There are limits to what national partiality can permit, and killing innocent people in an unjust war is beyond them.

Most people will no doubt find it absurd to propose in all seriousness that combatants coerced to go to a war that is objectively unjust could then be required by morality to do something as silly as to pretend to fight, or as treasonous as to desert via surrender. This may seem like moral theory gone mad, the recommendations of a theorist without the slightest sense of realism. This is a natural reaction but I suspect we have it primarily because, as citizens of a democratic country such as the US or Britain, we imagine that although our wars may sometimes be morally questionable, they are never so unjust as to warrant such unusual measures. Yet we might think differently if we were to consider how we might evaluate a Nazi soldier who had opted for one of these courses of action. It is not at all ridiculous to suppose that an intelligent and morally scrupulous young German who had been forcibly inducted into the Wehrmacht might privately have resolved that, although he would follow his army into combat, he would not kill an Allied soldier, even if it should cost him his life to keep that commitment, and that he would surrender to the Allies if the opportunity were to arise. I have no knowledge of any actual example of this sort, perhaps because such examples are likely to go unreported. But I would be shocked if there were no cases of this sort. I suspect, indeed, that many of us would like to believe that, if we found ourselves in this person's position, we would do exactly what I have described.

There are many examples of people who have chosen a certainty of execution rather than participate in an unjust war. One well-documented example is Franz Jägerstätter, an Austrian peasant farmer who refused on moral but not pacifist grounds to serve in the Nazi army, knowing that he would be executed as a result. Jägerstätter was a committed Catholic but found no support for his position among his coreligionists, including various members of the clergy, such as the Bishop of Linz, who all offered him the familiar forms of advice that still constitute the received wisdom on these issues: that he lacked the competence to judge the war unjust, that as a citizen he had no responsibility for the acts of the government and could therefore participate in the war with a clear conscience, and so on.[26] His response was one that I think many of us wish that we too would have the courage to give: "I cannot turn the responsibility [for my actions] over to the Führer."[27] On the eve of Jägerstätter's execution—he was beheaded—yet another priest came to remonstrate with him. The Mother Superior of an Austrian convent later gave this account of what occurred: "On the table before him [in his cell] lay a document; he had only to put his signature on it and his life would be saved. When the priest called his attention to it, he smilingly pushed it aside with the explanation: 'I cannot and may not take an oath in favor of a government that is fighting an unjust war.'"[28]

It is hard to imagine that any decent person could fail to admire this man. But would he really have been any less noble or admirable if he had signed the paper, donned the uniform of the Wehrmacht, and gone off with other Nazi soldiers, albeit determined not to contribute to their action but to impede it any way possible, and determined as well not to harm any Allied soldiers but to defect to them at the earliest opportunity? Such a course would not have involved wrongdoing (the Nazis had no right to a truthful declaration on whatever document they demanded that he sign) and would probably have yielded a significantly better outcome, not only for him and for those who loved him, but also for the anti-Nazi cause. It is conceivable that in Jägerstätter's case the risks involved in taking this course would have been too great, since had they discovered his defection the Nazis might have conducted reprisals against his family. But this is a contingent feature of the example and does not impugn the idea that devious forms of resistance of the sort I have suggested may in many cases be not inferior morally, and perhaps even superior, to martyrdom.

In summary, we have to recognize that the penalties for refusing conscription or for a soldier's refusal to fight in an unjust war are usually sufficiently significant to provide at least a partial excuse for entering an unjust war, in cases in which those pressures are present. If one is determined not to contribute to the advancement of the war's unjust aims, one may even be permitted to enter the war. If a soldier has entered an unjust war under extreme duress and then finds himself in a situation in which he will be killed unless he kills a just combatant in self-defense, the combined instances of duress may provide a full excuse for the killing. But in other cases, duress appears to provide only a partial excuse for killing people in the course of an unjust war.

3.3.3 Are Unjust Combatants Excused by Epistemic Limitations?

In the case of unjust combatants, duress as an excusing condition seldom operates in isolation. Epistemic limitation—factual and moral ignorance—is even more pervasive among unjust combatants than duress. Soldiers who fight in unjust wars tend to be poorly informed factually and usually have one or the other of two mistaken moral beliefs: either that their war is just or that, although their war is unjust, their participation in it is nevertheless morally permissible. What do these facts imply about whether and to what extent unjust combatants are excused?

If an unjust combatant correctly believes that it is morally imper-missible for him to fight and yet fights anyway, whatever excuses he might have are not epistemic. So assume that an unjust combatant mistakenly believes that it is morally permissible for him to participate in his country's war. It is a commonplace in epistemology that a person may be epistemically justified in having a belief that is in fact false. It is possible, therefore, that the unjust combatant's belief that he is morally permitted to fight is justified. But there are also *degrees* of epistemic justification. A person may be justified in having a certain belief, but only barely so. What this means is that while he is justified rather than unjustified in having the belief, the degree to which he can be justifiably confident in the truth of the belief is low. Alternatively, one might say that the degree of credence that the belief warrants is low. There are thus various possibilities in the case of the unjust combatant, assuming that his belief that it is permissible for him to fight is epistemically justified: his belief may be weakly justified, strongly justified, or justified to some intermediate degree. These possibilities are relevant to the question whether he is morally excused for fighting. For whether and to what extent he has an epistemically-based excuse for fighting depends on whether and to what extent his belief in the permissibility of his participation is epistemically justified.

Suppose that he is epistemically unjustified in having this belief—for example, because it is based on factual beliefs for which there is little or no evidence—but that he accepts it uncritically because the factual beliefs cohere well with the way his distorted ideology says that the world is. In that case, he has little or no epistemically-based excuse for participating in his side's unjust war.

Suppose, next, that his belief that he is morally permitted to fight is, though false, actually epistemically justified, but only barely so. That his belief that he is acting permissibly is justified is certainly an excusing condition, and a significant one. Yet given that the belief warrants only a low level credence, the excuse is weaker than it would be if the belief instead warranted a high degree of credence—that is, if he could justifiably have a high degree of confidence that his belief that he is acting permissibly is true.

There is, moreover, another factor here that is perhaps even more important than the degree of credence he is warranted in according to the belief. This is that the degree to which his justified belief excuses his objectively wrongful action depends on how much is at stake, morally, in the choice he must make between fighting and not fighting. Consider again the unjust combatant's belief that it is morally permissible for him to fight. Suppose that this is the belief on which he bases his decision to fight. If he did not have this belief, he would refuse to fight. The more that is at stake morally in the decision he makes based on this belief, the more important it is that his belief be true; and the more important it is that the belief be true, the less excuse he has if he gets it wrong and acts on the basis of a false belief. More specifically, the more that is at stake morally in the choice an agent makes on the basis of some belief, the higher the level of *justified* confidence the agent must have in the truth of the belief in order for the belief to ground an excuse of a fixed degree of strength, if the belief is in fact false.[29]

It may help to clarify that last claim to give a schematic example. Suppose a soldier is commanded to fight in an unjust war. He believes, however, and with a moderately high level of credence, that the war is just and that his participation in it is permissible. Suppose that he is in fact epistemically justified in having that belief and in according it that degree of credence. Next imagine two possible variants of the example. In one, the war is small, victory by his side would not be tragic, and in any case he will be deployed in an area in which there is very unlikely to be any fighting, so that his participation is unlikely to make any significant difference. In these conditions, his belief may provide a strong excuse for his participation. In the other possible variant, victory by his side would be a catastrophe from an impartial point of view and his participation would be likely not only to involve the killing of numerous enemy combatants but also to make a significant contribution to his side's war effort. In these conditions, his belief, although justified, would provide only a much weaker excuse for his participation. This is intuitively plausible. The same belief, with the same degree of justification, provides a stronger excuse when what is at stake is of lesser moral significance. When what is at stake is of greater moral significance, his belief must be better grounded to provide an excuse of equal strength if the belief turns out to be false.

It is important to be clear about the notion of "what is at stake morally." This is not just a matter of the moral gravity of what a person will do if he acts on the basis of an epistemically justified belief—for example, the moral gravity of killing innocent people, which is what a combatant will do if he fights in a war that he justifiably but falsely believes is just. What is at stake is instead comparative: it is the difference between what may happen if an agent acts one way and what may happen if he acts in another way. In the case of a soldier, what is at stake in whether or not he fights is the *moral* difference between the probable outcomes of both options. In this context, the notion of "what is at stake" presupposes uncertainty. Thus there are possible moral costs either way. When a soldier is deliberating about whether to fight in a war, and trying to determine whether participation is permissible, what is at stake morally is the moral difference between the two ways in which he might get it wrong: by fighting in a war that is unjust and by refusing to fight in a war that is just.

What makes the soldier's predicament so difficult morally is that in a choice between going to war and not going to war, there is usually a very great deal at stake, and the conditions in which he must choose are typically conditions of substantial factual and moral uncertainty, in which the justified level of credence in *any* set of relevant factual beliefs is quite low. What should soldiers do in these circumstances? Should they, for example, act on the basis of the factual and moral beliefs that have the highest justified level of credence?

I have no claim to expertise, or even competence, on issues of decision-making in conditions of uncertainty, on which there is a vast literature, but I will offer a few simple observations that I think are plausible, and that are specifically focused on the case of unjust combatants.[30] Suppose a soldier who voluntarily enlisted earlier is suddenly commanded to fight in a war that has begun quite unexpectedly. He has little leisure for reflection and the relevant facts are obscure. His government has asserted various factual claims that, if true, would support its further claim that the war is just. But these factual claims have been disputed or denied by many others, including experts among the soldier's own fellow citizens. The level of credence he is justified in having in either of the opposing sets of factual claims is thus quite low. It is clear, however, that his own country is not in danger. The theater of war is thousands of miles away in a remote country that he knows almost nothing about. He does know, however, that most of the people he would be fighting against are citizens of the country in which the war is being fought. What ought he to do?

He might reflect on his options in the following way. The war is either just or unjust, but he does not know which. Indeed, the one thing he does know is that he lacks relevant knowledge, both factual and moral. Suppose that as a morally scrupulous person, his primary concern is with the impact of his action on the people in the country in which the war is occurring: that is, the people he would be fighting for and those he would be fighting against. If, on the one hand, he refuses to fight and the war is in fact just, he will fail in his duty, as a soldier, to protect innocent people. He may even allow innocent people to be killed whom he could have saved. Yet, he might reflect further, if he refuses to fight, he will certainly be replaced by someone else who is likely to be as effective as he would have been. Perhaps the real victim of his refusal to fight would be the person who would replace him and be exposed to the risks of war in his stead.

If, on the other hand, he decides to fight and the war is in fact unjust, he will fail in his duty not to be an instrument in the service of unjust ends. He may also intentionally kill people who are innocent in the relevant sense as a means to those ends. Yet, he may reflect, if he were not to do these things, someone else would replace him and perhaps be even more efficient in killing innocent people and contributing to the achievement of the war's unjust aims.

In short, if he participates and the war is just, he may save innocent lives and make a small contribution to the achievement of a just cause. If he refuses to participate and the war is just, he will fail to save innocent lives and fail to contribute to the achievement of a just cause. If he participates and the war is unjust, he may kill innocent people and make a small contribution to the achievement of an unjust cause. If he refuses to participate and the war is unjust, he will have avoided killing innocent people and contributing to the achievement of an unjust cause. In the cases in which he participates, what he does would probably have been done by someone else had he not participated, and in the cases in which he does not participate, what he fails to do will probably be done by someone else instead. So it seems that where consequences are concerned, it makes little difference whether he participates or not.

But consequences are not all that matters morally. The soldier's options involve not just risks of harm to others but risks of his own *wrongdoing*. He faces *moral risks*, such as the risk of intentionally killing people who are in fact innocent, of wronging people and violating their rights. And there are two broad reasons why consideration of the moral risks the soldier faces may favor the refusal to fight.

One derives from general asymmetries in morality between doing and allowing and between intending and merely foreseeing. If the soldier refuses to fight and the war turns out to be just, he may *allow* some innocent people to be killed whom he could have saved—though this would not be intended and, as I noted, these people might well be saved by someone who replaces him. If he fights and the war turns out to be unjust, he may *intentionally kill* some people who have turned out to be innocent—though they might also have been killed by his replacement, or someone else, had he not fought. Most of us believe that in most contexts it is more seriously wrong to kill innocent people intentionally than it is to allow innocent people to be killed as an unintended effect of one's failure to act. Our negative duty not to kill, which is the correlate of people's negative right not to be killed, is in general stronger than our positive duty to prevent people from being killed, which is the correlate of people's positive right to be saved. If, as in this soldier's case, the factual claims that support the view that the war is just seem no more likely to be true than those that support the contrary view, it seems that the moral presumption is against fighting, for fighting risks intentionally killing people who are in fact innocent, while not fighting risks unintentionally allowing people who are in fact innocent to be killed.

The force of this point should not, however, be overstated. The claim that he risks intentionally killing innocent people is ambiguous. It could mean that he risks intentionally killing people he will know to be innocent. This is indeed specially objectionable but it is not what this soldier risks. Rather, he risks intentionally killing people who he will believe are not innocent but who are in fact innocent. This may still be more objectionable than killing such people foreseeably but unintentionally, but it is not so objectionable as intentionally killing people he knows to be innocent.

Another response to this point is to note that, while refusing to fight avoids a significant *risk* of killing people who are innocent, it may also involve a *certainty* of committing a punishable offense and failing to fulfill a professional obligation. The question is whether these latter considerations are sufficiently important morally to justify a significant risk (a roughly 50% subjective probability) of intentionally killing people who are innocent. In part for reasons given earlier concerning duress and the comparative weight of role-based duties, it is hard for me to believe that they are.

There is also a serious question whether a country and its military are really better served when soldiers unreflectively acquiesce in the demand to fight a war that turns out to be unjust than they would be if soldiers were instead to refuse to fight. Suppose that a significant number of soldiers in the Wehrmacht had refused their orders to invade neighboring countries so that what in fact became World War II had instead been only a small, local war that ended in an early defeat of the Nazis. Would that really have been worse for Germany than the actual war? Would it even have been worse for Germany than a Nazi victory? Were those few in the German military who resisted the Nazis really in default of their patriotic duties? If we answer those questions in the negative, then the failure to fulfill a professional obligation in this kind of case may be only a nominal failure, not a failure of substance. Those to whom the obligation was owed would have, on balance, no reason to regret that it was not fulfilled.

Another response is that if the soldier fights and the war turns out to be unjust, the people he kills will be strangers, whereas at least some of those he might prevent from being killed will be specially related to him in two ways: they will be his compatriots and his comrades in the military. If special relations have a moral role in this context, one might argue that saving comrades may substantially offset the wrongness of killing strangers. Yet since the soldier's comrades would by hypothesis also be fighting in an unjust war, they would presumably be liable to attack, so that to defend them might not be permissible, despite the special relation.

The second broad reason why the moral risks in this case seem to favor the refusal to fight appeals to considerations that are available to the soldier—indeed to all soldiers—independently of the facts about the particular war in which he has been commanded to fight. The first such consideration is that the purely statistical probability that a war is unjust is higher than the probability that it is just. This is true if either of two quite plausible assumptions is correct. The first of these assumptions is that while there can be wars in which each side fights unjustly—as Anscombe famously says, "human pride, malice and cruelty are so usual that it is true to say that wars have mostly been mere wickedness on both sides"—there nevertheless cannot be wars in which both sides fight justly—that is, in which both sides are fighting a just war.[31] This is the dominant view in the history of thought about the just war. After all, if both sides are in the right, how could either be justified in fighting the other? Suppose this common view is correct. Assuming that some wars are just on one side and unjust on the other, some unjust on both sides, but none just on both, it follows that collectives fighting in war have more often fought unjustly than justly, and that this must continue to be true.[32]

Some have argued, however, that it is possible for both sides in a war to be justified in fighting. This could be true if justification is subjective in nature. One side could be fighting an objectively just war and know that its war was just, while the other could be fully epistemically justified in believing that its war was just when it was actually objectively unjust. Both would be justified in fighting on a subjective account of justification. Yet to be subjectively but not objectively justified in this sort of case is no different from being objectively excused, since these are just different phrases employed by different theories to describe the same facts. The relevant question here is whether there are any *actual* cases in which all combatants who fight without a just cause are justified in subjective terms, or fully excused by epistemic considerations in objective terms. I will return to this later.

There have, however, been some in the just war tradition who have claimed that it is possible for both sides to be *objectively* justified in fighting. It is clearly possible for both sides in a war to have a just cause—provided that each is also pursuing an unjust cause. But there may also be cases in which neither of two sides is at fault and yet both have a just cause and are justified in fighting. There do seem to be cases at the level of individual action in which circumstances force two innocent and faultless people into conflict in such a way that each is justified in fighting the other, and indeed in which each is objectively justified in trying to *kill* the other. One example, as I noted in Section 2.2.2, might be a case of gladiatorial combat.[33] It is possible that there could be analogous cases involving states. Suppose that that is true. Even so, such cases would be very rare—just as the analogous cases involving individuals are very rare. And as long as there are fewer such cases than there are cases in which both sides fight unjustly, it is still true, as it is on the stronger assumption that wars that are just on both sides are impossible, that collectives have more often fought unjustly than justly, and that this will remain true in the future.

A second consideration that supports the view that, in conditions of uncertainty, the moral presumption is against fighting is that most people are strongly disposed to believe that their side in any dispute is in the right. Not only is it true that a war in which a soldier has been commanded to fight is statistically more likely to be unjust than just, but it is also true that he is highly likely to believe that it is just even when it is unjust.

These two considerations combine to suggest that soldiers should be skeptical of their own sense that their war is just, especially in cases in which the justification for the war is controversial. They should, however, be disposed to *trust* their judgment when they are inclined to believe that their war is unjust. Independently of the facts of the particular case, their judgment is supported not only by statistical probability but also by its being contrary to the natural bias in favor of believing that one is right. In the case of most soldiers, the evidence for their war's being unjust has to be unusually compelling to overcome this bias, and in general the best explanation of why it is compelling is that the war actually *is* unjust. Thus the mere presence of the belief that one's own side's war is unjust provides some support for the truth of the belief.

That the risk of being wrong is greater when a soldier believes his war is just than when he believes it is unjust is one reason why the moral risks are greater in a decision to fight than in a decision not to fight. When a soldier is uncertain about the morality of a war, the presumption should be that the *morally* safer course is not to fight.

A related point concerns a particular type of effect that a soldier's decision to fight or not to fight can have: namely, influencing the action of others. One risk that conscientious refusal to fight in a war carries is that one's action may encourage others to refuse as well, with catastrophic results if the war is in fact just. Yet because soldiers are strongly disposed to believe that their war is just, the risk that a soldier's misguided refusal to fight in a war that turns out to be just will influence others to do the same is slight. By contrast, the risk that a soldier's misguided decision to fight in a war that turns out to be unjust will influence others to do the same is greater, since the soldier's action would serve to confirm the natural bias of the others.

This is relevant to one of Vitoria's arguments for his view, cited above, that soldiers are permitted to fight at the command of a legitimate authority, provided they are not certain that the war is unjust. At one point, he goes further, claiming that "in defensive wars subjects are not merely permitted to follow their prince into battle even where the justice of the cause is in doubt, but are indeed bound to do so; and . . . the same is true also of offensive wars." In support of this view, he argues that "if subjects were unable to fight until they understood the justice of the war, the safety of the commonwealth would be gravely endangered." He then claims that "in cases of doubt the safer course should be followed; but if subjects fail to obey their prince in war from scruples of doubt, they run the risk of betraying the commonwealth into the hands of the enemy, which is much worse than fighting the enemy, doubts notwithstanding; therefore they had better fight."[34]

By "the safer course," Vitoria seems to mean the prudentially safer course, the course that is most conducive to the security of the soldier's community, *not* the *morally* safer course, the course that involves the least *moral* risk. On this point he was at variance with some of the more eminent of his successors in the just war tradition, including Grotius, who, although he uses the same form of words as Vitoria, clearly means something quite different. He writes "that whoever hesitates, when reflecting, in his decision to act ought to choose the safer course. The safer course, however, is to refrain from war." That by the "safer course" Grotius means the one with the lesser risk of wrongdoing is evident in his next paragraph, where he argues that

It is no objection that on the other side there is danger of disobedience. For when either course is uncertain that which is the lesser of two evils is free from sin; for if a war is unjust there is no disobedience in avoiding it. Moreover, disobedience in things of this kind, by its very nature, is a lesser evil than manslaughter, especially than the manslaughter of many innocent men.[35]

"Lesser evil" here clearly refers to the lesser *moral* evil, not to the less bad of the possible consequences. Although on the substantive point Pufendorf agrees with Vitoria, he follows Grotius on the matter of principle: "For all would agree that when the conscience hesitates between two considerations, it is safest in choosing that side from which there is less danger of sin."[36]

But even if we focus exclusively on prudential concerns—that is, on the safest course in Vitoria's sense—Vitoria's empirical claim is doubtful. When a country is being unjustly attacked or invaded, it is extremely unlikely that its soldiers will have significant doubts about whether it is permissible to fight in self-defense, either individual or national. How many recorded cases are there in which a significant proportion of soldiers have refused to fight on conscientious but not pacifist grounds in a war that was both wholly defensive and objectively just? I suspect that most people who are not professional historians would be hard pressed to cite a single example in all of history, and that most professional historians would not be able to do much better. And, as I noted, even if a soldier does believe that the war is unjust and refuses to fight, the chance that he will be setting an example that others will be tempted to follow is remote, principally because just wars of national defense are almost always *obviously* just. It therefore seems that Vitoria's concern is misplaced. It is simply not true that if soldiers believe that there is a presumption against fighting when they have significant doubts about the justice of a war in which they have been commanded to fight, that will imperil the security of their society against unjust foreign attack.

Notice that the case of the soldier that I have been discussing is not a case of self-defensive war. Rather, I stipulated that the war in which he has been commanded to fight is occurring in a distant country, and that most of the people against whom he would be fighting are inhabitants of that country. This was deliberate. Most people who might read this book are citizens of countries whose wars, if any, tend to be of this sort. But it is worth considering whether what I have thus far claimed about moral risk applies even in the case of defensive wars. Even if Vitoria were right that a country would be at greater risk of subjugation to or domination by a foreign power if its soldiers were to believe that they ought not to fight when they have significant doubts about the justice of their war, he is wrong, as Grotius and Pufendorf realized, to suppose that it can be permissible to pursue the prudentially safer course when it is also the morally riskier. Or perhaps one should say that he is wrong *if* we understand the evaluation of the moral risks to have already taken appropriate account of the relevant prudential considerations. So we should ask whether my claim that a soldier should be skeptical of his belief that his war is just applies even in the case of self-defensive war.

It seems obvious that a soldier is entitled to presume that a defensive war—a war fought against foreign forces, and fought at least initially and perhaps entirely within the borders of his own country—is a just war. It seems that soldiers are justified in believing with a high degree of credence that such a war is just and thus that it is morally riskier not to fight than to fight. If this is right, it seems that soldiers who fight in a defensive war that turns out to be unjust are nevertheless fully excused.

This is, however, an overly simplistic understanding of defensive war. It is, for one thing, not always clear what counts as a war of defense. When what is at issue is the right to the possession or habitation of disputed territory, what seems like defensive war to one side will look like aggression to the other, and vice versa. In general, moreover, if it is possible for a genuinely defensive war to be unjust, then at least in cases in which it is possible to know the facts that make the war unjust, it must be possible to fight in it without having an epistemically-based excuse, either full or partial. And it is indeed possible for defensive war to be unjust. A defensive war is unjust when the offensive war to which it is a response is a just war. As Emmerich de Vattel wrote, echoing the passage I quoted from Belli in Section 1.2, "if the enemy who wages offensive war has justice on his side, we have no right to make forcible opposition; and the defensive war then becomes unjust."[37] Most subsequent moral and legal theorists have agreed.

There are at least two types of offensive or aggressive war that are potentially just: preventive war and humanitarian intervention. These are forms of war that are not in the strict sense defensive: they are not responsive to an actual or imminent attack by another state. They are instead responsive, respectively, to a threat of attack that is not imminent, and to violations of human rights within the state that is attacked.

Consider first a just preventive war. Suppose that one state is engaged in planning and preparing for an unjust war against another, that the government of the state that is the potential victim has discovered the plans and preparations, that nonviolent methods have only a very low probability of being able to avert the war, and that if defensive action is deferred until the attack begins, or is about to begin, it will be less effective and more destructive than it would be if undertaken now, preventively. Suppose that in these conditions the state that is threatened launches a preventive war and assume for the sake of argument that this war is just. Assume further that the state that is preventively attacked could, rather than fighting back, renounce its plans for unjust war and offer adequate guarantees that it will not attack. But instead its government decides to fight a war that, though defensive, is unnecessary and unjust.

What ought its soldiers to do when ordered to fight in this defensive war and how ought we to think of them if they fight? Suppose that their government had carefully concealed its plans for unjust war from both its citizens and its soldiers, and that it now indignantly denies that it has had any such plans, which were discovered by the intended victim only through espionage, so that the evidence of the plan cannot be fully disclosed without revealing and thus compromising the sources of the intelligence. This is the most likely background to such a case, since overt preparations for unjust war forfeit the advantages of surprise and invite defensive preparations or even preventive attack. In these conditions, in which ordinary soldiers have no way of knowing about their government's plans and little reason to believe the allegations made by the state that has invaded their country, and in which their immediate deployment is necessary for successful defense, they may be epistemically justified in having a high degree of credence in the belief that their war is just and may thus have a strong or even full excuse for fighting.

This case seems to confirm the view that soldiers are entitled to presume that a defensive war is just and are therefore wholly or at least partially excused if a defensive war turns out to be unjust. There is, however, a second type of unjust defensive war that challenges this view—namely, defense against justified humanitarian intervention. When external intervention is necessary to stop a government from extensively violating the human rights of some group of its citizens, and when the intervention is proportionate to the gravity of the violations and the intended beneficiaries clearly welcome it, humanitarian intervention can be just. When this is so, military resistance to the intervention is objectively wrong.

In this kind of case, it is doubtful that soldiers can be epistemically justified in believing that participation in defensive war is permissible; it is, therefore, also doubtful that they have an epistemically-based excuse if they do participate. For if the violations of human rights are sufficiently extensive to justify military intervention, and sufficiently notorious actually to provoke it, it is extremely unlikely that soldiers will have been unaware of them, or therefore of the reason for the attack that they have been called upon to repel. They should know that their action shields the government in its violations of the human rights of their fellow citizens.

Matters of this sort are, however, never simple. The justification for humanitarian intervention is seldom uncontroversial and thus it is always possible that a soldier may be aware that his government is guilty of violating the human rights of the members of some domestic group and yet reasonably, though mistakenly, believe that the violations are insufficient to justify military intervention. When that is the case, he may have an epistemically-based excuse for fighting, the strength of which would depend upon the degree to which he is justified in believing that his defensive war is just, despite his government's wrongdoing.

It seems, in short, that the claims I have made about the moral risks involved in fighting in war do not apply, at least not with equal force, in the case of defensive war. But even in the case of apparently defensive war, there can be legitimate doubts about whether the war really is defensive and about whether, even if it is clearly defensive, it is just. So even when the war in which a soldier is commanded to fight seems to be entirely defensive, he cannot take it for granted that it is just. There is scope for epistemic error and if the war turns out to be unjust, he cannot count on being excused for participating in it.

Thus far I have considered the epistemically-based excuses that may be available to unjust combatants largely in the abstract. But we should ask, as we did in the case of duress, whether there are any defensible generalizations about the excuses that unjust combatants have in practice. Are many, or most, unjust combatants excused on grounds of nonculpable ignorance, and if so to what degree?

The general points I have made about what combatants can know independently of the facts about the particular war in which they have been commanded to fight are certainly relevant. Except in cases in which the war is clearly defensive and clearly not responsive to a justified instance of humanitarian intervention, soldiers can know that on a purely statistical basis their war is more likely to be unjust than just and that they will be strongly inclined to believe that it is just even if it is unjust. Assuming that these background considerations ought to dispose them to skepticism, and given that what is at stake in their decision is of the utmost importance morally, it seems clear that it is morally incumbent upon them to deliberate carefully and to be confident of their ability to rebut the apparent presumption against fighting before they commit themselves to fight. Yet it is highly doubtful that many do take seriously their moral duty to examine the reasons for and against their participation in the war.

Part of the evidence for this claim is empirical. It is found in the memoirs that soldiers write, the anecdotal accounts they give to journalists of why they joined, what their thoughts were when they were sent to fight, and so on. It is hard to find descriptions of prolonged and serious moral deliberation in these accounts. No doubt there are some, but I have not encountered them.

The other, and better, part of the evidence is the extreme rarity of instances in which a soldier or a group of soldiers refuses on conscientious grounds to participate in a war. There has certainly been no shortage of unjust wars, but cases of active-duty soldiers who have refused to participate in them are not common. There are three possibilities. One is that soldiers think carefully about the morality of the war but in the end conscientiously conclude that the war is just. While this is bound to happen in some cases, it cannot be the correct explanation in most cases. It is simply not credible to suppose that most soldiers who fight in unjust wars do deliberate carefully about the morality of the war but invariably get it wrong. Even someone with as little admiration for most people's capacity for moral reflection as I have would find it hard to believe that virtually everyone is that unconquerably obtuse.

The second possibility is that soldiers do deliberate carefully and succeed in many cases in recognizing that their war is unjust but are then consistently overwhelmed by duress or are too weak-willed or cowardly to refuse to fight. This too is implausible, if only because it makes no sense to suppose that people would bother to engage in the hard work of moral reflection unless they expected to be able to act on their conclusions. If they were motivated to deliberate by the desire to avoid wrongdoing, it could hardly be that this desire would then be wholly ineffectual in guiding their action in virtually all cases.

It seems, therefore, that the third possibility is what actually happens in most cases: soldiers simply do not often engage in scrupulous moral deliberation about whether their country's war is just or about whether they ought to fight in it. Yet after the fact they tend to claim a great variety of epistemically-based excuses. In discussing two notorious and egregious Nazi war criminals, Eichmann and Höss, Primo Levi rehearses the litany of excuses that he notes are claimed by all who are accused of wrongdoing in war.

In substance, these two defended themselves in the classical manner of the Nazi militia, or, better yet, of all militiamen: we have been educated in absolute obedience, hierarchy, nationalism; we have been imbued with slogans, intoxicated with ceremonies and demonstrations; we have been taught that the only justice was that which was to the advantage of our people and that the only truth was the words of the Leader. What do you want from us? How can you even think to expect from us, after the fact, a behavior different from ours and that of all those who were like us? We were the diligent executors, and for our diligence we were praised and promoted. The decisions were not ours because the regime in which we grew up did not permit autonomous decisions: others have decided for us, and that was the only way it could have happened because our ability to decide had been amputated. Therefore we are not responsible.[38]

Levi recounts these familiar excuses with scorn. Why? Not because they simply cannot apply to officials as highly placed as Eichmann and Höss, for Levi explicitly says that they are claimed by "all militiamen." (It is, however, worth noting that the epistemically-based excuses tend to have lesser application the higher a person is in the chain of command.) Perhaps Levi's sense that there is an element of bad faith in the assertion of these excuses derives from the fact that they can all to some extent be anticipated, predicted in advance. We have all heard these claims before—and so had all those who asserted them, long before they found it necessary to proclaim them on their own behalf. But the more these epistemic excuses are publicly asserted, the less available they become. The more often it is claimed that unjust combatants are excused by their ignorance, the less plausible it becomes for subsequent unjust combatants to plead ignorance as an excuse. If they know that their predecessors have pleaded ignorance as an excuse, they know that there are important issues of knowledge and responsibility in war. This makes it less plausible for them to plead ignorance as an excuse. If they were aware that there were important matters about which they were ignorant, why did they not seek to overcome their epistemic deficiencies before committing themselves to fight?

They say, for example, they believed their war was just; but they knew that the same was true of their enemy, and that it was unlikely that they could both be right. Why did this not give them pause? They say they were indoctrinated and conditioned to obey; but they knew when they joined that they would be, and knew when they set off to fight that they had been. They say their government deceived them; but they knew in advance that governments routinely deceive their citizens, especially in matters of war. People living under totalitarian or authoritarian rule know that their government censors, manipulates, and in general controls the media. If they know from this that their government does not trust them with the truth, they should expect to be lied to. Thus, when soldiers in a totalitarian or authoritarian state fight in an unjust war, their best excuse is likely to be duress. By contrast, soldiers in a democratic country with a free press may have a better excuse if they have fought in an unjust war on the basis of lies told them by their government. But even they may know that their government has fought wars for reasons that do not bear exposure and thus has lied to furnish an acceptable public justification. The *Pentagon Papers* revealed an assortment of lies told to rally support for the war in Vietnam; Reagan lied about the nature of the Contras and the sources of their funding in order to make war against Nicaragua; and members of the George W. Bush administration lied repeatedly about weapons of mass destruction in Iraq in order to justify the invasion and occupation of that country to the UN, the Congress, and the American public. The soldiers who will fight in the US's next war will have had access to these facts.

It matters, of course, what the recent history of a soldier's country is like, and what the character of its culture is. It is, for example, morally less risky for a soldier in Norway to obey an order to fight than it is for a soldier in the US to do so, and the Norwegian soldier will accordingly have a stronger epistemic excuse if the war in which he fights turns out to be unjust. But in general it seems that soldiers are unjustifiably complacent in their assumption that the wars in which they are commanded to fight are just. Indeed, whether they turn out to be just or unjust combatants is usually more a matter of luck than anything else. Given the gravity of what is at stake in a decision to go to war, there seem to be relatively few cases in which a soldier who becomes an unjust combatant can truthfully claim that he actually did all of the epistemic work that could reasonably be expected of him and thus has a full epistemically-based excuse for his participation in an unjust war. Most unjust combatants have been negligent with respect to what are, in the context, their rather stringent epistemic responsibilities and thus their ignorance, and the action based on it, are culpable to varying degrees, which is just to say that although their participation in an unjust war may be excused, the excuse is in general partial rather than full.

My argument that the moral risks involved in participation in war may exceed those of nonparticipation exerts pressure in the direction of a contingent form of pacifism. But this pressure can be resisted, and successfully overcome, when war is just. It can be overcome by careful attention to the facts and careful moral reasoning. There was little uncertainty, for example, that the Allied war against Nazi Germany, and the war against imperial Japan, were just wars.[39] In principle there can be cases in which a war is in fact just and yet most soldiers are not epistemically justified in believing that it is just, or are even epistemically justified in believing that it is unjust. The risk of this happening is greatest in countries in which the flow of information is tightly controlled and manipulated by the government. Yet in such countries there is little risk that a just war will in fact go unfought, since governments in these countries tend to supply motivation to their soldiers by duress rather than persuasion.

Before concluding this section on excuses, I will note a final point that, while somewhat tangential to our present concerns, is nonetheless sufficiently important to be worth a brief mention. This is that if we wish to prevent the initiation of unjust wars, one of the most important courses of action we can take is to try, so far as possible, to eliminate the epistemic excuses available to unjust combatants—or, in other words, to enable soldiers to have both a greatly enhanced understanding of the moral character of the war in which they are commanded to fight, and certain forms of legal support if their improved moral understanding leads them to engage in conscientious refusal to fight. I have elsewhere proposed that the best way to pursue this goal would be to establish an impartial international court whose function would be to interpret and administer a reformed and morally better-informed body of law devoted to matters of *jus ad bellum*. But it would take us too far afield to pursue this suggestion here. The important point for our purposes is that if we could offer soldiers a source of guidance about the morality of war that would be more impartial and more authoritative than their own government, this could provide a basis for holding them accountable for their participation in unjust wars—perhaps accountable in law but certainly accountable to their own consciences. This increased accountability could in turn give them an incentive to take their epistemic duties more seriously than they tend to do at present.

4

Liability and the Limits of Self-Defense

4.1 DIFFERENT TYPES OF THREAT

4.1.1 The Relevance of Excuses to Killing in Self-Defense

By fighting in a war that lacks a just cause, unjust combatants are acting in a way that is objectively wrong. Some moral theorists, including some theorists of the just war, have claimed that objective wrongdoing is sufficient for liability to defensive attack, provided that the attack is both necessary for the prevention or correction of the wrong and proportionate to the gravity of the wrong. Recall, for example, Elizabeth Anscombe's claim, which I cited earlier in Chapter 1, that "what is required, for the people attacked to be non-innocent in the relevant sense [that is, liable to attack], is that they should themselves be engaged in an objectively unjust proceeding which the attacker has the right to make his concern; or—the commonest case—should be unjustly attacking him."[1] If this view is correct, all unjust combatants are morally liable to attack in war, since they are engaged in a form of objective wrongdoing—pursuing unjust goals by military means—that is sufficiently serious to make them liable to attack as a means of preventing further wrongdoing of this sort.

Yet objective wrongdoing is not sufficient for liability in other areas; for example, it is not sufficient for liability to punishment in the criminal law. A person may violate the law and yet be exempted from punishment by an excuse that shows that she is not blameworthy for the act that violated the law. In the criminal law, in other words, certain excuses negate liability. And partial excuses may mitigate a person's liability for having violated the law, a consideration that may be taken into account in the sentencing phase of the trial.

A similar claim applies to moral liability to defensive violence. Suppose that a person who poses an objectively wrongful threat to another is excused, either wholly or in part, for doing so. His moral liability to defensive violence may be diminished as a consequence. This does not mean that it is impermissible for the person he threatens to defend herself against the threat he poses. But it can affect what counts as a proportionate defensive response. Suppose, for example, that a person is threatening to destroy one of your highly valued possessions. You could certainly stop him by breaking a bottle over his head and might be able to stop him by kicking him hard in the shin. Suppose that the value of the object is such that if he were fully responsible for his action, it would be proportionate to smash him over the head with a bottle. But in fact someone earlier put a drug in his drink without his being aware of it, and this, you realize, has weakened his control over his own action. He is partially, though perhaps not entirely, excused on grounds of diminished responsibility. In this case, it may be reasonable to suppose that smashing him with a bottle would be disproportionate, so that you have to settle for kicking him in the shin, despite the fact that this may be insufficient to prevent him from destroying your possession.

The principle to which I am appealing—that the extent to which a person is excused for posing a threat of wrongful harm affects the degree of his moral liability to defensive harm, which in turn affects the stringency of the proportionality restriction on defensive force—is considerably more controversial when what is at stake is the potential victim's life. I will therefore have to say more about the application of this principle to cases involving lethal threats as the argument of this chapter progresses.

The relevance of the principle for our purposes is that if it applies to killing in self-defense, then it also applies to killing in war. For one of the presuppositions of this book is that the justifications for killing people in war are of the same forms as the justifications for the killing of persons in other contexts. The difference between war and other forms of conflict is a difference only of degree and thus the moral principles that govern killing in lesser forms of conflict govern killing in war as well. A state of war makes no difference other than to make the application of the relevant principles more complicated and difficult because of the number of people involved, the complexities of their relations with one another, and the virtual impossibility of having knowledge of all that is relevant to the justification of an act of killing.

The basic forms of justification for the killing of persons, as I noted in Chapter 1, appeal to the victim's consent (actual and, perhaps, hypothetical), the victim's liability or desert, and the claim that killing is the lesser evil. Of these, only the latter two are applicable to killing in war, and of these the appeal to liability is significantly less controversial. (I mention liability and desert together because they are related, but no one supposes that the justification for killing enemy combatants is ever that they deserve to die; hence I will say nothing more about desert as a justification for killing.) The appeal to liability is the principal form of justification for the infliction of harm in the law: people are to be punished in the criminal law only when they have made themselves liable to punishment, not when punishing them would avert a greater evil, and people are forced to pay compensation in tort law only when they have acted in a way that makes them liable to compensate a victim, not when their paying compensation would be the lesser evil. And the appeal to liability is also the form of justification for harming and killing that is standardly recognized in common sense morality as governing lesser forms of conflict. Thus, for example, killing in self-defense is justified not when killing the attacker would be the lesser evil than allowing the potential victim to be killed, but when the attacker has acted in a way that makes him morally liable to defensive violence. The strategy of argument—the methodology—in this book is to extend this form of justification from these areas in which it is familiar and well understood to the context of war. The claim is that if a soldier is morally justified in killing a person in war, that is usually because the other person has acted in a way that has made him liable to be killed.

As I also noted in Chapter 1, the criterion of liability to attack in war is not merely that one poses a threat to another. At a minimum, the threat must be unjustified. But neither is the criterion of liability that one poses a threat to another through action that is objectively unjustified, as Anscombe claims. Rather, as I suggested earlier, it is a necessary condition of liability to defensive attack that one be *morally responsible* for posing an objectively unjustified threat. I will say more in defense of this claim later. But even if we add morally responsible agency as a condition of liability, and claim that the basis of liability to attack in war is posing a threat of unjustified harm in one's capacity as a morally responsible agent, we will still be omitting a crucial consideration. This is that while posing a threat of wrongful harm without either justification or excuse is a sufficient condition of liability to defensive force, it is not a necessary condition. For mere moral responsibility for an unjust threat of wrongful harm to another may be sufficient for liability to attack, even if one does not oneself *pose* the threat—that is, even if one is not oneself the agent of the threat. I will say more about this in Chapter 5.

Assume, then, that moral responsibility for an unjustified threat is the basis of liability to attack in war.[2] There are various forms and degrees of responsibility, and therefore also of liability. In particular, the degree of a person's responsibility for unjustifiably posing a threat of wrongful harm to others varies with the significance of any excusing conditions that may apply to his action. The more a person is excused for some objectively wrongful act, the less responsible he is for the consequences, and the less liable he may be to defensive action to prevent those consequences from occurring. If this is right, it could be highly relevant to the morality of killing in war. If, for example, an unjust combatant is fully excused for fighting in an unjust war, that may mean that his liability to defensive action is comparatively weak. In that case there might be a requirement that just combatants exercise certain forms of restraint in fighting against him. Or if there were no such requirement, the justification for attacking him without restraint might have to appeal at least in part to considerations other than his liability to attack, and those other considerations would have to be identified.

To try to elucidate the relation between excuses and liability, I will focus initially on cases of individual self-defense outside the context of war. Some of the examples I will use for purposes of illustration will presuppose that agents have knowledge that it is sometimes difficult to have even in cases of individual self-defense and that it is virtually impossible to have in the complex and confused circumstances of war. But it is helpful to try to get clear about what is at issue in simplified cases, even if they have certain idealized features, in order to know what to look for in the more complicated cases involving combatants in war that are our ultimate concern here. The conclusions we may draw from simplified cases of individual self-defense may have no direct application in war because the conditions for knowledge are so different. But it is important to identify the considerations that would be relevant in war if only we could have knowledge of them, in order to determine how we might most effectively try to compensate for the absence of that relevant knowledge.

It will help to have before us a set of distinctions among various different kinds of agent, to whom I will refer as "Threats," who pose a threat to others. I will define certain categories of Threat, offering one or more hypothetical examples of each. This will, I hope, introduce some conceptual clarity, which will then enable us to explore questions about whether, why, and to what extent different types of Threat are liable to defensive action, after which we can try to determine into which category or categories most unjust combatants fit, with the ultimate aim of better understanding their moral status in war.

4.1.2 Culpable Threats

I begin with the category at one end of the spectrum: *Culpable Threats*. These are people who pose a threat of wrongful harm to others and have neither justification, permission, nor excuse. They may intend the harm they threaten, or the risk they impose, or the threat may arise from action that is reckless or negligent. But because they have neither justification nor excuse, they are fully culpable for their threatening action. As such, they are fully liable to necessary and proportionate defensive action. A man who attempts to murder his wife so that he can inherit her money is a Culpable Threat. Not only the wife herself but any third party would be fully justified in killing this man if that were necessary to prevent him from killing her—or even just the surest means of saving her.

It is generally agreed that the proportionality restriction on killing a Culpable Threat is weaker than it is in other cases. Precisely because of the Culpable Threat's full culpability, it can be proportionate to inflict a significantly greater harm on a Culpable Threat if that is necessary to prevent him from inflicting a lesser harm on an innocent victim. The proportionality restriction is thought to be particularly weak in the case of lethal threats. It is, for example, often claimed that it can be permissible to kill any number of Culpable Threats when that is necessary to prevent them from killing a single innocent person. Others, though not as many, think that if a Culpable Threat intends to kill an innocent victim, it can be permissible to kill him if that is necessary to avert the threat no matter how low the probability of his succeeding in killing his victim would otherwise have been.

4.1.3 Partially Excused Threats

Culpable Threats are *fully* culpable; there are no excusing conditions that apply to their action. It is possible, however, to be culpable for an act while having a partial excuse. This is obvious, for when an excuse is only partial, some residue of culpability remains. There is therefore a large category of what I will call *Partially Excused Threats*: people who unjustifiably pose a threat of wrongful harm to others but whose action is excused to some extent, though not fully. A Partially

Excused Threat may have an excuse of any of the three broad types I identified earlier. A person might, for example, unjustifiably pose a threat to an innocent person only because he has himself been credibly threatened with some sanction if he fails to harm that person. If the level of duress to which he is exposed could be resisted by a person of ordinary fortitude, and in particular if it is insufficient to overwhelm his own will, his excuse is only partial, only mitigating. The strength of the excuse is a function of, among other things, the severity of the sanction and the magnitude of the harm he threatens to cause.

A person might also unjustifiably pose a threat to an innocent person by mistake, because he lacks relevant knowledge. But if his ignorance was avoidable—if, for example, he has been negligent in investigating the facts relevant to the permissibility of his action—his excuse is only partial. The same is true if he acts with a diminished capacity for responsible agency, but not in the complete absence of that capacity—as, for example, in the case of the person who threatens to destroy your valued possession. The drug he was involuntarily administered has impaired his capacity for self-control, but not eliminated it.

Partially Excused Threats are not necessarily less culpable than Culpable Threats. A Culpable Threat may, for example, be fully culpable for intentionally imposing a comparatively minor threat, while a Partially Excused Threat may be excused to some degree for negligently posing a greater threat. If the threat posed by the Partially Excused Threat is significantly greater, he may be more culpable than the Culpable Threat, despite the fact that his offense is negligent rather than intentional, and that he has a partial excuse. For the degree of an agent's culpability is a function of all these variables—whether the wrongful threat is intentional, reckless, or negligent, whether the agent has an excuse and how strong that excuse is, and the magnitude of the threatened harm—as well as others.

The proportionality constraint on defensive action against a Partially Excused Threat is more stringent than it is in the case of a Culpable Threat. This does not mean, of course, that it is always permissible to inflict greater harm on a Culpable Threat. What it means is that the extent of a Partially Excused Threat's liability is always discounted for his excuse—that is, that his liability would be greater without the excuse, if all other considerations remained the same. In other words, his liability would be greater if he were a Culpable Threat, and other things were equal.

As I noted earlier, the difference in liability emerges in the narrow proportionality constraint. Suppose that someone is attacking you and that if you do not defend yourself, you will be severely injured, though not killed. You have two defensive options. You can kill the Threat, thereby escaping entirely unharmed. Or you can incapacitate him in a way that will injure but not kill him—but only after he will have inflicted a lesser though still substantial injury on you. Suppose that if the person attacking you is a Culpable Threat, it would be proportionate to kill him. In that case, it may be permissible to kill him *rather than* incapacitate him at the cost of suffering a substantial injury—for example, a broken arm. Yet if you know that he has a partial excuse, it may be wrong for you to kill him—that is, you may be morally required to suffer the broken arm in order to avoid killing him. Suppose, for example, that he mistakenly believes that it is his duty to kill you. It is, in the circumstances, a natural mistake, but he could have avoided it if he had taken greater care in investigating the facts before he acted. If the excuse significantly diminishes his culpability, killing him may be disproportionate. In short, the harmfulness of the defensive action to which the Partially Excused Threat is liable varies with the degree of his culpability.

One may wonder why a wholly innocent victim might be required to share the cost of a Partially Excused Threat's wrongful action. Why should not the Threat be required to suffer the entire cost? Or suppose that you could also save yourself without killing the Threat, by breaking some other innocent person's arm. Why should *you*, among all the innocent people in the world, be singled out as the one who has to share the cost of his wrongful action with the Partially Excused Threat?

The answer, I think, is that for you the alternative to sharing the cost with the Threat is to *kill* him, and to do so intentionally, and the option of dividing the cost between the Threat and another innocent person requires you intentionally to break an innocent person's arm. In short, the explanation of why *you* have to share the cost appeals to the distinction between doing and allowing. To see this, suppose that a stranger is drowning and the only way you can save him would involve breaking your arm. Our general practice of refusing to make small sacrifices, such as sending money to Oxfam, to save people who will otherwise die, suggests that we do not believe that it is obligatory to *save* a stranger at the cost of suffering a broken arm. So the reason why you might be required to accept a broken arm for the sake of the Partially Excused Threat, who is not even innocent in the way the drowning stranger is, must be that what you must do to avoid it is to *kill* someone rather than merely to allow someone to die.

4.1.4 Excused Threats and Innocent Threats

In the next category are those who unjustifiably pose a threat of wrongful harm to others but are *fully* excused for doing so. The paradigm case of an *Excused Threat* is a person who acts under irresistible duress—that is, the sanction he faces, or the harm he will suffer, if he does not unjustifiably threaten someone else is so severe that it overwhelms his will, and would overwhelm the will of anyone else with a normal capacity for the exercise of willpower.

It is important to note that the claim that a person is fully excused for an act of objective wrongdoing implies only that the person is not culpable, that he or she is entirely blameless. It does *not* necessarily imply that the person is absolved of all *responsibility*. A person may be responsible for his objectively wrongful action even if he is not blameworthy. This is true, for example, in most if not all cases of what we call irresistible duress. When we say that duress is irresistible, we usually do not mean that literally. We concede that *some* people could and indeed would resist, and that it was physically and in some sense psychologically possible for the person who failed to resist to have resisted instead. There is therefore a basis for holding him responsible. But the standard of responsibility is not the standard of culpability. We do not accept that all those who are responsible for acting wrongly are also blamable. There are, of course, *some* cases in which what counts as a full excuse on an objective account of permissibility absolves a person not only of all culpability but also of all responsibility. But not all cases of full excuse are like this. I will say more about this later.

I have thus far focused on duress as an example of a full excuse. This was deliberate, for what I have called epistemically-based excuses pose a problem for the taxonomy of Threats. Consider a person who poses a lethal threat to another on the basis of factual and moral beliefs that he is fully epistemically justified in having—that is, he is justified in having these beliefs and in assigning them a degree of credence approaching certainty. But the beliefs are in fact false. If they were true, he would be objectively justified in killing the person he is now attempting to kill, who is in fact wholly innocent. On an objective account of justification, he is acting impermissibly but has a full epistemic excuse. But on a subjective account of justification, which makes a person's *justified* beliefs relevant to the permissibility of his action, this person acts permissibly and indeed justifiably, and therefore cannot have an excuse, for there is nothing for him to be excused *for*.

Call this person an *Epistemically Justified Mistaken Threat*. According to an objective account of permissibility, or an objective account of justification, he is an Excused Threat. But not according to a subjective account. It seems, therefore, that we need another label for such a Threat for those who accept subjective accounts of permissibility and justification. Let us say, then, that on a subjective account, he is an *Innocent Threat*. An Innocent Threat is someone who in objective terms acts impermissibly in posing a threat to another but also acts subjectively permissibly, or even with subjective justification. (This is in two respects an unfortunate label. First, the term "Innocent Threat" has several meanings in the literature, all different from the one I propose. Second, I have until now followed the just war tradition in using "innocent" to mean, roughly, "not liable." But it is possible—indeed I will argue that it is true—that some Innocent Threats in my sense *are* morally liable to defensive attack. But because the other labels I have considered are at least equally problematic, I will persist in using the term "Innocent Threat" in this particular technical sense.)

The categories of Excused Threat and Innocent Threat are therefore overlapping but not coextensive. According to both objective and subjective accounts of permissibility, a Threat who poses an objectively unjustified threat on the basis of irresistible duress is only an Excused Threat. But a person who poses an objectively unjustified threat on the basis of what the Scholastics called invincible ignorance is an Excused Threat according to an objective account but an Innocent Threat according to a subjective account.

When a Threat is excused on one account but acts permissibly on the other, the different labels refer to the same facts. In such cases of overlap, there can obviously be no substantive moral difference between an Excused Threat and an Innocent Threat. There are, however, relevant differences within the category of Innocent Threats (and, of course, corresponding differences within the category of Excused Threats, on an objective account). One such difference is that between those who act merely permissibly, with no positive moral reason, and those who act for a positive moral reason, and thus act with subjective justification. There are also relevant differences among those who intend to cause harm, those who knowingly but unintentionally cause harm, those who foreseeably risk causing harm, and those who cannot foresee that their action will cause harm. All such Threats may be acting in ways that are objectively impermissible but subjectively permissible.

It will be helpful to have particular examples that exemplify some of the various possibilities. Here are some cases that illustrate the distinctions that can be drawn.

> (1) *The Resident* The identical twin of a notorious mass murderer is driving in the middle of a stormy night in a remote area when his car breaks down. He is nonculpably unaware that his twin brother, the murderer, has within the past few hours escaped from prison in just this area, and that the residents have been warned of the escape. The murderer's notoriety derives from his invariable modus operandi: he violently breaks into people's homes and kills them instantly. As the twin whose car has broken down approaches a house to request to use the telephone, the resident of the house takes aim to shoot him, preemptively, believing him to be the murderer.

I will reserve the term "Epistemically Justified Mistaken Threat" for Innocent Threats who intend to kill someone whom they believe to be liable to be killed. The resident belongs in this category. He intends to kill someone who is in fact innocent in every sense, so his action is objectively wrong. But given his beliefs, which we may assume are epistemically fully justified, his action is subjectively not only permissible but justified.

> (2) *The Technician* A technician is guiding a pilotless drone aircraft toward its landing when it unaccountably veers off course in the direction of a group of houses in which he reasonably believes several families are living. He alters the drone's course in the only way he can, sending it where he knows it will kill one innocent bystander when it crashes. Although there was no reason for him to know this, all the families in fact moved out the day before, while the technician was still on vacation.

Because the plane would not have killed or injured anyone had he not acted, the technician's altering its course is objectively wrong. But his action is subjectively justified because his belief that the plane would otherwise have killed numerous people is fully epistemically justified and, if that belief were true, his act would be objectively justified. So just as the case of the resident is a case in which a person is subjectively justified in intentionally killing a person who is in fact innocent, so this is a case in which the technician is subjectively justified in foreseeably but unintentionally killing an innocent person.

(3) *The Conscientious Driver* A person who always keeps her car well maintained and always drives carefully and alertly decides to drive to the cinema. On the way, a freak event that she could not have anticipated occurs that causes her car to veer out of control in the direction of a pedestrian.

I will assume that on an objective account of permissibility, this conscientious driver is acting impermissibly. It is impermissible to drive, or to continue to drive, when one will lose control of the car and threaten the life of an innocent person. But of course she cannot know that these are the conditions in which she is driving. So while on an objective account of permissibility, she is an Excused Threat, on a subjective account, she is an Innocent Threat. She does not intend to harm anyone and cannot foresee that she will harm anyone, but she knows that driving is an activity that has a very tiny risk of causing great harm—so tiny that the activity, considered as a *type* of activity, is entirely permissible. But she has bad luck. Notice that although her action is subjectively permissible, it is not subjectively justified. She has no positive moral reason to engage in the activity that she knows has a tiny risk of unintentionally killing an innocent bystander.

(4) *The Ambulance Driver* An Emergency Medical Technician is driving an ambulance to the site of an accident to carry one of the victims to the hospital. She is driving conscientiously and alertly but a freak event occurs that causes the ambulance to veer uncontrollably toward a pedestrian.

This example is just like the case of the conscientious driver except that the ambulance driver has a positive moral reason to drive. She therefore has a subjective justification, and not merely a subjective permission, to act in a way that she knows has a tiny risk of causing great harm to an innocent bystander.

(5) *The Cell Phone Operator* A man's cell phone has, without his knowledge, been reprogrammed so that when he next presses the "send" button, the phone will send a signal that will detonate a bomb that will then kill an innocent person.

It is objectively wrong for the cell phone operator to press the "send" button. But he cannot know that. He is fully epistemically justified in believing, and with a degree of credence approaching certainty, that his pressing the button is entirely harmless. So if he presses it, he will be acting subjectively permissibly, though not with subjective justification, unless there is a positive moral reason to press it (such as the need to call the emergency number to report an accident). He is therefore an Excused Threat on an objective account, and an Innocent Threat on a subjective account. But unlike the resident, the cell phone operator does not choose to cause harm. And unlike the conscientious driver and the ambulance driver, he does not choose to engage in an activity that has a foreseeable risk of causing serious harm. Subjectively, his situation is not relevantly different from my situation right now, or yours. For after all, my computer could be rigged to detonate a bomb when I press the "tab" key. And even your book could be rigged to detonate a bomb when you turn the next page.

Because anyone who is an Innocent Threat on a subjective account is an Excused Threat on an objective account, while not all who are Excused Threats on an objective account are Innocent Threats on a subjective account, I will refer to the Threats in the five cases cited above as Innocent Threats rather than as Excused Threats. This makes it clear that the reason they are excused on an objective account and acting permissibly on a subjective account is that they are acting on the basis of epistemically justified but false beliefs. Although none of the five is blamable for posing an objectively unjustified threat, they nevertheless differ in the degree to which they are responsible for the threat they pose. Of the five, the one who bears the greatest responsibility for the threat she poses is the conscientious driver. Although she does not intend to harm anyone, she does know that her action carries a small risk of causing great though unintended harm. Although her act is of a type that is generally objectively permissible, and although she has taken due care to avoid harming anyone, she has had bad luck: the risk she knew her act carried has now, improbably and through no fault of her own, been realized. Because she knew of the small risk to others that her driving would impose, and because she nonetheless voluntarily chose to drive when there was no moral reason for her to do so—in short, because she knowingly imposed this risk for the sake of her own interests—she is morally liable to defensive action to prevent her from killing an innocent bystander.

In contrast to the conscientious driver, the resident, the technician, and the ambulance driver all act not merely subjectively permissibly but with subjective moral justification. Each justifiably believes that he or she has a strong moral reason to do exactly what he or she is doing, and that this reason is not outweighed by any countervailing reasons. But in each case, one or the other of these beliefs is mistaken. Although all of these three agents are blameless, it is reasonable to suppose that all are nevertheless responsible for their choices and that this responsibility, however minimal, is a basis for liability to defensive action. There are, however, differences among them that arguably make a difference to the degree of their responsibility. All three pose a lethal and objectively unjustified threat to a person who is in fact innocent. The resident threatens to kill a person intentionally, the technician threatens to kill a person foreseeably but unintentionally, and the ambulance driver took a risk of killing a person and now as a result of bad luck threatens to kill someone accidentally. If it is true, in general, that it is more seriously wrong to kill a person intentionally than to kill a person foreseeably but unintentionally, and more seriously wrong to kill a person foreseeably than to take a known risk of killing a person accidentally, then the resident chooses to take a greater moral risk in acting than the technician does, and the technician takes a greater moral risk than the ambulance driver. To choose to kill a person intentionally is to take a great moral risk. If one has bad luck and gets it wrong, so that one ends up having intentionally killed a person who is in fact innocent, the degree to which one is responsible for the death seems greater than it is if one has merely run a low risk of killing an innocent person accidentally and ended up killing her through bad luck. If moral responsibility for an objectively unjust threat is the criterion of liability to defensive action, and if the degree of a person's liability varies with the degree of her responsibility, then it seems that the resident is liable to defensive action to a greater degree than the technician, who is in turn liable to a greater degree than the ambulance driver.

4.1.5 Nonresponsible Threats

Like the conscientious driver, the cell phone operator acts in a way that is merely subjectively permissible rather than subjectively justified. There is no positive moral reason for him to press the "send" button on his phone. Yet intuitively he seems even less responsible for the threat he poses than the three Innocent Threats who act with subjective justification. The reason why this is so is that, unlike the others, he does not intentionally kill, knowingly kill, or even knowingly impose on others a risk of being killed. The threat he poses is not one that he could conceivably foresee; nor is there any association between the kind of act he does and the kind of threat he poses. What is singular about his case is not that he is nonculpably and invincibly ignorant of some relevant fact—a characteristic he shares with the other four Innocent Threats; it is, rather, that he is nonculpably and invincibly ignorant *that he poses any kind of threat or risk of harm to anyone.*

These facts absolve him of all responsibility for the threat he poses. He is what I call a *Nonresponsible Threat*: a person who without justification threatens to harm someone in a way to which she is not liable, but who is in no way morally responsible for doing so. (He remains, of course, an Excused Threat on an objective account and an Innocent Threat on a subjective account. There is thus some overlap not only between the categories of Excused Threat and Innocent Threat but also between those two categories and the category of Nonresponsible Threat.) If, as I have claimed, moral responsibility for an objectively unjustified threat to another is the basis of liability to defensive force, then the cell phone operator is not liable at all. If there is a justification for attacking or killing him in defense of the person he will otherwise kill by pressing the button on his phone, it must appeal to some consideration other than that he has acted in a way that makes him liable to defensive action.

The cell phone operator is a Nonresponsible Threat because he has no way of knowing that he poses a threat to anyone. In this respect he is relevantly like a person who merely by being in a public space has contracted a highly contagious and lethal disease, but is himself a symptomless carrier. But there are other ways in which people may pose a threat to others without being in any way morally responsible for doing so. One is to pose a threat without any exercise of agency at all, as in the cases discussed by Robert Nozick and Judith Jarvis Thomson in which a person is thrown from a height by someone else and threatens to land on and crush an immobilized person below.[3] Another example of this sort is a fetus whose continued growth inside a pregnant woman's body threatens her life. A different way in which one may pose a threat without responsibility is to act, or to move one's body, in the absence of any capacity for responsible agency. If it were possible, as it sometimes is in works of science fiction, for one person to use drugs or a device implanted in another person's brain to exercise complete control over that person's will, the manipulator could turn the person under his control into a Nonresponsible Threat.

It is worth noting a difference between the cell phone operator and Nonresponsible Threats of the other two types I have identified. The cell phone operator's complete absence of moral responsibility for posing a threat arises from the fact that he cannot know that he poses a threat. He nevertheless acts as a morally responsible agent. But Nonresponsible Threats of the other two types—those who pose a threat but not in their capacity as agents and those who have no capacity for morally responsible agency—are, *in posing a threat*, relevantly like a tumbling boulder or a charging tiger. The one does not act at all, while the other acts, but as a lower animal does, not as a responsible agent. What they do is not so much beyond the scope of moral evaluation as it is beneath it. It is neither permissible nor impermissible. Because what they do is not permissible, even subjectively, they cannot be Innocent Threats. Because it is also not impermissible, they cannot be Excused Threats. The cell phone operator, by contrast, acts objectively impermissibly and subjectively permissibly. It is only in cases of his sort that the category of the Nonresponsible Threat overlaps with those of the Excused Threat and the Innocent Threat.

According to common sense intuition, it is permissible to kill a Nonresponsible Threat if he would otherwise kill an innocent person, and perhaps even if he would only severely injure an innocent person. So the claim that a Nonresponsible Threat is not liable to defensive force is highly counterintuitive. I will therefore advance a couple of arguments in favor of the claim that a Nonresponsible Threat cannot be liable.

I claimed earlier in Section 3.1.2 that the explanation of why it is wrong to kill an innocent bystander in self-preservation begins with the fact that in general the presumption against killing a person is stronger than the presumption against letting a person die, and the presumption against intentional killing is stronger than that against unintended killing and much stronger than that against unintentionally allowing someone to die. If one's life is threatened by a Nonresponsible Threat, so that one must choose between intentionally killing the Threat and allowing oneself to be killed by him, the presumptions oppose killing in self-defense. To overcome or defeat the presumption against intentional killing, there must be some important moral difference between the Threat and oneself. The presumption could be overcome if the Threat had made himself liable to be killed. But there is no plausible basis for this claim. As I argued earlier, merely posing a threat to another is not sufficient for liability; neither is posing an objectively unjustified threat. In the case of a Nonresponsible Threat, his posing an unjustified threat to you is just a fact about his position in the local causal architecture and as such cannot cause him to forfeit his right not to be killed. The natural and understandable personal partiality of the person whose life he threatens is also insufficient to overcome the presumption against killing. If it were, it would generally be permissible to kill a single innocent bystander as a means of self-preservation. There is, in short, nothing that relevantly distinguishes a Nonresponsible Threat from an innocent bystander, and thus nothing in either case that can overcome the presumption against intentional killing.

It does not follow from the fact that a Nonresponsible Threat is not liable to defensive action that it can never be permissible to harm him in self-defense. On occasion, it can be permissible intentionally to harm even an innocent bystander as a means of self-preservation. The justification cannot, of course, be that the bystander is liable, for an innocent bystander is by definition not liable. But there can be a lesser-evil justification for intentionally harming an innocent bystander and the same kind of justification is available in some cases for harming a Nonresponsible Threat in self-defense. In general, whatever it would be permissible to do to an innocent bystander as a means of self-preservation it would also be permissible to do to a Nonresponsible Threat in self-defense, in relevantly similar conditions.

One might argue that there is a significant moral difference between killing an innocent bystander in self-preservation and killing a Nonresponsible Threat in self-defense—a difference that is related to but not identical with the obvious and perhaps necessary truth that a Nonresponsible Threat poses a threat while an innocent bystander does not. The difference is in the mode of agency: when one kills an innocent bystander in order to save one's own life, one uses her strategically, as an instrument in the service of one's own purposes, whereas when one kills a Nonresponsible Threat in self-defense, one does not use him to one's advantage but merely reacts to him and the problem he presents. Warren Quinn, who to my knowledge was the first to call attention to this distinction, though not in the context of self-defense, referred to these two modes of agency as "opportunistic agency" and "eliminative agency," and suggested that "it would not be surprising if we regarded fatal or harmful exploitation as more difficult to justify than fatal or harmful elimination."[4]

I suspect that Quinn is right that this distinction is of moral significance. Yet the fact that self-defense against a Nonresponsible Threat involves eliminative rather than opportunistic agency does not show that it is permissible, or that a Nonresponsible Threat may be liable to defensive action. For eliminative agency is often seriously wrong—for example, when a person murders his business rival because of the threat the victim's business poses to his own. It is therefore possible that the difference in agency shows only that, while killing a Nonresponsible Threat in self-defense is wrong, killing an innocent bystander in self-preservation is even more seriously wrong because it involves a more objectionable form of agency.

But in fact the appeal to the different modes of agency does not show even this. For there are cases in which killing an innocent bystander in self-preservation involves eliminative rather than opportunistic agency but still seems impermissible. Here are two examples, both involving what Noam Zohar calls an "Innocent Obstructor."[5]

> *Innocent Obstructor 1* One is running through the woods, trying to avoid being killed by a Culpable Threat. One comes to a high, narrow, and wobbly public bridge that one must cross to evade the Threat. There is, however, an innocent bystander sitting in the middle of the bridge with her legs dangling off, enjoying the view. If one runs onto the bridge, she will be shaken off and will plummet to her death.

> *Innocent Obstructor 2* The background details are the same as in Innocent Obstructor 1. But in this variant, merely running onto the bridge will not shake the innocent bystander off. Yet the bridge is too narrow for you to cross without her moving off it and there is insufficient time for her to move to allow you to escape. You must instead pause to shake the bridge vigorously to topple her off.

In the first of these cases one would kill the Innocent Obstructor as an anticipated side effect of one's effort to save oneself from the Culpable Threat. Although the killing would be unintended, intuitively it still seems impermissible. In the second case, the killing would be intended as a means, but one's agency would be eliminative rather than opportunistic. One would not be exploiting the innocent bystander's presence in order to save one's life. Yet to kill her is a clear instance of impermissibly killing an innocent bystander as a means of self-preservation.

Some proponents of the Doctrine of Double Effect would argue that even in the second case one need not intend to kill the innocent bystander and certainly need not intend her death. One might intend only to clear her out of one's path, and if she were to survive the fall uninjured, that would not thwart one's plan, which shows that her death is not within the scope of one's intention. And even if one must intend to topple her off the bridge as a means of clearing one's path, it remains true that one can intend to topple her off without intending to kill her and without intending that she die. Still, it is unlikely that many defenders of the Doctrine of Double Effect would think it permissible to shake the bridge to get her off it in these circumstances, even if one did not strictly intend to harm or kill her. It is certainly tempting to appeal to the distinction between eliminative and opportunistic agency in an effort to defend the intuition that intentionally killing a Nonresponsible Threat in self-defense is permissible while intentionally killing an innocent bystander in self-preservation is not. But there are no ways of understanding the concept of intention or of reinterpreting the Doctrine of Double Effect that are likely to help in this effort.

The comparison between intentionally killing the Innocent Obstructor and killing a Nonresponsible Threat in self-defense also provides some intuitive support for the claim that it is in general impermissible to kill a Nonresponsible Threat in self-defense because the Threat's lack of liability means that the main form of justification for self-defense does not apply. For it is intuitively plausible to claim that it is impermissible intentionally to topple the innocent bystander from the bridge, thereby causing her death, in order to facilitate one's escape. Yet there is no difference in the mode of agency involved in killing her and that involved in killing a Nonresponsible Threat. And it seems impossible to find a plausible basis for distinguishing between them on grounds of liability. It is clear that the Innocent Obstructor has done nothing to forfeit her right not to be intentionally killed. Is there, then, some difference between her and a Nonresponsible Threat that could ground the claim that the latter *has* forfeited his right? Is there, for example, some difference that could be relevant to liability between sitting quietly on a bridge and merely pressing the buttons on a cell phone, when there is no reason in either case for the person to suspect that either activity could be instrumental in bringing about another person's death? What seems relevant here is shared equally by both: a complete absence of responsibility for the predicament in which the person under threat finds himself. If we alter *that* factor in either case, we get an intuitively quite different result. If, for example, the woman on the bridge knew that a person would soon need to cross the bridge in order to evade a Culpable Threat, or if she planted herself there intentionally in order to prevent him from being able to cross, then it would be plausible to regard her as liable, *even though she would still be a bystander*—for status as a bystander is a matter of one's causal position, not of one's responsibility.[6] She would then be no more a threat than she is in either of the original cases, but she *would* be to some degree morally responsible for the threat one faced from the Culpable Threat, which her presence would impede one's ability to escape from. This supports the claim I made earlier: that what matters is not whether one *poses* a wrongful threat through one's own action but whether one is morally responsible for a wrongful threat.

4.1.6 Justified Threats and Just Threats

Primarily for the sake of completeness, it is worth noting two more categories of Threat, though neither is a category that could encompass unjust combatants, at least in a general way. Sometimes an agent acts with objective moral justification but nevertheless threatens to inflict wrongful harm on an innocent person—that is, harm that would *wrong* the victim, or contravene his or her rights. I will refer to such an agent as a *Justified Threat*. There are two general types of Justified Threat, and in both cases the form of justification that applies to the agent's action is a lesser-evil justification. In one case, the Justified Threat is objectively justified in intentionally infringing the right of an innocent person, a person who has neither waived nor forfeited her right. These are cases in which the innocent person's rights are straightforwardly overridden by more important countervailing considerations—for example, a case in which it is necessary to kill one innocent person as a means of preventing a much larger number of other innocent people from being killed by someone else. Anyone who is not a moral absolutist must believe that there are in principle such cases.

In the other case, the Justified Threat is objectively morally justified in acting in a way that infringes the rights of an innocent person as a foreseen but unintended effect. An example of a Justified Threat of this sort is the tactical bomber, a familiar figure in debates about the Doctrine of Double Effect and the relevance of intention to permissibility. The tactical bomber is fighting in a just war and has been ordered to bomb one of the enemy's more important military facilities. He knows that in doing so he will inevitably kill some innocent civilians who live nearby, but he also knows that the number of deaths he will cause is proportionate in the wide sense in relation to the importance of destroying the facility. His action is therefore objectively morally justified but will have as a side effect the killing of people who have done nothing to lose their right not to be killed. Like the person who intentionally kills an innocent person to save a much greater number of other innocent people, the tactical bomber justifiably threatens people who have done nothing to make themselves liable to be threatened.

The final category I will mention consists of those who are objectively morally justified in posing a threat of harm to which the potential victim is morally liable. Call such people *Just Threats*. The harm that a Just Threat would inflict would neither wrong the victim nor infringe his or her rights. The victim has no justified complaint about being harmed in the way threatened by the Just Threat. An obvious example of a Just Threat is someone who responds with necessary and proportionate defensive force to an attack by a Culpable Threat.

While I suggested that unjust combatants are neither Justified Threats nor Just Threats, that claim may be slightly misleading. Because unjust combatants are engaged in a general form of action—fighting in a war that is unjust because it lacks a just cause—that is objectively wrong, it is not possible that they could be Justified Threats or Just Threats through the course of a war. Yet there can be some occasions even during an unjust war when unjust combatants may act not only objectively permissibly but even with objective justification. This can be the case, as I noted in Section 1.3, if just combatants are pursuing their just cause by impermissible means, such as intentionally attacking people who are innocent in the relevant sense. If a soldier on the opposing side, who is fighting in an unjust war, attacks the just combatants to prevent them from killing innocent people, he may then be acting with objective moral justification against people who are liable to be attacked.[7] On that occasion, then, he may have temporary status as a Just Threat. I say "may have" rather than "has" because even while he is doing one act that is morally justified, and perhaps even morally required, he is also engaged in a temporally extended course of action that is wrong: fighting in an unjust war. Because of this—that is, because after he has prevented the just combatants from doing wrong, he will revert to the pursuit of his own ongoing wrongful course of action—he remains a legitimate target of attack. His moral status is curiously mixed. Even while he is doing one act for which there is objective justification, he does not cease to be engaged in another course of action that is wrong.

The set of categories I have outlined—Culpable Threats, Partially Excused Threats, Excused Threats, Innocent Threats, Nonresponsible Threats, Justified Threats, and Just Threats—is not exhaustive. There are various other possibilities, such as the category of persons who, acting in a way that is objectively permissible but not objectively justified, pose a threat of wrongful harm to another. There are also those who pose a threat of wrongful harm through action that is objectively justified but subjectively impermissible. I will not consider these and other possibilities that are of no obvious relevance to the moral status of combatants in war.

4.2 LIABILITY TO DEFENSIVE ATTACK

The next issue to consider is whether and to what extent Threats of the different types I have identified are morally liable to defensive attack. I will assume that it is uncontroversial that when an agent is to some degree culpable for posing a threat of wrongful harm to another, that agent is liable to defensive attack. Culpable and Partially Excused Threats are, therefore, liable to defensive attack. Liability is, however, a matter of degree and the degree of a Partially Excused Threat's liability depends on the strength of the excusing conditions that apply to his or her action. As I noted before, degree of liability is manifest in the stringency of the narrow proportionality constraint. The stronger a Partially Excused Threat's excuse is—the more it approaches a full excuse—the more stringent the proportionality constraint becomes. If the excuse is trivial, the Partially Excused Threat is barely distinguishable from a Culpable Threat and is liable to virtually the same degree of harm to which he would be liable in the absence of the excuse. If, by contrast, the excuse has nearly the force of a full excuse—if, that is, it is almost fully exculpating—then the degree of harm to which the Partially Excused Threat is liable, or the degree of harm that it would be proportionate to inflict via defensive action, is only marginally more than it would be permissible to inflict on an Excused Threat in the same circumstances.

Excused Threats who are not also Innocent or Nonresponsible Threats are liable, though to a reduced degree relative to Culpable and Partially Excused Threats. If an excuse is sufficient to absolve a person not only of all culpability for posing an objectively wrongful threat but also of all responsibility, then the Excused Threat is also a Nonresponsible Threat. If, however, the excuse absolves the agent only of culpability and not of all responsibility, and if responsibility for a wrongful threat is the criterion of liability to defensive attack, then the Excused Threat must be liable to some degree. This seems intuitively right in the paradigm case of an Excused Threat: namely, a person who acts under irresistible duress. As I noted, duress is never literally irresistible; hence, while that excuse may render a person altogether blameless, it does not render him wholly nonresponsible.

Similarly, Innocent Threats who are not also Nonresponsible Threats are liable to defensive action. Again this follows from the fact that they are morally responsible for posing a wrongful threat (if this were not so they would be Nonresponsible Threats), together with the assumption that responsibility for a wrongful threat is the criterion of liability to defensive attack. There is a clear intuitive basis for this judgment in the case of someone like the conscientious driver, who chooses for nonmoral reasons of her own to act in a way that she knows imposes a tiny risk of great harm to innocent people. If she has bad luck and will now accidentally kill an innocent person unless defensive action is taken against her, she seems liable to necessary and proportionate defensive action. Since what is at stake is the life of an innocent bystander, proportionate harm could include death.

If moral responsibility for a wrongful threat is a sufficient condition of liability to defensive action, it is a necessary truth that all Innocent Threats who are not also Nonresponsible Threats are liable. What may be disputed is whether some of those I have identified as Innocent but not Nonresponsible Threats are really not Nonresponsible Threats. This is particularly true in the cases of the technician, the resident, and the ambulance driver, all of whom act with subjective justification. For simplicity, I will focus mainly on the case of the resident, who is what I have called an Epistemically Justified Mistaken Threat. To strengthen the challenge to my earlier claim that he is not a Nonresponsible Threat, let us assume that the members of his immediate family—his wife and small children—are with him in the house when the murderer's identical twin is approaching. In that case his shooting the twin, though objectively wrong, is not only subjectively morally justified but is even subjectively morally *required*. His situation, let us assume, is subjectively indistinguishable from that of a person whose house really *is* being approached by an escaped mass murderer in the middle of the night. Assume that such a person, in shooting the genuine mass murderer, would be a Just Threat. Our original resident's situation is, on these assumptions, subjectively indistinguishable from that of a Just Threat. The resident and the Just Threat respond in exactly the same way to subjectively identical circumstances. How, then, can the resident, and Epistemically Justified Mistaken Threats in general, be liable? Is it really sufficient for liability that they voluntarily choose to harm or kill someone and have the bad luck to be objectively mistaken, when a Just

Threat makes the same choice in indistinguishable conditions, yet has the good luck to be correct, and is therefore not liable? Can whether someone is liable really be just a matter of luck?

It cannot be *merely* a matter of luck. A person cannot become liable to defensive action without having engaged in some form of voluntary action that had some reasonably foreseeable risk of creating a wrongful threat. But when two people have acted in the same way, it can then be a matter of luck that one becomes liable to defensive action while the other does not.[8] What we are liable to is a function of what happens as a result of our action, which is a matter over which we have imperfect control. In many cases this seems intuitively acceptable. In the case of the conscientious driver, for example, either the driver will kill the pedestrian or the pedestrian, or some third party, will kill the driver in self- or other-defense. The harm threatened by the driver, which is a type of harm that one foreseeably risks inflicting on others when one drives, cannot be divided between the two of them, or among all those who, like the conscientious driver, chose to drive for reasons that were optional. All of the cost must go either to the driver or to the pedestrian. Since the driver chose to impose the risk for reasons of her own, it is fair that she should suffer the cost rather than imposing it on the pedestrian. Yet there are indefinitely many drivers who imposed the same risks that she did but had better luck. That she is liable and they are not is a matter of moral luck. Yet she acted in the knowledge that bad moral luck was a possibility.

Some people will, however, think that the conscientious driver cannot be held responsible for what happens as a result of events that were entirely unforeseeable. And even more people will think that the resident cannot be held responsible for the consequences of action that would be morally required if his fully epistemically justified beliefs were true. Some people, in other words, will think that the conscientious driver is a Nonresponsible Threat, and even more will think that the resident is. The idea that Innocent Threats who are subjectively justified in acting, and perhaps even those who are only subjectively permitted, are actually Nonresponsible Threats will not seem *morally* implausible to most people. This is because most people assume that it is permissible to kill a Nonresponsible Threat in self- or other-defense. On this assumption, it is permissible to kill the conscientious driver and even the resident in self- or other-defense, even if they bear no responsibility for the wrongful threat they pose, just as it is permissible, on this view, to kill the cell phone operator if there is no other way to prevent him from pressing the "send" button.

But for those who believe that there is no basis for the claim that a Nonresponsible Threat is liable to defensive attack, and who also believe that an appeal either to liability, consent, or lesser evil is necessary to override the presumption against the intentional killing of a person, the idea that the conscientious driver and the resident are Nonresponsible Threats is counterintuitive, since it seems to imply that it would be wrong for the pedestrian to kill the driver in self-defense, and that it would be wrong for the identical twin to kill the resident in self-defense. For if neither the driver nor the resident is liable, and since neither can be killed on the basis of a lesser-evil justification, there seems to be no plausible justification for killing them in self-defense.

But even if we believe, as I do, that there is a basis for liability in such cases as those of the conscientious driver and the resident, we have to concede that it is slight. And in cases such as these in which the moral asymmetry between the Threat and the potential victim is so slight, it may be that the Threat's liability is insufficiently significant to be morally decisive. In most cases in which killing in self-defense is justified, the presumption against intentional killing is easily overridden by the liability of the Threat; but when the degree of the Threat's responsibility, and therefore liability, is negligible, it may be insufficient to override that presumption. Perhaps it is a mistake to suppose that in such cases the slight or negligible liability of the Innocent Threat is morally decisive, so that while the innocent victim is entitled to kill the Threat in self-defense, the Threat has no right of self-defense against the victim. And perhaps it is also a mistake to suppose that when there is no basis for liability on the part of the Threat (that is, in cases involving Nonresponsible Threats), the presumption against intentional killing is morally decisive, so that it is impermissible for the innocent victim to defend herself. Perhaps the proper resolution in these cases is different. It may be that in cases in which there is little moral difference between the Threat and the potential innocent victim, it is too simplistic to suppose that *some* degree of responsibility, however slight, on the part of the Threat makes it justifiable for the victim to kill in self-defense, whereas when there is no basis for the attribution of responsibility, the victim must allow herself to be killed. We should consider whether there is another way of resolving these conflicts that recognizes the essential moral equality of the parties involved.

Suppose for the sake of argument that one or more of the following claims is true.

- Nonresponsible Threats are not morally liable to defensive attack, but the idea that the innocent victim must simply submit to being killed is unacceptable.
- All Innocent Threats, both those who act subjectively permissibly and those who act with subjective justification, are Nonresponsible Threats and are not liable to defensive attack, but the idea that the innocent victim must simply submit to being killed is unacceptable.
- Most Innocent Threats are not Nonresponsible Threats but the degree to which they are responsible is too slight for conflicts between them and their potential innocent victims to be resolved decisively in favor of the victim.

How, given one or more of these assumptions, should such conflicts be resolved? I can think of three possible modes of resolution. There may be others. In briefly sketching the three, I will, for convenience, focus mainly on unavoidable conflicts between Nonresponsible Threats and their potential innocent victims.

(1) One possibility is to divide the unavoidable harm between them. Suppose, for example, that instead of killing a Nonresponsible Threat in self-defense, the potential victim can save her life by nonlethally injuring the Nonresponsible Threat, though only at the cost of suffering a comparable nonlethal injury herself. If she follows that option, she and the Nonresponsible Threat, both of whom are entirely innocent people, will share the misfortune of their having come into unavoidable conflict. That may seem a fairer (if not altogether realistic) way of resolving the conflict than insisting that because the Nonresponsible Threat is not liable, the moral presumption against intentional killing requires that the victim allow herself to be killed.

Suppose, however, that the harm cannot be divided. In practice, it seldom can be. It may still be possible, though, to follow a decision-procedure that treats both innocent parties fairly by giving them each an equal chance of surviving. The potential victim might, for example, be morally required to use a randomizing device, such as a coin toss, to determine whether to kill the Nonresponsible Threat or to allow herself to be killed. It is, of course, entirely fanciful, indeed ridiculous, to imagine that anyone who was about to be killed would or could do such a thing. But if such a procedure really were the morally ideal solution, it would be important to know that, if only so that the knowledge could guide the design of institutions that might promote such resolutions at a different level of action. Or it might be that disinterested third parties, who would not be acting under such extreme pressures, could intervene in the knowledge that only a random selection would be fair. If we thought that the Threat was not entirely nonresponsible, but was liable to some slight degree, the ideal solution might be a weighted lottery that would give the Threat a lower chance of survival, with the reduction in probability being proportionate to the degree of his liability.

(2) A second possibility is that in cases in which there is little or no moral asymmetry between a Threat and the potential innocent victim, we should see each as objectively permitted to engage in self-defense against the other. Suppose, for example, that the innocent person who will be killed if the cell phone operator presses the button on his rewired phone can save herself only by killing him before he presses the button. One might argue that although the cell phone operator has done nothing to make himself liable to be killed, morality does not require the potential victim to allow herself to be killed. She has a right not to be killed that she is permitted to defend against infringement even by a Nonresponsible Threat. So she is morally permitted to kill him. But because he too has a right not to be killed that he has done nothing to forfeit, he retains his right of self-defense and would be permitted to kill her in preemptive defense, if that were possible. Let us refer to this kind of case, in which each party to a conflict is objectively permitted to try to kill the other in self-defense, as a "symmetrical defense case."

I suspect that there are symmetrical defense cases. I have elsewhere argued that the conflict between a Justified Threat and an innocent victim who will be killed as a side effect of his action if she does not kill him in self-defense is such a case.[9] But there are problems in regarding at least some conflicts between Nonresponsible Threats and innocent victims, and between Innocent Threats and innocent victims, as symmetrical defense cases. One such problem is that one must explain how the presumption against intentional killing is overridden in the absence of either liability on the part of the Threat or a lesser-evil justification. Another is that Nonresponsible Threats do not seem to threaten their victim's *rights* when the threat they pose does not derive from their agency at all. So insofar as the justification for self-defense by the victim depends on the assumption that she is thereby defending her rights against infringement, it will not extend to these cases.[10]

(3) The third and final possibility I will mention is that in cases in which there is little or no relevant moral asymmetry between the Threat and the potential victim, we should be guided by a convention designed to bring about the fewest killings of innocent people if people were to follow it over time. Gerhard Øverland has defended such a proposal.[11] He argues, in effect, that the best convention for regulating conflicts between Threats who are morally innocent and potential victims who are morally innocent is to permit the victim, but not the Threat, to kill in self-defense, on the ground that it is the Threat who has initiated the conflict. He offers two reasons for thinking that this convention would result in fewer innocent people being killed, and thus would be accepted ex ante by hypothetical contractors: (i) that initiators of conflict are more likely to be culpable than those who react to a threat from another; hence when mistakes occur this rule is more likely to penalize the guilty and less likely to lead the genuinely innocent to fail to defend themselves; and (ii) that locating conventionally-based liability with the initiator will help to deter people from becoming Threats, even ones who are morally innocent. Another reason he does not mention is that because one person can threaten many but cannot threaten fewer than one, it may be that each of us is more likely to be a potential victim of a Threat who is morally innocent than to be such a Threat. This, however, ignores the fact that there are cases in which one potential victim is threatened by more than one Threat—a familiar phenomenon in war. But the convention is supposed to govern all cases involving Threats who are morally innocent, including cases of individual self-defense, so if in general there are more cases in which one innocent person threatens many than cases in which many threaten one, it may still be true that each of us is antecedently more likely to be the victim rather than the Threat in cases in which there is little or no moral difference between them. (Alternatively, however, we could have a more fine-grained convention that would permit victims to engage in self-defense when they outnumber Threats who are morally innocent, but not when they are outnumbered by those Threats.)

There are naturally problems with this proposal as well. One is that, like the previous suggestion, it too requires an explanation of how it could be acceptable to have a convention that permits people intentionally to kill innocent people rather than to allow other innocent people (themselves) to be killed. Perhaps it could be claimed that the presumption against intentional killing is overridden by hypothetical consent, by the presumed rationality of agreeing to abide by such a convention. Another problem, though, is that this proposal does not respond to the concern that led to the search for an alternative way of resolving these conflicts: namely, that it seems unfair, when both parties to a conflict are entirely innocent, that one party should be morally required to bear the full cost—death—while the other suffers nothing at all.

I will return to the discussion of these three proposals for resolving conflicts in which there is little moral difference between the Threat and the victim, and to their applications and the plausibility of their implications, in the following section.

4.3 THE MORAL STATUS OF UNJUST COMBATANTS

I have argued that Culpable Threats, Partially Excused Threats, and Excused Threats and Innocent Threats who are not also Nonresponsible Threats are all liable to defensive attack. Culpable Threats are fully liable and the degree of harm that it would be narrowly proportionate to inflict on them in self-defense is determined entirely by the magnitude of the expected harm they threaten to cause (unless, perhaps, there is contributory fault on the part of the victim). Narrow proportionality in defense against a Partially Excused Threat is determined in part by the magnitude of the harm to be averted but also by the strength of the excusing conditions that apply to the Threat's action. The stronger the excuse, the more stringent the restriction. The proportionality constraint is even more stringent in self-defense against Excused Threats and Innocent Threats. In general, among Threats who are liable, the grounds for liability are weakest in the case of Innocent Threats (who are, of course, Excused Threats with a full epistemically-based excuse according to an objective account of permissibility). The basis for their liability is simply that they know they are intentionally harming, or foreseeably harming, or imposing a risk of harm, and also know that it is possible that those they harm may be innocent. Nonresponsible Threats are not liable at all.

All unjust combatants who are actually or potentially engaged in fighting are aware that they are intentionally attacking some people, risking harming others, or at least are committed to doing so. They can therefore be Nonresponsible Threats only if they altogether lack the capacity for morally responsible agency. There are, possibly, some who meet that description. I will discuss them at the end of the chapter. What this means is that there is a basis for liability in the case of virtually all unjust combatants.

This is true even if some unjust combatants are fully excused on grounds of irresistible duress. For, as I noted, duress can absolve a person of all culpability but does not absolve him of all responsibility. Even if unjust combatants are Innocent Threats who act with subjective justification, there is a basis for the attribution of liability in their prior choice to join or to allow themselves to be conscripted into the military, knowing that there was a risk that they would be ordered to fight in an unjust war, and knowing as well that they might mistakenly regard that war as just.

There is, indeed, some reason to think that the liability of combatants is *strict*, in the sense that they can be liable to attack even if they have done nothing objectively wrong, at least as yet. Suppose, for example, that many people in a particular society join the military for good moral reasons. Their country has been peaceable for decades but nevertheless has hostile neighbors. They want to be able to defend it effectively if it is attacked. So they join and begin to train for the defense of their country. Soon thereafter, their government begins to conspire to launch an unjust aggressive war against a neighboring country in two years' time. The plans and preparations for this war are highly secret: no one in the general population or in the lower ranks of the military knows anything about them. But they are discovered by spies of the country that is the intended victim. The government of this latter country knows that it cannot prevent this war by diplomatic or other peaceful means and that to wait until the attack is imminent before responding militarily would be tantamount to accepting defeat. Its only chance is preventive war. But preventive war would involve attacking the potential aggressor's soldiers, who know nothing of their government's plans and are engaged exclusively in activities of the sorts in which soldiers engage in peacetime: training, drilling, and so on. Are these soldiers *liable* to preventive attack? I think that even in this case, in which the soldiers have as yet done nothing wrong, there are grounds for holding them liable. They earlier made a voluntary choice that in effect committed them in a public way to obedience, and those to whom they owe obedience will, unless prevented, order them to fight in an unjust war in which it is reasonable to expect that they will participate. These two factors—that they chose to make themselves instruments of their government and that their government will otherwise use them to fight an unjust war—make them share moral responsibility for the threat their country poses to its neighbor, and this in turn makes them liable even to preventive attack when that is necessary to avert the threat.[12]

The justification for attacking unjust combatants in war would, however, be highly problematic if unjust combatants were Innocent Threats and if the first of the three alternative modes of resolution discussed in the previous section turned out to be the morally most appropriate way to resolve conflicts between Innocent Threats and their innocent potential victims. No one would or could fight a war on the basis of a strategy that sought to apportion the harms suffered on both sides according to some formula for justice in the distribution of harm, such as a weighed lottery. So if unjust combatants were Innocent Threats and that were the right way to deal with Innocent Threats, wars that we now regard as just wars would all have been fought in an unjust manner.

Many people would, however, welcome the suggestion that unjust combatants are Innocent Threats and that conflicts between Innocent Threats and their victims must be treated in the second alternative way suggested above, as symmetrical defense cases. This is, indeed, one way to interpret what, in Section 2.3, I referred to as the "epistemic argument". If all unjust combatants were Innocent Threats, and if conflicts between Innocent Threats and their potential innocent victims were symmetrical defense cases, the moral equality of combatants would be vindicated.

This suggestion was easy to refute because the moral equality of combatants asserts the universal equality of status among combatants, yet it is uncontroversial that not *all* unjust combatants are Innocent Threats. Some fight in full awareness that their war is unjust because it lacks a just cause. But the moral equality of combatants embraces them as well. Still, if most unjust combatants were Innocent Threats, or even if only a great many were, that would provide some partial support for those who think that participation in a war is not wrong just because it lacks a just cause.

Yet I think it is clear that at most only a small proportion of unjust combatants qualify as Innocent Threats, in the sense in which I am using that term. For few, if any, fight on the basis of factual and moral beliefs that are fully epistemically justified—that is, beliefs to which they are justified in according a high degree of credence and that, if true, would make their action objectively justified. This is shown by the considerations I discussed in evaluating the moral risks involved in fighting in war. I argued in Section 3.3.3 that given that what is at stake morally in a decision to go to war is of the highest importance, soldiers have a stringent moral responsibility to seek to overcome the epistemic constraints that typically characterize their situation. If they were to do that, there would be various highly relevant considerations that would be available to them independently of the facts about their particular war. Among the facts they could know, as I pointed out earlier, is that at least half the time that soldiers go to war they fight unjustly. With a bit more thought they could discover that the proportion of just to unjust wars is probably not even 50–50, that there are probably fewer just wars than there are unjust wars. So unless they are confident that their war is purely self-defensive and is not a response to a justified instance of humanitarian intervention, they ought to be skeptical. Yet they also know that most soldiers in situations relevantly like their own are not skeptical but instead believe that the war in which they fight is just—indeed that soldiers are almost as likely to have that belief when their war is unjust as they are when it is just. They can probably see that the soldiers against whom they would be fighting are equally convinced that *their* war is just, and they know that it is very unlikely that both sides are right. Soldiers can understand many of the reasons why other soldiers are so often misled about the morality of the wars in which they fight. For they know that soldiers tend to defer to the authority of their government, that governments often lie, and so on. In particular, they can know just from looking around at their fellow soldiers that soldiers very seldom even try to fulfill their rather exacting epistemic duties. So it is hardly surprising that they so often get it wrong.

What this means is that soldiers should know that there is a high risk of getting it wrong. In this respect, fighting in war is quite different from engaging in individual self-defense. In individual self-defense, there is little reason to be on guard against mistaking a wholly innocent or unthreatening person for a Culpable Threat. It is for this reason that the examples in the literature—such as my case of the resident and the twin, or the case in which someone mistakes an actor rehearsing a murder scene for a genuine murderer—are contrived and unrealistic. But soldiers would know, if they gave the matter only a little thought, that they have compelling reasons to be on guard against the high risk of mistaking an unjust war for a just war. They cannot assume that they are uniquely exempt from the characteristic tendency among soldiers to ignorance and delusion about the moral character of the wars in which they fight. It should be apparent to them that unless they give very careful consideration to what they are being ordered to do, whether they end up as just combatants or unjust combatants is mainly a matter of moral luck. If they fail to take these and other considerations into account, they are negligent. What counts as negligence in the formation of belief is sensitive to context, but in this context the demand for epistemic justification is high. That so few soldiers ever refuse to fight in wars that are unjust strongly suggests that unjust combatants are quite generally negligent about their epistemic responsibilities. But if they are negligent, they are not Innocent Threats.

All of the foregoing claims, most of which merely rehearse points made earlier in the section on moral risk, are quite general and make no reference to the particular war in which a soldier might be commanded to fight. But many wars that are unjust have characteristic properties that should arouse suspicion in anyone ordered to fight in them. One wonders, in retrospect, how Nazi soldiers who fought in Poland, France, Denmark, Russia, and the many other countries they unjustly invaded could possibly have imagined that they were fighting in a just war. In general, wars fought abroad on the territory of a state that has not itself invaded another state are likely to be unjust wars of aggression, particularly if the enemy combatants are citizens of that state and live and circulate among civilians there without being betrayed to their adversaries—civilians whom the invading soldiers might be told that they are defending. It is, of course, entirely possible that such a war is an instance of justifiable humanitarian intervention or preventive war, but in that case the burden of justification lies with the invading soldiers' government and, at least in the case of humanitarian intervention, the evidence necessary to establish a convincing justification should be publicly available. It is also a cause for suspicion if, in the world as it is now, a country resorts to war without seeking authorization from the United Nations. Of course, none of these features, or even all of them in conjunction, is an infallible indicator of an unjust war. But they do raise doubts that must be rebutted before a soldier can claim epistemic justification for the belief that his war is just. If a soldier decides to fight in a war that has some or all of these features and the war turns out to be unjust, he is very unlikely to count as an Innocent Threat.

The conclusion that I draw from the foregoing discussion is that the great majority of unjust combatants are neither Excused Threats nor Innocent Threats, but Partially Excused Threats. The many excuses that I cited earlier as having frequent application to the action of unjust combatants do function to mitigate the culpability of these combatants for fighting in an unjust war. In this respect, Walzer is right: the vast majority of unjust combatants are not criminals, in either a moral or a legal sense. But their excuses are seldom full excuses; nor do their epistemic limitations often rise to the level of subjective justification.

There are interesting theoretical questions here that I will not pursue in depth because the cases in which they arise are insufficiently common to affect the practical implications of my argument. One such question is whether a number of partial excuses can add together to provide a full excuse. Suppose, for example, that an unjust combatant is immature, so that his capacity for morally responsible action has not reached its peak, and that he fights under moderate duress and in a state of ignorance for which he is partially though not fully excused. Might these excuses combine to make him an Excused Threat? It seems clear that they combine to diminish his culpability by more than any one of them does on its own, but it is doubtful that they combine to yield a full excuse. This is because each leaves grounds for blame that do not seem to be wholly canceled or eliminated by the others. But even if they did together provide a full excuse, that would not relieve this combatant of liability, since even a full excuse would absolve him only of culpability, not responsibility.

A related question is whether two or more distinct excuses, each of which is a full excuse, could combine to exempt an agent not only from all culpability but also from all responsibility. Suppose, for example, that an unjust combatant fights both with a full epistemically-based excuse (which, on a subjective account of permissibility, is a subjective permission) and also under irresistible duress. Is he then not only an Excused Threat and an Innocent Threat but also a Nonresponsible Threat? I do not know how to answer this question, but for our purposes that does not matter. If I was right to claim earlier that each of these conditions is quite rare on its own, it seems that instances in which both conditions are present together must be so rare as to be of little or no practical concern—a conclusion that is reinforced by the fact that an unjust combatant with more than one full excuse would in any case not be identifiable as such in combat.

If, as I have argued, the overwhelming majority of unjust combatants are Partially Excused Threats, then just combatants are entitled to act on the *presumption* that the unjust combatants they face in combat are Partially Excused Threats. In practice, it would be unreasonable for them to do otherwise, in the absence of more detailed knowledge about a particular unjust combatant or group of unjust combatants. Some unjust combatants may, perhaps, benefit from this presumption, for there are certainly some unjust combatants who are Culpable Threats who have enlisted and gone to fight in the absence of duress and in full awareness that their war is unjust. If their adversaries respect the presumption, this may lead to their being treated less harshly than they are liable to be treated. In other cases, however, it may lead to unjust combatants' receiving treatment that is harsher than that to which they are liable. These differences are unlikely to be detectable on the battlefield, because virtually all unjust combatants are liable to attack and the differences I am describing are therefore only differences in the application of the narrow proportionality restriction. If, acting on the presumption that all unjust combatants are Partially Excused Threats, a just combatant inflicts a harm on an unjust combatant that would be proportionate if the latter were a Partially Excused Threat but is objectively disproportionate because he is in fact an Innocent Threat, the objective disproportionality would be indiscernible by anyone other than an omniscient observer, of which there are none.

I mention this in-practice-irrelevant detail only to emphasize an important theoretical point, which is that in claiming that just combatants are entitled to presume that all unjust combatants are Partially Excused Threats, I am not "collectivizing" the moral status of unjust combatants. No individual combatant gets his moral status merely from membership in a collective. If an unjust combatant is not a Partially Excused Threat but is treated as if he were one, and if this treatment is worse than what his actual status demands, then he has probably been treated unjustly. But the just combatant who has treated him this way has acted with subjective justification, and the responsibility for his objective error almost certainly lies more with the unjust combatant than with the just combatant. Just combatants are, of course, morally required to do the same epistemic work that unjust combatants are (and in most cases probably fulfill the requirement no better than unjust combatants do, which is to say that they are generally just combatants only by virtue of having had good moral luck). Yet their epistemic obligations are primarily concerned with determining the moral character of their war, not with determining the moral status of individual adversaries on the battlefield. To require the latter would be to require the impossible; hence they must be guided by broad presumptions.

4.4 LIABILITY AND PUNISHMENT

Although the vast majority of unjust combatants are Partially Excused Threats, some are Culpable Threats, others are Excused or Innocent Threats, and a few may be Nonresponsible Threats. Apart from those who are Nonresponsible Threats, unjust combatants in all these categories are liable to defensive attack to one degree or another. This is because all are responsible to one degree or another for posing an objectively wrongful threat of harm to others. But if they are liable to defensive force, might they also be liable to punishment?

There is no necessary connection between liability to defensive force and liability to punishment. This is in part because one's being liable to defensive force is compatible with one's being fully excused for the action to which the defensive force is a response. Both Excused Threats and Innocent Threats are, on an objective account of permissibility, fully excused for the wrongful threats they pose. What this means is that they are absolved of all culpability, or blameworthiness. But they remain responsible for the threats they pose. Innocent Threats, for example, act in the knowledge that they are harming someone and that there is a risk that the person they are harming is entirely innocent, or that they are imposing a risk of harm on innocent people. The risks are sufficiently slight that we do not blame them if they have bad luck and those risks eventuate in harm. But we hold them liable to defensive force nonetheless because they have chosen to act in the awareness of those risks.

Liability to punishment, unlike liability to defensive force, presupposes culpability. Excused Threats and Innocent Threats are therefore not liable to punishment. They are either fully excused or are acting subjectively permissibly; either way, they are absolved of all culpability and it would therefore be unjust to punish them for their objective wrongdoing. But the same is not true of Culpable Threats and Partially Excused Threats. They are wholly or partially culpable for posing an objectively wrongful threat to others and therefore could in principle be liable to punishment, particularly, of course, if they succeed in harming or killing innocent people. If most unjust combatants are Partially Excused Threats, and some much smaller proportion are Culpable Threats, the question arises whether they ought to be punished in the aftermath of a war. I will argue that, at least at present, there are decisive reasons, mostly of a pragmatic nature, not to hold unjust combatants liable to punishment.

Assuming that most unjust combatants are Partially Excused Threats, the case in favor of punishment appeals, not so much to retribution, but to deterrence. At least since the end of World War II, the aim of preventing wars from occurring has assumed an importance in the international law of war at least equal to that of the aim of constraining the conduct of wars when they occur. Hence the insistence of the UN Charter that the *only* legal occasion for the resort to war in the absence of authorization from the Security Council is self-defense or collective defense against aggression by another state—that is, when war has effectively already begun. Because our current legal instruments are comparatively crude and rudimentary, it may be best, for pragmatic reasons, to aim broadly at the prevention of war. Yet in more favorable conditions what we ought to aim for is the prevention of *unjust* wars. And one way to try to do that is to try to deter soldiers from participating in unjust wars by threatening them with punishment if they do. If a government contemplating the initiation of an unjust war were fearful that at least some of its soldiers might resist the order to fight because of their own fear of punishment, this could help deter the government from risking a challenge to its authority from within its own military.

At present, however, there is no impartial international court that could conduct trials of combatants who have fought in an unjust war. Because no government could try its own soldiers for fighting in a war in which it had commanded them to fight, the idea that unjust combatants are liable to punishment could lead to trials by victorious powers of the individual soldiers of their defeated adversary. Since there are probably more unjust wars than just wars, and because any country that fights a war declares itself to be in the right, the victorious power that would prosecute allegedly unjust combatants would be more likely to be a vengeful aggressor prosecuting just combatants who had opposed it. In cases in which it seems likely from the outset that the unjust side will win the war, the fear of being "punished" after the war could combine with the fear of being killed in the war to deter people from fighting in a just war against the aggressor.

Even when it is the side with the just cause that emerges victorious, the prospect of punishment for genuinely unjust combatants could have various bad effects on the conduct of the war. Unjust combatants who feared punishment at the end of the war might be more reluctant to surrender, preferring to continue to fight with a low probability of victory than to surrender with a high probability of being punished. (The just side could, of course, offer an amnesty, but it would undermine the point of threatening unjust combatants with punishment if they could predict that the threat would have to be withdrawn to induce them to surrender.) And they might also reason that if they face mass punishment in the event of defeat, they have little to lose from abandoning all restraint in the effort to win. They might reason, for example, that if they will be punished in any case if they are defeated, and if the prosecutors are unlikely to have knowledge of their individual acts, each might have nothing to lose, but perhaps something to gain, from the commission of war crimes or atrocities that would increase their chance of victory and thus of immunity to punishment.

Even if there were a just and impartial international court, there would still be powerful objections to any attempt to punish unjust combatants merely for fighting in an unjust war. Even if they are a minority, some unjust combatants are not culpable. And among those who are culpable, some are significantly more culpable than others. Collective punishments would therefore be unjust. Individuals would have to be tried to determine whether they were culpable and if so to what degree. But it would be entirely impossible, for obvious reasons, to provide fair trials for all the members of an army. It might be feasible to try some small proportion of the unjust combatants who would be selected randomly for prosecution, but this would not only involve comparative unfairness but would also dilute the deterrent effect of threatening punishment. This is especially true on the assumption that most of those tried and convicted would have substantial excuses, so that their sentences would have to be comparatively mild. A threat in advance of war to impose quite mild sanctions on a randomly selected and rather small proportion of unjust combatants in the war's aftermath would be unlikely to have any significant deterrent effect. So even if it could be imposed in a fair and feasible manner, punishment of unjust combatants would be a waste of resources that could surely be put to better use in the *post bellum* period.

It is also worth noting that the intended deterrent effect of punishment would not be on those who would be punished. For when a war is over, most combatants tend to return to civilian life. They are likely to be out of the military, or too old to serve, by the time the next war starts. In this respect, unjust combatants are quite different from ordinary criminals and terrorists, who may be strongly disposed to recidivism. So if the aim of punishment would be deterrence, the punishment would probably be unjust, for those punished would not be responsible for the threats that might later be posed by the different and unidentifiable individuals whom the punishment would be intended to deter.

I prefaced my arguments in this section by saying that *at present* there are decisive reasons not to hold unjust combatants liable to punishment. But it is possible that conditions could change in a way that would make it desirable to threaten unjust combatants with punishment. One reason that I have not yet mentioned why it would be unwise to threaten unjust combatants with punishment now is that, although there is a law of *jus ad bellum*, there is no authoritative interpreter of that law that soldiers can consult in advance of going to war. When the legal authorities in a soldier's society order him to fight in a war, international law fails to provide him with any source of guidance that might authoritatively controvert his government's assertions about the legality of the war. If the war turns out to be unjust and illegal, the law cannot fairly hold him liable when it has failed to be clear about what it demands of him.

I suggested earlier, at the end of Section 3.3.3, that one important step we can take in preventing unjust wars is to seek to mitigate or eliminate the conditions that tend to excuse participation in them. This is particularly true of the epistemic excuses. If international law could find a way to put soldiers on notice that the war in which they have been commanded to fight, or in which they are at present fighting, is an illegal war and that they can be held legally accountable for participating in it, this would significantly facilitate our ability to threaten them with punishment without unfairness.

4.5 THE RELEVANCE OF EXCUSES TO THE DISTRIBUTION OF RISK

Excuses reduce the degree of a person's responsibility for action that is objectively wrong. This is true even of partial excuses. If, as I have claimed, moral responsibility for an objectively wrongful threat is the criterion of liability to defensive force, it seems that diminished responsibility should entail diminished liability. Diminished liability, in turn, is manifest in the increased stringency of the narrow proportionality constraint. It follows that the stronger a Threat's excuses are, the more stringent the proportionality constraint is in governing the harm it is permissible to cause him in self-defense. To most of us, this is intuitively clear in cases of individual self-defense, or at least in cases not involving lethal threats. If a person's action threatens to injure you in some comparatively minor way, and if he is a Culpable Threat, it seems that it would be proportionate for you to inflict an even greater harm on him than he would otherwise inflict on you if that is necessary to defend yourself. But that degree of harm might be disproportionate if he is, for example, an Excused Threat. If he is in no way culpable, the degree of his liability is lower and defensive force may be proportionate only if it inflicts on him no more harm, or perhaps even less harm, than he would otherwise inflict on you.

The same is true in war, though of course in conditions of war the relevant information about an individual unjust combatant's excuses will almost certainly be lacking. Still, if what I have argued thus far is right, we know that most unjust combatants are at least partially excused for the wrongful threats they pose to others. Since the dominant view is that unjust combatants do not act wrongly at all, anyone who has been persuaded by my argument that most unjust combatants are in fact Partially Excused Threats should be intuitively disposed to find their excuses greatly mitigating. That is, if in the past one has regarded unjust combatants as acting objectively permissibly but has now been persuaded that they act objectively wrongly, one will naturally take them, in general, to be entirely or almost entirely excused. But in that case one should conclude that their liability to attack is correspondingly diminished, so that what counts as proportionate force in fighting against them may be significantly constrained relative to what is commonly believed.

The contrast between the two views is striking and worth emphasizing. The view about the moral status of unjust combatants that I am defending parallels the common view about individual self-defense. It holds that unjust combatants are liable to attack because they are responsible for an objectively wrongful threat, yet concedes that because they generally have excuses, their liability is diminished so that the narrow proportionality restriction on defense against them is stricter than it would be in the absence of excuses. The prevailing view, by contrast, holds that even though unjust combatants act objectively permissibly, it is nevertheless permissible to kill them intentionally at any time no matter what they are doing. The suggestion that just combatants might be morally required to exercise restraint in fighting against unjust combatants, or at least against some of them, is thus quite a radical departure from the prevailing view.

Yet this view is not entirely unprecedented in the just war tradition. In his treatise "On the American Indians," Vitoria argued that if those he referred to as "the barbarians" attack the Spanish because of unfounded but excusable fear, "the Spaniards must take care for their own safety, but do so with as little harm to the barbarians as possible, . . . since in this case what we may suppose were understandable fears made them innocent. . . . This is a consideration which must be given great weight. The laws of war against really harmful and offensive enemies are quite different from those against innocent or ignorant ones."[13]

There are contemporary cases in which it is possible to have knowledge that makes it reasonable to act on different presumptions in fighting against different groups of combatants. During the Gulf War of 1990–1, forces of the US-led coalition were sometimes engaged in battle against the Iraqi Republican Guard—an elite, well-paid, and loyal force—yet at other times fought against units composed almost entirely of recent conscripts who had been coerced by threats to themselves and their families to take up positions in the desert. Although there were presumably some members of the Republican Guard who fought only from fear of what would be done to them if they did not, and some conscripts who were eager to defend the Ba'athist regime, it was reasonable for coalition forces to act on the presumption that any excuses available to members of the Republican Guard were comparatively weak, while those that applied to the action of the conscripts were quite strong. If that is correct, then the proportionality constraint on what could permissibly be done to the conscripts was stricter than it was in its application to action against the Republican Guard. In effect, the proportionality restriction imposed a *requirement of restraint* on coalition forces in at least some of their engagements with units composed mainly of conscripts that did not apply, or at least not to anything like the same extent, to their engagements with the Republican Guard.

Michael Walzer rejects this view. Here is what he says about this example.

Imagine a battle in which American forces are about to turn the flank of a Republican Guard division, and some regular army [i.e., conscript] units are rushed into place to protect the flank. It isn't an actual case, but it could easily have happened; it isn't a weird hypothetical. So, how would McMahan explain to the American soldiers that they have to use minimal force and accept greater risks over there, even while they are fighting as harshly as is "necessary" over here? I would like to listen to his talk to the soldiers. I don't believe that he could make the case. What he regards as significant differences of responsibility between the Guard and the regular army just aren't going to make a difference on the battlefield—because of what battlefields are like.[14]

I suspect that most people share Walzer's view. Interestingly, Walzer himself parts company with some people when he acknowledges that soldiers *are* required to exercise restraint, and to accept greater risks to themselves, to avoid harming *civilians*, or to reduce the harm they cause to civilians as a side effect of their military action. He claims that it is a condition of permissibly causing harm to civilians as a side effect of military action that the combatant "seeks to minimize it, accepting costs to himself." Thus, "if saving civilian lives [that is, by not killing civilians] means risking soldiers' lives, the risk must be accepted."[15] In this he and the recent *U.S. Army/Marine Corps Counterinsurgency Field Manual* are in agreement, as the latter also asserts that "combat, including counterinsurgency and other forms of unconventional warfare, often obligates Soldiers and Marines to accept some risk to minimize harm to noncombatants."[16] Suppose, then, that we convert the example Walzer gives into "a weird hypothetical" example by imagining that the regular army units are not composed of conscripts but that they do drag innocent civilians onto the battlefield with them to use as shields—that is, in the hope that the presence of the civilians will make the American soldiers reluctant to attack them. Walzer must accept that in these circumstances any commander would be morally required to explain to his forces that they must exercise restraint and accept greater risks over there, on the flank where the civilians are, even though they may fight without restraint over here, where the Republican Guard are. The presence of the civilians has to make a moral difference on the battlefield, no matter what battlefields are like. So whatever this commander would say to his forces is what I might say to soldiers preparing to attack a unit of conscripts who are on the battlefield only as a result of extreme duress—with this difference: I would say to them, not that those they are about to attack are a mix of highly blameworthy combatants and wholly innocent civilians, but that those they are about to attack are almost as innocent, in the relevant sense, as most civilians are—indeed, that they *were* innocent civilians until just a short while ago, when they were driven from their homes and onto the battlefield by threats to themselves and their families. I would say that, in an important sense, they did not choose to be here, and that we should accordingly do our best to subdue them while causing as little harm to them as possible, even if that means accepting greater risks to ourselves.

There are, of course, different forms and degrees of risk that just combatants might take in seeking to reduce the harm they cause to unjust combatants whom they recognize as having strong excuses. The exercise of restraint might increase the risk to their own safety, or the safety of their comrades, or it might increase the risk of failure in the achievement of their just cause. The *Counterinsurgency Field Manual* acknowledges both risks and states that "combatants are not required to take so much risk that they fail in their mission or forfeit their lives."[17] Strictly interpreted, however, this is not a significant limitation. For what it says is simply that if the exercise of restraint is certain to cause them to fail in their mission or to lose their lives, then there is no requirement of restraint. The quoted passage thus leaves it open that they could be required to exercise restraint in ways that would significantly reduce the probability of succeeding in their mission, or significantly increase the probability of their being killed.

The suggestion that just combatants could be required to jeopardize the success of their mission in order to reduce the harm they would inflict on unjust combatants is substantially less plausible than the suggestion that they should accept greater risks to their own lives in order to do so. For just warfare is much more than the mere exercise of rights of individual self-defense by just combatants. If the point were just to preserve the lives of the just combatants, the best course in most cases would be for them simply to stay at home. But they deliberately put their lives at risk for a reason: to achieve their just cause. In most cases, the importance of achieving the just cause has such great weight in *in bello* proportionality calculations that the partial excuses of unjust combatants have scarcely any effect on those calculations at all. If unjust combatants are even minimally culpable, as I have argued that virtually all are, then they are liable to attack and the great value of achieving the just cause may simply overwhelm any claim they might have to be treated with restraint—even though that claim might be decisive if less were at stake.

The basic idea here is probably clear but it is sufficiently important to bear some elaboration. The proportionality restriction that is relevant here is not the familiar wide *in bello* restriction that governs the amount of harm it may be permissible to inflict on innocent bystanders as a foreseeable side effect of action intended to attack a military target. It is instead the narrow restriction that governs the degree of harm that it is permissible to inflict on a person who is responsible for an objectively wrongful threat, as a means of averting that threat. This latter restriction is sensitive to a variety of factors. These include (1) the magnitude of the wrongful harm to be prevented, (2) the effectiveness of the defensive act in averting the harm, (3) the magnitude of the harm inflicted on the wrongdoer, and (4) the degree of his responsibility for the threat he poses. The relevant point here is that when the first of these is very great, variations in the fourth are likely to have comparatively little significance, provided that the Threat is morally responsible, and particularly if he is culpable to some extent, as most unjust combatants are. In war, of course, the second factor tends to weigh against the proportionality of the harm inflicted defensively, for the killing of any particular unjust combatant is unlikely to make a significant contribution to the achievement of the just cause. Yet in war the incapacitation of unjust combatants, usually by killing them, is almost always a necessary means of achieving the just cause. That is the nature of war. Those pursuing an unjust cause deploy armed forces to achieve their goal by force. The victims must fight back to prevent themselves from being compelled to surrender whatever it is their enemies want. Successful opposition to the enemy's unjust cause involves incapacitating enough of the enemy soldiers to prevent them from being able physically to compel the yielding up of whatever it is their side wants. So if what is at stake is of the greatest importance for many people, if success requires killing, and if those killed are not only responsible but also culpable for the wrong they are doing, then the degree of their culpability is unlikely to affect whether killing them as a means of preventing that wrong is proportionate in the narrow sense. They have, it seems, no justified complaint about being killed, if sparing them would have diminished the prospect of success in achieving the just cause. Any complaint on their behalf invites the harsh response that they could have avoided being killed if they had considered more carefully what they were ordered to do, and refused to do it.

It seems that the claim I have made—namely, that the narrow *in bello* proportionality constraint on acts of war by just combatants is more restrictive when unjust combatants have significant excuses—has practical application primarily, and perhaps only, in cases in which all that is at stake is the security of the just combatants themselves. That is, the requirement of restraint by just combatants applies primarily when the issue is simply their own self-defense. If that is right, then what seemed like a radical claim has quite limited practical significance. This is because it is seldom the case that all that is at stake in a confrontation between just combatants and unjust combatants is the survival of those individuals. If just combatants exercise restraint and fewer unjust combatants are killed, those who might have been killed instead survive to continue to promote their side's unjust cause. And if more just combatants are killed than otherwise might have been, their deaths weaken their side's ability to achieve its just cause.

There are, however, some cases in which it is reasonable to believe that efforts to spare unjust combatants would have virtually no effect on the probability of success in achieving the just cause, but would increase the risks faced by just combatants themselves. This might be true, for example, in cases of radically asymmetrical warfare, when victory by the side with the just cause is more or less assured in advance. And it might also be true when there is a high probability of being able to render unjust combatants *hors de combat* without killing them, for example by incapacitating them through nonlethal injury, or by inducing them to surrender so that they can be taken captive. It is in such conditions that the unjust combatants' excuses could impose a requirement of restraint on just combatants—that is, a requirement to take greater risks with their own lives and well-being in order to reduce the harm they would otherwise inflict on unjust combatants.

My earlier comments about fighting with restraint against Iraqi conscripts during the Gulf War can now be clarified in the light of this significant qualification. Coalition forces would not have been required to fight with restraint against Iraqi conscripts if that would have jeopardized their ability to restore the sovereignty of Kuwait. But there may well have been cases in which, rather than using maximum force against the positions held by units composed largely of conscripts, coalition forces could have restrained their firepower and been more patient in offering opportunities for surrender, even though it might have been costlier in various ways and physically riskier to do so.

4.6 CHILD SOLDIERS

I have argued that most unjust combatants are Partially Excused Threats—that is, that they typically have many excuses that mitigate their culpability for posing an objectively wrongful threat to others, but that in most cases some element of culpability remains. In part because of that residue of culpability, the effect of their excuses on the stringency of the narrow proportionality restriction is largely negligible in cases in which the exercise of restraint by just combatants would compromise the effectiveness of their efforts to achieve their just cause. The situation would be somewhat different, however, if it were a reasonable presumption that unjust combatants are either Excused Threats or Innocent Threats. For in that case, although they would be morally responsible for wrongfully posing a threat, they would not be culpable, and that might significantly diminish their liability to defensive attack. And if unjust combatants could reasonably be regarded as Nonresponsible Threats—that is, if they were not only not culpable but not even morally responsible for their action—then they would not be morally liable to attack at all and any justification for attacking them would have to be of a different form, such as a lesser-evil justification.

There are surely some unjust combatants who are Excused Threats, Innocent Threats, or even Nonresponsible Threats. But in almost all conflicts in war, they constitute at most a tiny minority and as individuals they cannot be identified and singled out for different treatment. The same is true of those unjust combatants who are Culpable Threats. Hence, as I claimed earlier, it is reasonable, and unavoidable, for just combatants to act on the presumption that unjust combatants are Partially Excused Threats. Yet there may be some cases in which that presumption does not hold. In some instances it may be reasonable to suppose that most or even all the members of some military unit against which one must fight are Excused Threats, Innocent Threats, or perhaps even Nonresponsible Threats. This could be the case if, for example, one were at war with people who deploy units consisting largely or entirely of child soldiers.

Child soldiers are quite common in some areas of the world, particularly Africa, Asia, and South America. The conditions that lead to their deployment are often, indeed usually, quite horrific. The process often begins with abduction. A group of armed men enters a village and gathers the inhabitants together in an open public space. A child of perhaps 10 years of age is selected and ordered to take a gun and kill his friend, or perhaps one of his parents. The first such child may hesitate or refuse, and is instantly shot dead. Another is then brought forward and given the same order. Those subsequently chosen are less likely to refuse. After a sufficient number of children have been put through this ordeal in full view of the entire village, they are taken away at gunpoint to a camp where they are to be turned into soldiers. Actually though, the process has already begun. It began with the coerced killings in the village, which have various effects: making the killer feel irredeemably corrupted, making him an outcast from his community, binding him to his abductors, and so on. A similar strategy was used in the Nazi concentrations camps. In his final reflections on his experiences in Auschwitz, Primo Levi wrote of those prisoners who became collaborators with the Nazis that "the best way to bind them [was] to burden them with guilt, cover them with blood, compromise them as much as possible, thus establishing a bond of complicity so that they [could] no longer turn back."[18] It is surprising how this one arcane and unfamiliar element of human psychology seems somehow naturally accessible to otherwise ignorant and psychologically insensitive men. At the camp, the abducted children are further brutalized, indoctrinated, and trained, perhaps for several years. Finally, they are given light automatic weapons and administered drugs that further anesthetize their consciences and subdue their fears, and are sent to fight for an unjust cause, often in an indiscriminate manner.[19]

The reigning theory of the just war draws no distinction between child soldiers and other combatants. For according to that theory, child soldiers are liable to attack like all other combatants merely by virtue of posing a threat to others. Whether and to what extent they are morally responsible for their action is irrelevant, as is the fact that they are children. It is permissible to do to them whatever it would be permissible to do to adult combatants. Yet the process described above by which children are turned into child soldiers is not unusual or atypical. Children who have been subjected to these horrible abuses have unusually strong excuses of all the broad types identified in Section 3.2. Abduction and brutal mistreatment constitute duress through the implicit threat, to which explicit threats are usually added, of even greater harm in the event of disobedience; physical isolation and indoctrination produce profound ignorance; and youth, psychological manipulation, and drugs together diminish their capacity for responsible agency. I earlier expressed skepticism about the idea that partial excuses of various kinds could combine to form a full or complete excuse, but the number, variety, and strength of the excuses that typically apply to the action of child soldiers are such as to make it tempting to suppose that they are in general Excused Threats, if not Nonresponsible Threats. Certainly if there is any identifiable class of soldiers of whom it might be reasonable to *presume* that *all* are Excused Threats or perhaps even Nonresponsible Threats (on the ground that *most* really are), it is the class of child soldiers.

I think, however, that we should resist the suggestion that it is a reasonable presumption that child soldiers are Nonresponsible Threats. While some child soldiers are as young as 10, or even 8, they have also been forced to adapt to their circumstances and usually, as a consequence, have become precociously mature in various ways. In any case, no one really supposes that a child of 10, even one who has been subjected to terrible abuse, is wholly lacking in moral responsibility for his action. No parent, for example, regards her child as an automaton. If her child torments the cat, she regards that differently from the way she does the dog's efforts to harm the cat.

The great majority of child soldiers are, however, older than 10, and most are in their teens. In law, the category of child soldiers includes all those below the age of 18, which is the generally recognized age at which adulthood conventionally begins. Domestic law recognizes that in general people below the age of 18 have a lesser capacity for morally responsible agency than adults do; hence they are held to different legal standards and are generally punished less severely than adults for the same offenses; yet they are not treated as lacking the capacity for moral responsibility and are not exempted from punishment altogether. Indeed, if we believe that most 10-year-olds have some capacity for morally responsible agency, we should accept that most teenagers have that capacity to an even greater degree.

When child soldiers have been abused by those they serve, when they are threatened with terrible harms for refusing to fight, when they know they will be drugged before being sent to fight, when, as is often the case, their past missions have involved assaulting villages and killing unarmed villagers—in these conditions, they should be able to infer that those who command them are not trustworthy and that the likelihood that they are doing wrong is very high. Their best excuse is probably neither epistemic nor, except in the case of the very youngest, that their capacity for responsible agency is diminished, but that they act under great and in many cases irresistible duress. The reasonable presumption in the case of child soldiers seems to be that they are either Excused Threats or Partially Excused Threats, and that even in the latter case their excuses, though partial, are unusually strong.

As with adult unjust combatants, their excuses may not significantly affect the narrow proportionality calculation when the exercise of restraint in fighting against them would decrease the probability of defeating the unjust aims of those for whom they fight. But when just combatants could use lesser force against child soldiers without seriously compromising their ability to achieve their just aims, they may be morally required to fight with restraint, even at greater risk to themselves. This may be only partly because of the child soldiers' excuses. For it also seems important that these soldiers are *children*—that is, individuals who have hardly had a chance at life and have already been terribly victimized. There is, of course, little difference in this respect between an 18-year-old regular combatant and a 17-year-old child soldier. But when child soldiers are conspicuously young, there is moral reason to exercise restraint simply because of their special vulnerability to exploitation and loss. Just combatants should show them mercy, even at the cost of additional risk to themselves, in order to try to allow these already greatly wronged children a chance at life.

I personally find this highly intuitive and hope that others do as well. Contrary to Walzer's skepticism about the possibility of convincing soldiers to fight with restraint against some enemy combatants even while fighting without restraint against others, I suspect that any commander would earn the respect of his troops if he were to order them to take additional risks to try to drive back, incapacitate, subdue, or capture child soldiers, while sparing their lives.

5

Civilian Immunity and Civilian Liability

5.1 THE MORAL AND LEGAL FOUNDATIONS OF CIVILIAN IMMUNITY

In 1955, Graham Greene published an eerily prescient novel about the beginnings of American military involvement in Vietnam. The narrator, a civilian, is with a soldier when they discover the bodies of a woman and a small child who have been shot: "The lieutenant said, 'Have you seen enough?' speaking savagely, almost as though I had been responsible for these deaths; perhaps to the soldier the civilian is the man who employs him to kill, who includes the guilt of murder in the pay envelope and escapes responsibility.'"[1]

This is in some ways a curious suggestion. Because pacifists are few, and the doctrine of the moral equality of combatants is almost universally accepted among those who are not pacifists, few people think that there is any reason for soldiers to feel guilt for doing what they are paid to do, even when that involves fighting in an unjust war. Soldiers may feel guilt if they have committed atrocities in war, as some have done in Greene's story, but it would seldom be reasonable for them to suppose that the commission of war crimes was among the assignments that the civilian population expected them to fulfill to earn their pay envelope. And civilians do not in general think of themselves as shielded from guilt for an unjust war by the intervening agency of the soldiers—paid agents whose dirty hands enable the civilians to keep theirs clean. They very rarely feel any personal guilt, remorse, or even responsibility for the events in a war that their country is fighting, even if it is exposed as unjust, particularly if the war is occurring in a geographically remote area. And this is not because they think their soldiers obligingly relieve them of responsibility or guilt by taking it upon themselves. Rather, the general view, shared by civilians and soldiers alike, is that neither civilians nor soldiers are morally responsible, much less guilty, for unjust wars or for acts of war (other than war crimes, for which individual soldiers *are* held responsible) committed in the course of an unjust war.

Most of us accept not only that ordinary civilians are not responsible when their country fights an unjust war but also that they are not legitimate targets in such a war. If these two claims are right, they ought, in my view, to be connected. I have argued that the criterion of liability to attack in war is moral responsibility for a wrong that may be permissibly prevented or corrected by means of war, or by an act of war. If that is right, the claim that civilians are not legitimate targets in war should follow from the claim that they are not responsible for a wrongful war or for the wrongful acts of which it is composed. Yet according to the currently orthodox theory of the just war, the two claims are unconnected. Proponents of the orthodox theory generally accept that civilians are not morally responsible for their country's unjust war, but even if they accepted that civilians were morally responsible, they would reject the inference that the civilians' responsibility would make them legitimate targets.

The reigning theory of the just war follows international law in its understanding of the requirement of discrimination. It holds that in war all combatants are legitimate targets of attack, while no noncombatants, or civilians, are. That is, the requirement of discrimination as commonly understood contains both a permission and a prohibition. The permission is to attack enemy combatants, at any time or place while war is in progress, provided they have not been rendered *hors de combat* via surrender, wounding, or capture. The prohibition is of intentional attacks on noncombatants or civilians.

I have argued that it is a mistake to suppose that there is such a permission. Not all combatants are legitimate targets of attack in war. Unless they fight by wrongful means, just combatants do nothing to make themselves morally liable to attack. They neither waive nor forfeit their right not to be attacked. They are not, therefore, legitimate targets. It would be gratifying if we could revise the orthodox requirement of discrimination by rejecting the permission but retaining the prohibition. We might claim, in other words, that although it is permissible for just combatants to attack unjust combatants, it is impermissible for unjust combatants to attack just combatants, and impermissible for either to attack civilians. And we could try to defend this claim by appealing to the principle that all those (except perhaps Nonresponsible Threats) who pose an objectively unjust threat are legitimate targets in war, while those who pose no threat at all are not.

There are, however, two problems with this reformulated requirement of discrimination and the principle underlying it. One is that the underlying moral principle does not rule out all intentional attacks against civilians. As we saw earlier in Section 1.2, some civilians, such as scientists whose discoveries have applications for weapons technologies, contribute directly to the country's ability to wage an unjust war; indeed their contributions may be more threatening to just combatants and those they protect than the contributions of most unjust combatants. There are, moreover, other ways in which some civilians are relevantly similar to some soldiers with respect to posing an unjust threat. Consider a soldier whose country is fighting an unjust war but who will not be deployed for combat for at least two years because his special expertise is required for a vitally important project that is wholly unrelated to the war that is in progress. According to virtually all just war theorists, this soldier, by virtue of having an official role in the military, poses a threat and is therefore a legitimate target. But compare him to a cadet in his final year at one of this same country's military academies, who will be deployed for combat in just a few months. This cadet is still a university student; he is not yet a soldier and is not considered by just war theorists to be a legitimate target. But he poses a more immediate unjust threat than the soldier who will not be deployed for at least another two years. The same is true of other people who are currently noncombatants but will nevertheless be deployed for combat within a year: a student in his final year at a state university who is enrolled in the Reserve Officers' Training Corps (ROTC), a civilian who has been conscripted but has not yet reported for duty, a student in his last month of high school who will join the army in a month because the country has universal conscription, and so on. It seems that any plausible basis for the claim that the soldier who will not be deployed for two years poses a threat must imply that these various civilians pose a threat as well.

The second problem with the reformulated requirement of discrimination is that it makes *posing* a threat a necessary condition of liability to attack in war, though there are many cases in which a person is intuitively liable to attack because of his moral responsibility for an unjust threat, even though he is not the agent who poses the threat. Here is a hypothetical example. Suppose that the Sheriff in a small town in the rural South during the late nineteenth century finds his position under threat by the new Mayor. For many years the Sheriff, a highly respected figure, has exercised almost complete control over the town, while the former mayor served as a mere figurehead. But the new Mayor has decided to change that and has begun to assert his authority in ways that threaten to reduce the Sheriff to a subordinate and largely powerless position. So the Sheriff decides to have the Mayor killed. He summons an uneducated 18-year-old farmhand whom he knows to be one of his admirers and tells him a great many alarming but false stories about the Mayor that together make a strong case for assassination. The Sheriff temporarily deputizes the farmhand, pays him a handsome deputy's salary, swears him to secrecy, and subtly but unmistakably threatens him with retribution if he either fails to carry out the killing or confesses to it later. The farmhand has serious doubts about the morality and legality of what he has been ordered to do but the combination of duress, the Sheriff's authority, and his own uncertainty about the facts compel him to attempt to carry out the plan. But the conversation between the Sheriff and the farmhand was overheard and has been reported to the Mayor. The Mayor arms himself and sets off to confront the Sheriff but instead finds himself confronted by the farmhand. Suppose that the Mayor cannot defend himself by shooting the farmhand, who is shielded behind a tree. But the Mayor sees the Sheriff in the distance. The Sheriff is too far away to be summoned and thus cannot intervene to prevent the farmhand from shooting the Mayor, even if he wanted to. But the Mayor correctly believes that the farmhand will feel himself released from his assignment if the Sheriff is dead. He therefore has only one means of preventing himself from being unjustly killed, and that is to shoot the Sheriff.

If he shoots the Sheriff, this will not be an instance of killing in self-defense, in the strict and literal sense, for the Sheriff poses no threat to him. The Sheriff is what I have elsewhere called a "Culpable Cause" of the threat from the farmhand—that is, he is morally and causally responsible for the threat the Mayor now faces, but only through action that lies in the past and cannot now be prevented.[2] (If the Sheriff were in a position to countermand the order to kill the Mayor before the farmhand fired, then perhaps he would remain a part of the threat to the Mayor and killing him could count as self-defense; but at the point at which the Mayor must act, there is nothing the Sheriff can do to prevent the farmhand from acting.) Still, it seems that the same considerations that justify killing in paradigm cases of justified self-defense also apply in this case. Through his own culpable action, the Sheriff has made it unavoidable that either he or the Mayor will be killed; but the Mayor can determine which of them it will be. It would be unjust for the Mayor to have to pay the cost of the Sheriff's wrongful action and it is therefore permissible for him to shift that cost to the Sheriff himself, even though this requires killing him. The Sheriff can have no morally justified complaint about being forced to suffer the costs made inevitable by his own wrongful action. He has, in short, made himself liable to be killed. That the action through which he did it lies in the past rather than in the present or the immediate future, as in cases of self-defense, is morally irrelevant.

Doubts about whether it is permissible for the Mayor to kill the Sheriff as a means of self-preservation might be dispelled by considering that, if the farmhand were to kill the Mayor, the Sheriff would, if the facts were known, be found guilty of murder as an accessory. He would be morally liable to punishment, and legally liable even to the death penalty, though any functions that punishment could serve would be significantly less important than the effect that killing him ex ante would have: namely, preservation of the Mayor's life. It is therefore hard to believe that the Sheriff cannot be liable to harm ex ante as a means of preventing the wrong for which he would be liable to punishment ex post.

Next consider a variant of this example in which the Mayor can preserve his own life by killing either the Sheriff or the farmhand. If he shoots the farmhand, that will be an act of self-defense against an objectively wrongful threat, since the farmhand directly threatens his life. Even if we concede that it is permissible for the Mayor to kill the Sheriff if that is the only means by which he can preserve his life, those who consider that *posing* a wrongful threat is a more solid foundation for liability than merely being morally responsible for such a threat should believe that the Mayor ought, in this version of the case, to kill the farmhand rather than the Sheriff. But for most of us that is counterintuitive. All the initiative has come from the Sheriff. The farmhand, by contrast, is a reluctant and largely innocent dupe who has been deceived, manipulated, and coerced as a means of achieving the Sheriff's goal. He too is a victim of the Sheriff. If one of them must be killed as a means of preventing the killing of the Mayor, justice requires that it be the Sheriff.

I argued earlier, in Section 4.1.5, that merely posing an objectively unjustified threat without being in any way morally responsible for that is insufficient for liability to defensive action. I am now claiming that moral responsibility for an unjustified threat that one does not oneself pose is sufficient for liability to harm as a means of protecting the person wrongly threatened. If this is right, what matters is moral responsibility for an objectively unjustified threat. In some cases whether a person is the agent of a threat can affect the degree of his responsibility for that threat, but the act of posing the threat has no relevance to liability apart from the contribution it makes to the person's moral responsibility for the threat.

The moral of these stories for the problem of responsibility in unjust wars should be obvious: civilians can be related to unjust combatants in ways that are closely analogous to the relation between the Sheriff and the farmhand. They can be Culpable Causes of unjust wars and of unjust acts of war. They can be instigators of unjust wars, or aiders and abettors who share responsibility for unjust acts of war perpetrated by unjust combatants. To deny that this could ever make them liable to suffer the effects of certain acts that diminish the threat posed by unjust combatants is to treat liability in war altogether differently from the way that we commonly treat liability in other contexts. In criminal law, for example, when a perpetrator is liable for a crime, accessories, including instigators and aiders and abettors, are derivatively liable. If their culpability is greater than that of the perpetrator, as in the case of the Sheriff and the farmhand, their liability may be greater as well.

The orthodox understanding of the requirement of discrimination—that all combatants or soldiers are legitimate targets while no noncombatants or civilians are—cannot ground either liability to attack or immunity from attack in war in what people *do*. It is false that all soldiers pose a threat, and false that no civilians do. It is obviously false that all combatants are morally responsible for an objectively unjustified threat, and false that no civilians are. What, then, is the basis of the orthodox view that all combatants are morally liable to attack while all civilians are morally immune from attack?

The answer is that liability and immunity are, on the orthodox theory of the just war, functions not so much of action as of *membership*. There is no explanation of how all combatants could be liable to attack while no civilians are other than the idea that in war both liability and immunity are *collective*. Soldiers are liable to attack simply because they are members of the military and thus have combatant *status*, irrespective of what they might be *doing*. And civilians are immune from attack because they are not members of the military and thus have noncombatant status, provided that they do not do the one thing that would shift them into the category of combatants—namely, take up arms and fight. (This final qualification shows that even on the orthodox view, combatant status is not entirely divorced from what a person does.

Although fighting in a war is not necessary for combatant status, it can be sufficient for a combatant's liabilities, if not for a combatant's privileges.)

The idea that people can be liable to attack, or immune from attack, merely by virtue of their membership in a group, particularly when membership is involuntary, or largely involuntary, is both false and morally repugnant. As Primo Levi, perhaps the most insightful and articulate of the survivors of Auschwitz, put it: "I do not understand, I cannot tolerate the fact that a man should be judged not for what he is but because of the group to which he happens to belong."[3] The word "happens" is crucial. Sometimes a voluntary choice to become a member of a group can be a basis of liability, particularly if the terms of membership include either tacit or explicit consent to accept responsibility for the collective action of the group or if membership in the group involves a foreseeable risk of becoming an unjust threat to others—as I noted in the brief discussion of liability to preventive attack in Section 4.3.

Without a substantial element of voluntary choice, however, mere membership in a collective, even a military organization, cannot be a basis of liability. And, more relevant to our purposes at this point, mere membership in a group cannot shield a person from moral liability if that person acts in a way that would otherwise incur liability. As I have noted, both instigating unjust action and aiding and abetting such action are sources of liability to punishment in criminal law, and there is no reason why they cannot also be a source of liability to harm from action that defends an innocent victim from an unjust threat posed by the perpetrator. If accessories can be liable to harm from defensive action in the context of individual self-defense, there is no reason why this cannot also be true in war.

Doctrines of collective immunity are corollaries of doctrines of collective liability, or liability by membership. They stand or fall together. And we had better hope that they fall. For notions of collective liability are at the heart of alleged justifications for terrorism that are not mere appeals to the lesser evil. Terrorists are very often morally motivated—indeed highly motivated and strongly convinced of the rectitude of their action, as the phenomenon of suicide bombing attests. They are therefore unlikely to think of themselves as attacking and killing people who are morally innocent. Rather, they persuade themselves that those whom they kill are liable to attack by virtue of their identity as members of an evil group, and that they are therefore not wronged when they are killed as a means of intimidating other members of that group. Those who engage in the commission of genocide are likely to anesthetize their consciences with similar thoughts. Such thoughts have become all too familiar in the wake of the mass atrocities of the twentieth century, but they were not always so readily accepted. In her history of genocide in the twentieth century, Samantha Power comments on the Allied response to initial reports of the Nazi genocide against the European Jews that "the vast majority of people simply did not believe what they read; the notion of getting attacked for being (rather than for doing) was too discomfiting and too foreign to process readily."[4]

I will assume, then, that no one can be liable to be harmed *merely* by virtue of membership in a group and that the same arguments that establish this claim also show that no one can be morally immune from being harmed simply by virtue of membership in a group, such as the group of civilians. It is therefore in principle possible for a civilian to become liable to be harmed in war, though only on the basis of what he or she as an individual does. In the remainder of this chapter, I will explore the idea of civilian liability in war. I will not examine at any length the other types of justification for harming or attacking civilians, such as consequentialist justifications or nonconsequentialist lesser-evil justifications, though various such justifications have been proposed.

It is, however, worth pausing briefly to take note of a few justifications for killing civilians that are not based on claims about individual liability. These justifications have a surprising source: George Orwell. First in a review, written in 1944, of a book by Vera Brittain denouncing the bombing of civilian targets, and then in a column responding to criticisms of the review, Orwell advanced four distinct considerations that favor the bombing of civilians in war. Three are given in the following short passage from the book review.

War is not avoidable at this stage of history, and since it has to happen it does not seem to me a bad thing that others should be killed besides young men. I wrote in 1937: "Sometimes it is a comfort to me to think that the aeroplane is altering the conditions of war. Perhaps when the next great war comes we may see that sight unprecedented in all history, a jingo with a bullet hole in him." We haven't yet seen that (it is perhaps a contradiction in terms), but at any rate the suffering of this war has been shared out more evenly than the last one was [*sic*]. The immunity of the civilian, one of the things that have made war possible, has been shattered. Unlike Miss Brittain, I don't regret that. I can't feel that war is "humanised" by being confined to the slaughter of the young and becomes "barbarous" when the old get killed as well.[5]

The main suggestion advanced here is egalitarian: when suffering and death are inevitable, it is better if they are distributed equally throughout all segments of the population rather than being concentrated among the members of one group, which Orwell identifies as "the healthiest and bravest of the young male population."[6] Yet this suggestion ought to have little appeal even to the staunchest egalitarians. For it elevates the concern with outcomes, evaluated from an impersonal perspective, altogether above considerations of justice. A precisely parallel argument would applaud measures to ensure that in inner-city gang warfare, the casualties are shared equally between the gang members and resident bystanders.

A second suggestion seems essentially retributive—namely, that it would be nice to see warmongers reap the harvest of the wars for which they agitate. It is just possible, however, to interpret the image of the jingo with the bullet hole not as an image of a villain who has got his just desert but as a suggestion that it is more just if those who are responsible for instigating unjust wars pay the cost of their own wrongdoing than if those costs go to soldiers who had no part in starting the war. If it is plausible to read Orwell this way, then this sentence in the passage is just a colorful way of making the point that civilians can be liable by virtue of the contributions they make to an unjust war.

The third suggestion, made in passing in a single clause, is that the doctrine of civilian immunity has facilitated the fighting of wars by enabling civilians to advocate and support the fighting of wars with a secure sense that they themselves will be spared the awful effects. I will return to this idea later in the chapter. While I accept that, in general, civilians may not be harmed or killed as an intended means of deterring future wars, I also accept that the deterrent effect that casualties among civilians can have does count as a good effect in calculations of wide proportionality.

Orwell's fourth suggestion occurs in the response to his critics. There he writes that "we can't yet calculate the casualties of the present war, but the last one [World War I] killed between ten and twenty million young men. Had it been conducted, as the next one will perhaps be, with flying bombs, rockets and other long-range weapons which kill old and young, healthy and unhealthy, male and female impartially, it would probably have damaged European civilisation somewhat less than it did."[7] Orwell's reason for this claim is that the disproportionate killing of young males reduces the reproductive capacity of the society. Since I doubt that anyone will regard this as an impressive reason for killing civilians in war, I will merely note that Michael Walzer has recently cited the same consideration—the value of communal survival—as the principal reason for *upholding* the principle of civilian immunity. He writes:

Whatever happens to these two armies, . . . the "peoples" on both sides must be accommodated at the end. The central principle of *jus in bello*, that civilians can't be targeted or deliberately killed, means that they will be—morally speaking, they have to be—present at the conclusion. This is the deepest meaning of noncombatant immunity: it doesn't only protect individual noncombatants; it also protects the group to which they belong.[8]

Whatever its plausibility, this is a highly unorthodox interpretation of the requirement of discrimination in war. Walzer's claim is that the deepest reason why it is forbidden to kill civilians in war is not that they retain their right not to be killed and thus are not legitimate targets—though that is also a reason—but that killing civilians threatens the ultimate collectivist value: the survival of the collective in all its many dimensions.

The concern with the survival of collectives is a concern with consequences. I believe that the deepest meaning of the requirement of discrimination has nothing to do with collectives or consequences but is instead a matter of respect for individual rights. If civilians may not be attacked or harmed in war, it is because they have done nothing to lose their right not to be attacked, not because their survival as individuals is necessary for or constitutive of collective survival. In any case, as Orwell notes, the killing of soldiers can be as inimical to collective survival as the killing of civilians. But if the intentional killing of civilians is wrong primarily because they retain their rights and thus are not liable to attack, then it is possible that they, or some of them, could become legitimate targets by acting in ways that entail a forfeiture of their rights, thus rendering them liable to suffer certain harms. Some of these ways of acting are, it seems, compatible with their remaining civilians and retaining their status as noncombatants. If that is right, the broad, general principle of civilian immunity is false as a matter of basic morality.

To facilitate the discussion of the moral status of civilians in war, it will be helpful to introduce a couple of terms of art. I will refer to civilians in a country that is fighting a war that is unjust because it lacks a just cause as "unjust civilians," and to civilians in a country that is fighting a just war as "just civilians." In subsequent discussions of civilian liability, I will, for reasons of economy, sometimes refer to unjust civilians simply as "civilians." The context should make it clear whether "civilians" refers to unjust civilians, just civilians, or all civilians on both sides.

Notice that these definitions are not exhaustive of civilians in countries at war; they omit the class of civilians whose country is fighting a war that has a just cause but is nevertheless unjust overall because it also seeks the achievement of an unjust cause that is unnecessary for the achievement of the just cause. In cases in which it is better from an impartial point of view that the war be fought, and civilians lack the ability to alter its aims, it may be permissible for them to support it, even when it is impermissible for the government to pursue this set of aims because it has the option of pursuing only the just aim.[9] Again, I leave these cases aside.

If civilians can be liable to suffer certain harms in war, there will be a broad asymmetry between just and unjust civilians that parallels that between just and unjust combatants. In general, only unjust civilians may be liable, though there may be an exception in the case of just civilians who are somehow responsible for their country's pursuit of its just cause by impermissible means. But although in general only unjust combatants and unjust civilians can be liable, there is a significant difference between the two groups. As I argued in Chapter 4, most unjust combatants are liable to intentional attack in war. But the vast majority of unjust civilians are not. Although the reasons why they are not may seem obvious, it will be important to make them clear as our discussion proceeds.

5.2 THE POSSIBLE BASES OF CIVILIAN LIABILITY

What are the possible bases of civilian liability in war? It is perhaps worth noting at the outset that few writers have seriously contended that civilians bear responsibility for an unjust war initiated by their government on the ground that citizens *authorize* the acts of their government. Hobbes argued, on the contrary, that because people have no right to act wrongly under the law of nature, they cannot transfer that right to the sovereign. And Locke made the same point: "For the People having given to their Governours no Power to do an unjust thing, such as is to make an unjust War, (for they never had such a Power in themselves:) They ought not to be charged, as guilty of the Violence and Unjustice that is committed in an Unjust War, any farther, than they actually abet it."[10]

But civilians can abet the prosecution of an unjust war. And they can be complicit in instigating it. There is in fact a broad range of different ways in which civilians might be implicated as accessories in an unjust war. A civilian may have a high degree of responsibility for an unjust war, or may share responsibility for the war to a degree that is virtually negligible. And many civilians bear no responsibility at all.

Here is an actual case that illustrates the way in which civilians may bear a high degree of responsibility for an unjust war. In 1954 the United States organized and directed an invasion of Guatemala that overthrew the democratically elected government and effectively turned the country into a torture dungeon run by a series of terrorist military dictators for the following four decades. One key factor in precipitating the coup was the intense pressure exerted on the Eisenhower administration by executives from United Fruit Company, a politically powerful organization with extensive holdings in Central America and a variety of close connections to the US government. The company wanted the government overthrown because the Guatemalan president, Jacobo Arbenz Guzmán, had nationalized some of United Fruit Company's uncultivated lands in order to distribute them to the local peasantry, paying what the company had declared they were worth for tax purposes. Whether this small war that had such devastating long-term consequences would have occurred without the intervention by United Fruit Company is of course debatable, but at least one CIA operative, Howard Hunt, who was one of the directors of the invasion and later became chief of covert operations under President Nixon, has claimed that the role of United Fruit was decisive.[11]

There are numerous other kinds of action through which civilians may bear responsibility, to varying degrees, for an unjust war. They may seek to arouse support for the war, either through persuasion or demagoguery, by writing books, articles, or editorials, by giving speeches or sermons, or by promoting the war on television or radio. (Kenneth Pollack's book, *The Threatening Storm: The Case for Invading Iraq*, published in 2002, was apparently quite influential in generating support among policy-makers and the public for the war that continues as I write.) They may lobby their political representatives, or vote for the candidate or party that promises war. These are all ways in which civilians may intentionally promote the fighting of an unjust war, but there are even more ways in which they may contribute to such a war without intending to—for example, by working in sectors of the economy that are directly or indirectly involved in the production of weapons or other materials or technologies that are necessary or useful for waging war, by providing money through taxes without which the war could not be fought, and so on.

Civilians may also bear responsibility through omission. When their government is proposing to fight an unjust war, or is in the midst of fighting such a war, citizens may have a duty to oppose it. If they do have such a duty but they instead acquiesce in their government's action, they bear some responsibility for that action. The responsibility may be greater the more control the citizens have over their government; hence responsibility and liability may be greater among the citizens in a democracy than among those in a dictatorship—though citizens in a dictatorship may also have a duty not to acquiesce in being governed by a dictator, especially when the dictatorial regime is fighting or preparing to fight an unjust war. The primary difference is that the dangers that citizens in a dictatorship face in opposing their government are generally greater and thus weigh more heavily against the duty of opposition.

In principle it is possible that even foreign civilians may have a duty to oppose another state's unjust war and thus may share responsibility for the war if they fail to oppose it effectively. In general, of course, the duties of individuals with respect to the acts of states other than their own are few and minimal. Citizens have special responsibility for unjust wars fought by their own state for the simple reason that it is *their* institutions that are then malfunctioning—institutions that operate on the basis of their labor, through their financial support, and ostensibly with their consent and for their benefit. In many cases they neither consent nor benefit but they do not deny that the institutions are theirs, that they and not others are the ones who are ruled by them and participate in their functioning. As I claimed earlier, these facts give them a special responsibility to ensure that the institutions are not a source of unjust harm to others whom the institutions do not serve.

Yet imagine a case in which a totalitarian state has wrongfully invaded a neighboring state. Its own citizens are subject to violent repression for the slightest expressions of dissent; hence the costs of protest within the country are prohibitive. Only exceptionally heroic people will protest, and they are too few to have any effect. But there is a powerful state whose economic support is vital to the totalitarian state. This powerful state is a democracy whose citizens can express their views without fear of reprisal and whose government is responsive to those views. A mass protest by these citizens would be without cost to them and would have a high probability of success in forcing a stop to the aggression. But suppose they do nothing. In these circumstances, it seems reasonable to say that the citizens of the foreign democracy bear greater responsibility for the unjust war fought by the totalitarian state than that state's own civilian citizens do.

One objection to the idea of responsibility by omission in this sort of case is that a person can be responsible by omission for the occurrence of an event only if there is something she could have done to prevent that event. But no individual civilian can possibly prevent her government from fighting an unjust war; therefore she can have no responsibility for that war by virtue of failing to act to prevent it.

This objection raises difficult questions about coordination problems in collective action. I have no satisfactory answers to those questions. But I will venture a couple of simple, naïve observations. Coordination problems are particularly intractable when it takes many people acting together to produce significant good consequences, each individual's contribution to the outcome is insignificant, yet each individual incurs a significant cost in contributing. In this kind of case, the incentives for each person favor inaction. But in the example I cited, the citizens in the foreign democracy can act without significant risk to themselves to protest their government's support for the country fighting the unjust war. If enough do their part, they can together stop the war. Each therefore has a moral reason to protest and if too few protest for their action to be effective, many of those who could have contributed to stopping the war but failed to protest will bear some responsibility for the war's continuation.

One must, however, be cautious in making claims about responsibility through omission. For each person, there are indefinitely many serious wrongs that he or she could contribute to preventing. Indeed, for each citizen, there are indefinitely many wrongs that are being committed, or have been or may be committed, by her own government that she could contribute to stopping, preventing, or rectifying. Even if she devotes every waking moment to addressing some of these wrongs, there will remain indefinitely many others that she could be addressing instead. Suppose, for example, that an American citizen spends virtually all of her time working to reduce carbon emissions by the US and thus to slow the pace of climate change. In order to protest an unjust war that the US is either fighting or preparing to fight, she would have to neglect some of her commitments in the work she is doing on climate change.

If she decides to pursue her work on climate change and leave the task of opposing the war to others, she does not, it seems, thereby incur even a slight degree of responsibility for the unjust war. I will not attempt to formulate the conditions in which a citizen may become responsible and therefore perhaps liable for certain of her government's wrongful acts or policies by failing to oppose them. For present purposes it is perhaps enough to note that these conditions are unlikely to be simple and will not imply that every citizen who fails to oppose her country's unjust war must share in the responsibility for it.

It is also questionable whether voting is a basis of liability. Suppose, as we imagined in Chapter 2, that our government conducts a referendum on whether to go to war. The war the government proposes is objectively unjust but I vote in favor of it. The proposal to go to war is overwhelmingly approved and we proceed to fight an unjust war. Does my having voted for the war give me a share of the responsibility for it? Some people believe not only that one cannot be responsible for an event by omission unless one could have prevented it, but also that one cannot be responsible for an event by commission unless one has made a causal contribution to the event's occurrence. And it may seem that in this case my voting has made no causal contribution to war, which would have occurred just the same had I not voted at all or had I even voted against it.

It seems, however, that this cannot be right. Suppose the situation is that we, the citizens, have arranged not only to have the referendum but also to make the implementation of the results of the voting automatic. If the vote goes against the war, then as soon as all the votes are submitted and tallied electronically, there will be an announcement that there will be no war. If the vote is in favor of the war, a signal will automatically be sent to activate a large number of robots, which are preprogrammed to fight the war without any human involvement. If we vote overwhelmingly in favor of the war, which is then fought, it seems that, on the assumptions stated in the previous paragraph, no one has any responsibility for this war, since each person's vote made no causal contribution to it. Since at least some of us must be responsible for this war, it seems that either causation is not necessary for responsibility or else each voter, or at least each person who voted in favor of the war, contributed causally to the war by voting.

One might locate causation in the decision to hold the referendum, or in the setting up of the automated implementation of the decision taken through the vote. But suppose that the referendum can be attributed to the efforts of the opponents of the war, who thought that having the vote was the best way to thwart the efforts of the war's proponents, and that the automated activation system, and indeed the robots themselves, were designed and built by only a few people. It seems absurd to say that responsibility for the war lies only with the opponents of the war, or with only a few scientists and technicians.

5.3 CIVILIAN LIABILITY TO LESSER AND "COLLATERAL" HARMS

I have suggested that there are ways in which civilians can be accessories to the fighting of an unjust war, and in that way share responsibility for the war. Responsible civilians are therefore potentially liable to certain forms of action that might be necessary to prevent or correct the wrongs involved in the war. But this leaves it open what they might be liable to. There can be forms of liability in war that fall well short of liability to military attack. It might be, for example, that many unjust civilians bear sufficient responsibility for their country's unjust war to be liable to suffer the effects of economic sanctions. Suppose such sanctions were imposed not only to weaken the country's military productivity but also to make conditions of life harsher for the civilian population, in the hope of prompting the civilians to pressure their government to sue for peace. Many adult civilians may have had enough of a role in the initiation of the war to have no valid complaint about being subject to these hardships. If so, this would be an important element in the moral justification for the imposition of the sanctions.

This is not to say that the use of economic sanctions in a just war is morally unproblematic. No matter how carefully economic sanctions may be directed against those who are liable—insofar as these people can be identified at all—their effects tend to be diffuse, in part because it is difficult to contain the effects of any kind of economic damage, but also because the government can often channel the harmful effects away from the liable so that they fall instead mainly on those who are not liable. Since those who are liable have generally become so through collusion with the government, the government has an incentive to protect them in this way. For example, during the dozen years between the Gulf War and the current Iraq War, the Ba'athist regime of Saddam Hussein ensured that the burden of the economic sanctions mandated by the UN fell disproportionately on the country's poor and powerless

Shiite majority, who had had little influence on the actions of the government to which the sanctions were a response. In exactly what way the intervening agency of the government in cases such as this is relevant in determining whether sanctions are proportionate in the wide sense is an issue I will not take up here.

Civilian complicity in an unjust war may also be relevant to the justification of the intentional destruction of civilian property as a means of applying pressure to a government and its civilian supporters. Some NATO attacks against targets in Serbia during the Kosovo war were apparently of this sort. Less controversially, the contributions that civilians may make to an unjust war can make them liable to suffer various burdens in the immediate postwar period. For example, even fairly minimal forms of responsibility for an unjust war may render civilians liable to contribute to the payment of reparations to the victims of their country's unjust war. Many civilians may also bear sufficient responsibility for an unjust war and thus for the chaotic and fragile conditions that prevail in its aftermath to be liable to occupation until those *post bellum* conditions can be stabilized. It seems, for example, that most adult German civilians were not wronged by being subject to temporary occupation following the Allied victory in World War II, though many were wronged by individual acts done impermissibly in the course of the occupation.

There is another form of civilian liability that has been little discussed. Normally the claim that people are liable to be harmed is invoked to justify what is done to them intentionally. Yet as I noted in Section 1.3 in introducing the distinction between narrow and wide proportionality, people can also be liable to suffer harms inflicted on them unintentionally, as a side effect of action intended to achieve other aims. Sometimes when a person is harmed either accidentally or as a foreseen but unintended effect, he is not thereby wronged. For he may have acted in such a way as to have deprived himself of any justified complaint against being harmed in that way. As I also noted, if intention is relevant to the permissibility of action, a fixed degree of responsibility for a wrong may be sufficient for a person to be liable to suffer a certain harm as a side effect of the means of preventing that wrong even if it is not sufficient to make him liable to the intentional infliction of the same harm as a means of preventing the same wrong.

The following example indicates the intuitive plausibility of the idea that people's responsibility can be relevant to the permissibility of harming them foreseeably but unintentionally. Suppose that we are fighting a just war and that there are two equally important military targets in the territory of our adversary. One is located well within the enemy's borders, while the other is right on the enemy state's border with a neutral country. Suppose that there is a small village just beside each target that would be destroyed along with the target. The village beside the target inside the enemy country has 200 inhabitants, all of whom are known to be supporters of their country's war and to have contributed to it and benefited from it in various ways, while the village beside the target on the border has only 150 inhabitants. Yet the second village is on the other side of the border: its 150 civilians are all neutrals. Suppose that we have the capacity to bomb only one of these targets.

If other things are equal, we ought to bomb the target in the interior of the enemy country rather than the one on the border. For the civilians who would be killed in that attack are responsible to at least some degree for their country's unjust war, and thus for the necessity of our bombing military targets in their country, while the civilians in the neutral country presumably bear no responsibility for the unjust war at all. This consideration is sufficiently significant to outweigh the difference in numbers. Because many of them are at least to some degree responsible for their government's action, it is better to kill more unjust civilians as a side effect than to kill fewer nonresponsible neutral civilians as a side effect.

Next consider a couple of actual examples. First, during the Kosovo war, NATO forces attacked and destroyed various "dual-use" elements of the Serbian infrastructure: assets that were of use both for civilian and military purposes, such as bridges, power plants, communications facilities, and so on. The widespread enthusiasm among Serbian nationalist civilians for the expulsion of Albanians from Kosovo was undoubtedly among the factors that emboldened the Milosevic regime to act and arguably made many Serbian civilians liable to the deprivations they suffered as a side effect of the destruction of infrastructure (on the charitable assumption that the intention was to prevent only the military rather than the civilian use of the assets that were destroyed).

Second, in the summer of 2006, members of Hezbollah fired thousands of rockets into northern Israel from launch sites in southern Lebanon. The rockets were not aimed at military facilities but were instead intended to kill civilians, though they were so crude that they landed more or less randomly, killing surprisingly few people relative to the number that were fired. Some of the launch sites were within

Lebanese villages, so that when Israel sent jets to destroy them in order to prevent further attacks, many Lebanese civilians were killed. That much seems to be part of the historical record. But let us now make some assumptions that may not be true. Suppose that in at least some cases the civilian villagers could have protested and prevented the rockets from being launched from within their village but did not, not because they were intimidated by Hezbollah but because they approved of the attacks on Israel and were averse to obstructing them. In that case at least some of those harmed when Israel destroyed the launch sites may have been liable to suffer those harms. Although they were not liable to intentional attack, they may have had no legitimate complaint about being harmed as a side effect. For by hypothesis—again, I do not claim that this was actually the case—they contributed to making retaliatory attacks necessary for the defense of innocent people by allowing the initial wrongful attacks to be launched from sites located near where they lived.

5.4 CAN CIVILIANS BE LIABLE TO INTENTIONAL MILITARY ATTACK?

It may be relatively uncontentious that civilians can make themselves liable to pay reparations or to suffer the burdens of economic sanctions or even military occupation. It is considerably more controversial to suggest that considerations of civilian liability can have a role in determining the permissibility of military action that foreseeably harms civilians as a side effect. Yet the examples I have cited suggest that it is intuitively quite plausible to suppose that it is easier to justify causing civilians "collateral" harm when they bear some responsibility for the wrong that makes military action necessary than when they do not. But it is here that most of us draw the line. Just war theory, international law, and common sense intuition coincide in condemning intentional military attacks on civilians in war (though perhaps not quite categorically, as there is no consensus in the US, even now, that the bombings of Tokyo, Hiroshima, and Nagasaki were wrong).

Yet the account of liability to attack in war that I have defended cannot rule out the possibility that civilians may be liable to intentional attack. Taken in the abstract, this may not seem altogether counterintuitive. Suppose, for example, that Guatemalan soldiers in 1954 could have prevented the overthrow of their legitimate government by attacking and killing the group of United Fruit Company executives who were instrumental in initiating the coup. If that had been the only means of preventing the coup, it does not seem to me counterintuitive to suppose that it would have been permissible. And the most plausible way to defend that judgment is to appeal, not to the claim that killing the executives would have been the lesser evil, but to the claim that they had made themselves liable to attack by their role in instigating an unjust war. Even if killing the executives had not been the only option—if, for example, fighting a defensive war against the invading forces would have had an equal probability of success—killing the executives might have been morally better, because of their responsibility, than sacrificing the lives of a significant number of young Guatemalan soldiers who had done no wrong, in an effort to repel the invasion.

But this example is unusual in various respects. First, civilians who are not in government are very rarely able to influence the resort to war to anything like the degree to which the United Fruit Company executives did. Second, the part of the story that is purely imaginary—that the coup could somehow have been averted, and with certainty, by killing the executives—is fanciful and contrived. In practice it is never possible to prevent unjust wars by attacking civilians in this way.

There is, however, another actual example in which the claim that civilians have made themselves liable to military attack may not be entirely counterintuitive. There are ways in which civilians may culpably threaten the same rights that are threatened by an unjust war. The Israeli settlers in the occupied West Bank, for example, threaten Palestinians with dispossession of the land on which they and their ancestors have lived for generations. The right to occupy and retain possession of the territory on which one's nation has lived for generations is internationally recognized as a fundamental right, even though there are disputes about whether it is a collective or an individual right. Defense of the right of people to prevent themselves from being dispossessed of the lands where they and their ancestors have lived is almost universally regarded as a just cause for war, as is the recovery of such lands, provided that no other people have established a stronger moral claim to them during the period since they were taken. The threat that the settlers pose to the Palestinians—knowingly and deliberately—is precisely the threat of establishing a rival moral claim to Palestinian lands that have been under Israeli occupation since 1967. When a community has lived continuously in an area for an extended period, when they have built towns, neighborhoods, and an infrastructure supporting their life there, when their children and their children's children have been born and lived all their lives there, the people acquire a moral entitlement to remain. All of us live on land that was at one time stolen by our ancestors from people of a different nationality who had inhabited it previously. But in most cases, the moral claims of the nations who were long ago forcibly dispossessed have now lapsed because the continuous occupation and development of the land by others has given them a stronger claim. Rights to the recovery of stolen land thus contain an implicit statute of limitations.

The strategy of settlement in the Occupied Territories is a strategy of annexation through the acquisition of moral rights deriving from continuous habitation and development. The settlers are thus active participants in the theft of the Palestinian lands by the means I have described—not just conscious and willing participants but enthusiastic and indeed fanatical instigators and perpetrators of the strategy by which the theft is being accomplished. If a nation may justly go to war against those who forcibly seek to expel it from its national territory, why may not the Palestinians use military means, if necessary, against those who seek to expel them from their national territory, not directly by force of arms, but by a slower yet perhaps even more effective means, supported by a tacit promise of military protection if it is needed?

Some might argue that the settlers are not in fact civilians. They are citizens of a state with universal conscription and extensive reserves, many have ties with the military, and virtually all are heavily armed. Yet none of these considerations undermines their status as civilians. Reservists are civilians during the long periods in which they are not in active service and the settlers are no more heavily harmed than a great many American civilians.

One might also argue that the settlers cannot be legitimate targets of military attack because they belong in an entirely different category from combatants: they are criminals whose wrongful action makes them liable to police action but not to acts of war. Yet their crime is not an ordinary domestic crime but something very like the international crime of aggression, a crime that, when committed by soldiers, justifies defensive war. Perhaps it is true that the best response to the threat they pose would be for the Israeli police to seek to arrest and permanently expel them. But as long as it remains clear that this will not happen, the question remains what the Palestinians might be permitted to do in defense of their territorial rights, and what it might be permissible for international agents to do on their behalf. In either case there would be no difference in substance between police action and military action. So the moral issue remains whether the settlers are morally liable to attack as a means of expelling them or of preventing the expansion of the settlements.

The Israeli settlers are similar to the United Fruit Company executives in several morally significant respects. The unjust threat their action poses to others is serious and they are responsible, and indeed culpable, to a high degree for posing the threat. It is true that, unlike the executives, the settlers, if unopposed, do not threaten people's *lives*, and this is relevant to whether attacking them militarily could be proportionate in the narrow sense. Their action also differs from that of the executives, however, in that it is not at all fanciful to suppose that the wrongs that they have committed could begin to be corrected, and those they are continuing to commit stopped, by means of military action. Nor would the Palestinians, after forty-one years of occupation, be obviously deluded to believe that military action is necessary for the defense of their rights (though I in fact think that this belief is mistaken). In that case it may be plausible to suppose that at least some of the settlers have made themselves liable to military attack, particularly if they would resist nonmilitary but forcible efforts to expel them by violent means. I say that only "some" are liable because there are of course many among the settlers who are wholly innocent, in the sense of not being liable to any form of harm from action intended to restore the West Bank to its rightful inhabitants. Thus the instances in which Palestinians have infiltrated a settlement at night and killed children sleeping in their beds are instances of murder for terrorist purposes and nothing more.

These cases suggest that the idea that civilians can in principle be liable to military attack is not altogether intuitively implausible. But this conclusion is of limited practical significance because the cases are highly anomalous in various respects. As I noted, both the executives and the adult settlers bear a high degree of responsibility, both causal and moral, for serious wrongs. In the case of the executives, I simply stipulated that killing them would be effective in averting an unjust coup and I also assumed that it could be done without harming the innocent as a side effect. In the case of the settlers, it is independently plausible to suppose that military action, properly conducted, could dislodge them and prevent their return, and it is a feasible requirement of permissible military action against them that their children be allowed to leave before it would begin. That suggests that the wide proportionality restriction might be easily satisfiable.

But the moral constraints that might be satisfied in these cases are impossible to satisfy in virtually all actual cases of intentional military attacks against civilians. It is rare for any civilian to bear a significant degree of responsibility for an unjust war, or for any of the particular acts of war of which the war is composed. In all unjust wars, many civilians bear no responsibility whatever. Children are the most obvious examples and they are present wherever wars are fought. In some unjust wars, many civilians do bear some responsibility but the degree to which most of them are responsible is very slight. Most civilians have, on their own, no capacity at all to affect the action of their government. They may pay their taxes, vote or even campaign for particular political candidates (sometimes on the basis of general sympathy with their overall positions on matters of policy but seldom because of their advocacy of war), participate in the culture from which the country's political leaders have emerged, fail to protest their country's unjust war, perhaps because they correctly believe that to do so would be ineffective, or perhaps because they approve of the war, and so on; but none of these things, nor even all of them together, is ordinarily sufficient for the forfeiture of a person's right not to be attacked and killed. Military attack exceeds what a person may ordinarily be liable to on the basis of these comparatively trivial sources of responsibility.

This is to say, in effect, that most intentional attacks on civilians violate the narrow proportionality requirement that is internal to the notion of liability. They almost invariably violate the wide proportionality requirement as well. Even when there are some civilians in a society who bear a significant degree of responsibility for an unjust war, they are difficult to identify with confidence and even when they are they rarely concentrate themselves together in isolation as a target for a discriminate and proportionate attack. Rather, responsible civilians are usually interspersed among a larger number of wholly innocent civilians and therefore cannot be attacked militarily without disproportionate harm to the innocent as a side effect.

Perhaps most important of all, military attacks against civilians generally cannot be an effective means of pursuing a just cause. Even when there are civilians in a society who bear a significant degree of responsibility for an unjust war, and even when they can be identified and attacked in isolation, they cannot be liable to attack unless attacking them can make an effective contribution to the achievement of a just cause. Unlike unjust combatants, civilians do not generally *pose* a threat of wrongful harm; but unless they are themselves the immediate source of a threat, killing them cannot be directly effective as a means of averting a wrongful threat in the way that killing in self-defense is. (The Israeli settlers are a conspicuous exception.) Killing in self-defense is almost necessarily effective: a person who poses a threat through his action can no longer pose that threat if he has been killed. But the contributions that civilians make to the threats their state poses in war often lie in the past and can no longer be prevented. Civilians often contribute, as I noted, mainly as Culpable Causes, instigators who make little or no continuing contribution. In general, therefore, the only way that killing civilians can serve as a means of averting an unjust threat is indirectly, through affecting the action of others—typically by causing the remaining civilians to fear that they too will be killed unless the war comes to an end, thereby prompting them to exert pressure on their government to surrender.

Because attacking civilians generally has to operate in this way, through its effects on the wills of others, it is a tactic of notoriously uncertain effectiveness. Its use by the British against the Germans in World War II was largely ineffective, as was its use by the Germans against the British. In both cases there is indeed evidence to suggest that it was instead counterproductive, provoking indignation and hatred that stiffened resistance rather than undermining civilian morale. It is even disputed whether the obliteration of the cities of Tokyo, Hiroshima, and Nagasaki was effective in coercing the Japanese to surrender, for many historians have argued that it was really the declaration of war against Japan by the Soviet Union on August 8, 1945, the day before the atomic bombing of Nagasaki, that was actually decisive in breaking the will of the Japanese government.

It is a corollary of the fact that the killing of civilians generally depends for its effectiveness on influencing the action of others that it generally involves what I earlier followed Warren Quinn in calling "opportunistic" agency—that is, it involves using people strategically in harmful ways as a means of achieving one's ends. That attacking civilians usually operates opportunistically seems to combine synergistically with the fact that civilians generally bear only a low degree of responsibility for the acts of their government to make the intentional killing of civilians in war an especially objectionable means of advancing a just cause.

It must be conceded, however, that at least some of the constraints I have mentioned admit of some flexibility. Sometimes, for example, people make themselves liable to be used in harmful ways, even fatally used. Suppose, for example, that the only way the Mayor in the earlier example could save himself was to shoot the Sheriff, who was poised above the farmhand, causing the Sheriff's body to fall on and thereby incapacitate the farmhand. It is plausible to suppose that it would be permissible for the Mayor to kill the Sheriff in this way, and that the reason it would be permissible is that the Sheriff had made himself liable to be killed in that way.

More importantly, even the constraint concerning the degree of a person's responsibility can, in certain cases, be highly permissive. In particular, that the degree of a person's responsibility for an unjust threat is very low does not entail that he cannot be liable to defensive killing—that is, it does not entail that killing him must be disproportionate to his potential liability. The problem is that liability is not like desert in being determined only by what one has done; one's liability to harm is also a function of the harms that others will suffer, and for which one will bear some responsibility, if one is not harmed. Recall the discussion in Section 4.2 of cases in which it is unavoidable that one of two people will die and in which one of the two bears a slight degree of responsibility for this fact while the other bears no responsibility at all. It seems that in cases such as this, even a slight degree of responsibility for a situation in which someone must die, and especially a very slight degree of culpability, can be sufficient to override the presumption against intentional killing. A degree of responsibility or culpability that would be too slight to be of any significance if the issue were punishment can be decisive when the issue is defense.

One might concede that there can be rare cases—such as those discussed in Section 4.1.4 (the resident, the conscientious driver . . .)—in which it can be permissible for a person who is in no way liable to be harmed to kill a person who is responsible, though only to a slight degree, for an unjust threat to his life. But one may be skeptical about whether this concession has any bearing on the ethics of killing in war. To see that it does, at least in principle, recall the hypothetical example in Section 5.2 in which the question of whether the country will resort to war is to be resolved by plebiscite, the votes in favor of war win overwhelmingly, and an unjust war fought by robots is automatically initiated. Suppose that the victims of the robot attack cannot defeat the robots but can attack the civilian population of the country that has launched the unjust war. Suppose further that it is reasonable for them to believe (and is also true) that if they kill enough civilians, that will motivate the survivors to rescind the vote and recall the robots.

Intuitively it seems permissible for the victims of the unjust war to begin to attack and kill the civilians, not because, or only because, this is the lesser evil, but because the civilians have made themselves liable to military attack. Yet the degree of each individual civilian's responsibility for the unjust war seems slight. The causal contribution of each civilian seems negligible and the mere act of casting a vote in favor of an unjust war seems no worse than what civilians do in actual cases when they vote for a candidate committed to a war platform.

Some people are scornful of contrived hypothetical examples of this sort so it may help to offer a less pure but more realistic example. Suppose that the mistaken factual beliefs about the bombing of Hiroshima that many Americans cherish were true, and that various other circumstances were different from the way they in fact were. Suppose that the actual history of the bombing was as follows. Instead of insisting on unconditional surrender, the US demanded surrender but offered to allow the Japanese to retain the Emperor and keep various elements of the Shinto system in place. When this offer was refused, the US then detonated an atomic bomb over an uninhabited island to demonstrate the effects of the new weapon it threatened to use as an option of last resort if the Japanese continued to reject the demand for surrender on the terms described. Although refusing to enter the war against the Japanese, the Soviets offered to intercede on their behalf in a negotiated surrender but their offer was rejected with contempt. The Japanese cabinet remained unified in opposition to surrender on any terms, leaving the US with only two options for forcing the Japanese to surrender: either drop an atomic bomb on a Japanese city or conduct a land invasion of Japan. Suppose that an invasion would have caused many casualties among Japanese civilians as side effects, would have required the sacrifice of perhaps as many as 100,000 American soldiers, but would have had no higher probability of success than bombing a city. Finally, many civilians in Hiroshima bore more than a negligible degree of responsibility for their country's acts of unjust aggression that had made the defeat of Japan a moral necessity. It was, after all, *their* government, expressing the beliefs and values of their culture, and acting with their support, that had conducted the imperial campaigns against what they themselves saw as inferior Asian races. The US therefore had three options: (1) sacrificing a large number of young American men torn from their peaceful lives by Japanese aggression, (2) intentionally killing a comparable number of Japanese civilians, many of whom bore some responsibility for that aggression, and (3) allowing the aggression to go undefeated. It is not implausible to suppose that, in *these* conditions, it would have been permissible to bomb Hiroshima—not because, or simply because, the bombing would have been the lesser evil, but because many of the civilians bore some responsibility for the fact that it was now unavoidable that a large number of people would die, and this made them *liable* to intentional attack, *given that* the only other options would have involved the unjust killing of a comparable number of people who bore no responsibility at all.

One might point out that in Hiroshima, as in all cities, there were a great many civilians who were entirely free of any liability to harm and therefore that in intentionally attacking civilians there, the US must have been guilty of intentionally attacking a large number of innocent people even if it was also attacking some who were liable. Yet this objection can be addressed in the same way that the more familiar problem of killing innocent civilians as a side effect of attacking combatants is typically addressed, by claiming that the killing of the innocent is unintended, so that while it may make the action disproportionate, it does not make it indiscriminate.

One may be tempted to respond that this makes no sense in the case of deliberate attacks on civilians, since one cannot discriminate at all between those who are liable and those who are innocent, and so cannot intend to attack only the former. By contrast, when one attacks combatants, knowing that one will also kill civilians, one can identify the combatants and make them the focus of one's intention. But to see that this response is mistaken, suppose that a pilot is commanded to bomb a concentration of combatants in which there are a few innocent civilians intermingled. He can identify the combatants by their uniforms and the civilians by the absence of a uniform and can intend, in dropping his bomb, to kill only the combatants. But his ability to distinguish visually between the combatants and the civilians is irrelevant to what his intentions are. Suppose that he has flown over once to confirm the proportion of combatants to civilians, to ensure that the attack will be proportionate in the wide sense. When he flies back, he discovers that the combatants have all changed into civilian clothes, or that the civilians have been forced to don uniforms. His inability now to pick out the civilians from among the combatants cannot affect the intention with which he will drop his bomb. So it seems coherent to suppose that one could drop an atomic bomb on a city intending to kill only those civilians who bear responsibility for their country's aggression while foreseeing that one would also kill others who are innocent as a side effect, even if one has no idea which are which. Provided that one has a rough idea of the proportion of innocent civilians to liable civilians, one can determine whether a successful attack would be proportionate in the wide sense.

Many of us will still feel considerable intuitive unease about the idea that it could ever be permissible to attack a large concentration of civilians in war, whatever the expected consequences of refusing to do so might be. There is, perhaps, a way to draw back from embracing the permissibility of bombing a city while nevertheless recognizing that individual civilians may be liable to attack if they bear a significant degree of responsibility for an unjust war. This is to argue that there is a threshold of responsibility below which responsibility for an unjust threat, while perhaps sufficient for liability to lesser forms of harm, is insufficient for liability to intentional, potentially lethal attack. One could, on this view, concede that the United Fruit executives were liable to intentional attack while denying that civilians whose only contributions to an unjust war are that they have voted, campaigned for political candidates, paid taxes, participated and even rejoiced in the culture that has spawned the unjust war, and so on, can ever forfeit their right against military attack merely by acting in these ways.

The idea that responsibility can ground liability only if it exceeds a certain threshold is, in theoretical terms, neither ad hoc nor arbitrary. If there is a standing moral presumption against the killing of a person, and in particular against the intentional killing of a person, it should be unsurprising if it takes more than a modicum of responsibility to override it. But though the idea of a threshold of responsibility is appealing, I think it is an overly simplistic way of trying to explain the impermissibility of bombing a city in a country fighting an unjust war. If there were such a threshold for liability, it seems that the conscientious driver would have to be below it. Although the degree of the driver's *causal* responsibility for the threat to the innocent pedestrian is much higher than that of almost any unjust civilian for the threat to any of his enemies, the degree of the conscientious driver's *moral* responsibility is much lower. However one might understand the permissibility of his action in objective terms, it is clear that he does not act culpably. Yet civilians who actively support an unjust war do often act culpably, even if their causal influence is negligible. But if the conscientious driver were below a threshold of responsibility, he would not be liable, so that the best way to understand the conflict between him and the pedestrian would be as a symmetrical defense case. Since this is not the best way to view that conflict, we should not accept the idea of a threshold of responsibility.

The idea that there is such a threshold is excessively reductionist. The reason why it is impermissible to bomb a city, even when many of its inhabitants bear some responsibility for an unjust war, cannot be reduced to only one of the factors that are relevant to liability. The reason why it is not permissible to attack large concentrations of civilians derives from the *combined* force of these various factors. That most unjust civilians are at most responsible to only a low degree for their country's unjust war, that attacks against civilians generally involve the opportunistic use of people as mere means, that they are virtually always of highly uncertain effectiveness because their relevant effects are not immediate but must come indirectly through the wills of others, that responsible civilians are virtually always intermingled with wholly innocent civilians—it is these factors together that explain why civilians are almost never liable to intentional military attack, and why even when some are liable it is still generally impermissible to attack them. These factors together constitute the real basis of the *moral* immunity of civilians, which has nothing to do with mere civilian status.

5.5 CIVILIAN LIABILITY AND TERRORISM

If the argument of the previous section is correct, civilian immunity is contingent rather than absolute. While it could probably never be permissible in practice to destroy a city, there are likely to be some occasions on which some civilians may be liable to intentional military attack, and on which it may be permissible to attack them. Imagine such an occasion, which has these features: (1) there are a number of unjust civilians present who as individuals bear a substantial degree of moral responsibility for their county's unjust war, (2) intentionally attacking them would have a high probability of preventing the wrongful killing of an equal or greater number of wholly innocent people on the other side, and (3) there are few if any genuinely innocent civilians nearby, so that an attack on these civilians would be proportionate not only in the narrow sense but in the wide sense as well. Yet suppose this attack would have to achieve the effect of saving the innocent lives by creating fear among the victims' fellow citizens: perhaps other civilians, or perhaps members of the military or the government—it does not matter. What is necessary to raise the question I will address is that this would be an attack against civilians that would be intended to operate causally by terrorizing and intimidating others, coercing them to meet the attackers' demands. The question is whether this attack would be an instance of terrorism.

There is a facile answer to this question that appeals to definitional considerations. As terrorism is usually defined, it involves intentionally attacking civilians as a means of pursuing political or ideological goals. There are many problems with such a definition, one of which is that it implies that various essential aspects of police work count as terrorism. When those who give this definition of terrorism come to realize that it has this implication, they usually try to patch up the definition by stipulating that intentional attacks on civilians for political reasons do not count as terrorism unless they are unlawful or unauthorized. But introducing that qualification into the definition entails that acts that count as terrorism now would cease to be terrorism if they were legalized, for whatever reason. And that obscures what is distinctively wrong about terrorism. It is better to say that terrorism involves intentionally attacking people who are innocent, in the generic sense of not being liable to attack, usually to intimidate or coerce others who are related to them in certain ways, as a means of achieving certain broadly political goals. But if terrorism is defined as intentionally attacking the innocent, then attacks on civilians who are not innocent but are liable to intentional attack cannot be acts of terrorism.

Although I think we would achieve greater moral clarity by understanding terrorism in this way, the actual use of the term is such that most people would view the case I have described as a clear instance of terrorism. If we accept that the meaning of "terrorism" tracks the use of the term in common discourse, then the substantive view I have defended implies that terrorism can be permissible even in situations that are not cases of supreme emergency. What is more, some of the claims I have made about civilian liability bear a disturbing resemblance to claims that some terrorists have made. It is worth quoting at length from Osama bin Laden's 2002 "Letter to the American people" in order, first, to note the similarities but, second, and more importantly, to explain why the similarities are deceptive and why the position for which I have argued provides no justification for the acts of contemporary terrorists. Here is what bin Laden wrote:

You may . . . dispute that [the various accusations and grievances just stated do] not justify aggression against civilians, for crimes they did not commit and offenses in which they did not partake: This argument contradicts your continuous repetition that America is the land of freedom . . . Therefore, the American people are the ones who choose their government by way of their own free will; a choice which stems from their agreement to its policies. Thus the American people have chosen, consented to, and affirmed their support for the Israeli oppression of the Palestinians, the occupation and usurpation of their land, and its continuous killing, torture, punishment and expulsion of Palestinians. The American people have the ability and the choice to refuse the policies of the Government and even to change it if they want. The American people are the ones who pay the taxes which fund the planes that bomb us in Afghanistan, the tanks that strike and destroy our homes in Palestine, the armies which occupy our lands in the Arabian Gulf, and the fleets which ensure the blockade of Iraq. These tax dollars are given to Israel for it to continue to attack us and penetrate our lands. So the American people are the ones who fund the attacks against us, and they are the ones who oversee the expenditure of these monies in the way they wish, through their elected candidates. Also the American army is part of the American people. . . . The American people are the ones who employ both their men and women in the American forces which attack us. This is why the American people cannot be innocent of all the crimes committed by the Americans and Jews against us.[12]

These assertions provide support for my earlier claim that terrorists are unlikely to think of themselves as killing innocent people. Indeed, it is in some ways rather encouraging that bin Laden has sought to justify his action within a familiar and plausible framework of moral justification. For he is not claiming, at least in these passages, that it is permissible to kill Americans simply because God commands Believers to do so, or because of their identity as citizens of the United States. He is arguing instead that it is permissible to kill Americans because of what they have *done*.

Still, his claims are mere caricatures of reasonable claims about civilian liability. As I noted earlier, only unjust civilians can be liable to attack in war. This means, in effect, that it is a condition of the permissibility of attacking civilians that there be a just cause for war. It is insufficient to have only unspecific and tendentious grievances about oppression and occupation of lands in the Arabian Gulf, still less to complain about bombings in Afghanistan that were conducted only in response to attacks on US embassies in Africa and on the World Trade Towers perpetrated by associates of bin Laden himself who operated from bases in Afghanistan. One cannot intentionally kill thousands of American civilians and then claim that those who are next on the target list become liable to be killed by paying for the weapons that their government uses to try to defend them.

Although I have conceded that it is possible for a person to be liable to be killed on the basis of only a low level of responsibility, in general it is necessary that a person bear a high degree of responsibility for a wrong in order to be liable to be killed as a means of preventing or correcting that wrong. It is, again, reassuring that bin Laden seems to recognize that whether a civilian can be liable for the action of her government depends on the degree to which she is able to influence that action. But causal influence and responsibility do not operate in the way bin Laden supposes. By his standards, any time a democratic government acts wrongly, each of its citizens becomes a legitimate target of killing on the ground that he or she has "the choice to refuse the policies of the Government and even to change it."

Of the factors that I claimed in the previous section are relevant to civilian liability, the one that seems to be most important in excluding civilian liability in most cases is the effectiveness condition. Even when civilians bear some significant degree of responsibility for the wrongful action of their government, they become liable to attack only if the harm they would suffer would be narrowly proportionate in relation to the harm that would thereby be prevented. That Bin Laden altogether ignores this condition is perhaps not surprising, since he can hardly take pride in the effectiveness of the mass killing of civilians on September 11, 2001, in expelling American forces from the Middle East.

It is important to note that the foregoing discussion of civilian liability has been concerned solely with *moral* immunity and *moral* liability. Although I have argued that in principle, and even rarely in practice, some civilians can be liable to military attack, this has no direct bearing, at least at present, on whether the law of war should allow exceptions to the current prohibition of intentional attacks against civilians. In current conditions, the law of war cannot aspire to congruence with the morality of war. It must be formulated with a pragmatic concern for the consequences of its implementation. And pragmatic considerations argue decisively for an absolute, exceptionless legal prohibition of intentional military attacks against civilians.[13] The moral permission to attack civilians can apply only to just combatants and even in their case it applies only very rarely. If the appropriately limited moral permission were to be legally recognized, the temptation to attack civilians in war is so great that just combatants would inevitably abuse the permission, while unjust combatants, imagining themselves to be just combatants, would liberally avail themselves of it as well. While absolute civilian immunity is false as a moral doctrine, it remains a legal necessity.

Notes

CHAPTER 1

1. See Ray Monk, *Ludwig Wittgenstein: The Duty of Genius* (New York: The Free Press, 1990), pp. 110–66. The two quoted passages are from pp. 114 and 154, respectively.
2. David Edmonds and John Eidinow, *Wittgenstein's Poker* (New York: Ecco, 2002), pp. 89–90.
3. Monk, *Wittgenstein*, p. 111.
4. Ibid., p. 112. Italics in the original.
5. Ibid.
6. Michael Walzer, *Just and Unjust Wars* (New York: Basic Books, 1977), p. 21. Compare Henry Sidgwick's claim that "the rules which civilised opinion should attempt to impose on combatants . . . must abstract from all consideration of the justice of the war." (*The Elements of Politics* [London: Macmillan, 1891], pp. 253–4.)
7. George F. Fletcher and Jens David Ohlin, *Defending Humanity: When Force is Justified and Why* (New York: Oxford University Press, 2008), p. 20.
8. Walzer, *Just and Unjust Wars*, pp. 34 and 41.
9. Ibid., p. 146.
10. Compare Judith Jarvis Thomson, *The Realm of Rights* (Cambridge, MA: Harvard University Press, 1990), p. 122. I draw the distinction differently from the way she does. On her definition, violations are a species of infringement. On mine, violations and infringements are mutually exclusive.
11. G. E. M. Anscombe, "Mr. Truman's Degree," in her *Ethics, Religion, and Politics*, Collected Philosophical Papers, vol. iii (Minneapolis: University of Minnesota Press, 1981), p. 67.
12. Thomas Nagel, "War and Massacre," *Philosophy and Public Affairs* 1 (1972): 123–43, p. 139. Also see Anthony Kenny, *The Logic of Deterrence* (London: Firethorn Press, 1985), p. 10; George I. Mavrodes, "Conventions and the Morality of War," *Philosophy and Public Affairs* 4 (1975): 117–31; Robert K. Fullinwider, "War and Innocence," *Philosophy and Public Affairs* 5 (1975): 90–7; Jeffrie G. Murphy, "The Killing of the Innocent," *The Monist* 57 (1973): 527–50; and John Finnis, Joseph M. Boyle, Jr., and Germain Grisez, *Nuclear Deterrence, Morality and Realism* (Oxford: Clarendon Press, 1987), pp. 86–90.
13. Nagel, "War and Massacre," p. 139.
14. Walzer, *Just and Unjust Wars*, p. 145.

15. Nagel, "War and Massacre," p. 140. Compare Murphy, "The Killing of the Innocent," pp. 532–4.
16. Walzer, *Just and Unjust Wars*, p. 146.
17. Pierino Belli, *A Treatise on Military Matters and Warfare* (Oxford: Clarendon Press, 1936), Pt. ii, ch. 2, p. 65. John Locke, *Two Treatises of Government*, ed. Peter Laslett (Cambridge: Cambridge University Press, 2002), p. 402.
18. See e.g. Henry Shue, "Do We Need a 'Morality of War'?", in David Rodin and Henry Shue, eds., *Just and Unjust Warriors: The Moral and Legal Status of Soldiers* (Oxford: Oxford University Press, 2008), pp. 87–111.
19. Hugo Grotius, *De Jure Belli Ac Pacis, Libri Tres*, vol. ii (Oxford: Clarendon Press, 1925), p. 593 (Bk. ii, ch. 26, §vi, 1).
20. Ibid. (Bk. ii, ch. 26, §VI, 2).
21. For a detailed and fascinating discussion of this case, see George P. Fletcher, *A Crime of Self-Defense: Bernard Goetz and the Law on Trial* (Chicago: University of Chicago Press, 1990).
22. Walzer, *Just and Unjust Wars*, pp. 251–68. For an illuminating discussion of the supreme emergency exemption, see Daniel Statman, "Supreme Emergencies Revisited," *Ethics* 117 (2006): 58–79.
23. In two earlier articles, I argued, without distinguishing between the narrow and wide proportionality requirements, that the only good effects of war or an act of war that count in the proportionality calculation are those that are either constitutive of the just cause or instrumental to its achievement. I am greatly indebted to Joshue Orozco for demonstrating that I was wrong about that, and for identifying the source of my mistake, which was my failure to distinguish between good effects that can be intentionally pursued by means of war and good effects that can weigh against and cancel out the bad effects of war. I continue to maintain that in the narrow *ad bellum* and *in bello* proportionality requirements, in which what is at issue is whether harms inflicted on those who are potentially liable exceed what the victims might be liable to, the only good effects that weigh against the harms inflicted are those that are constitutive of or instrumental to the achievement of a just cause. But this restriction does not apply to the wide requirements. The mistake identified by Orozco is in "The Ethics of Killing in War," *Ethics* 114 (2004): 693–733, and in "Just Cause for War," *Ethics and International Affairs* 19 (2005): 1–21.
24. Adam Roberts and Richard Guelff, eds., *Documents on the Laws of War* (Oxford: Clarendon Press, 1982), p. 416.
25. Francisco de Vitoria, "On the Law of War," in Anthony Pagden and Jeremy Lawrance, eds., *Political Writings* (Cambridge: Cambridge University Press, 1991), p. 303.
26. Francisco Suárez, "On War" (Disputation xiii, *De Triplici Virtute Theologica: Charitate*), in *Selections from Three Works* (Oxford: Clarendon Press, 1944), pp. 845–6. Emphasis added. I will here add a brief confession.

When I began to think and write about the morality of war in the 1980s, and published a brief rejection of the moral equality of combatants in 1991 and a more extensive argument against it in 1994, I had the impression that I was chipping away at the foundations of a unified and monolithic tradition of thought about the just war. To my embarrassment, it was not until I met Gregory Reichberg in Oxford in 2005 that I realized, under his tutelage, that I was not a revolutionary at all but a reactionary, and that I have been busy reinventing the wheel (or the flat tire, as those will think who believe we have done well to evolve beyond the views of the classical theorists). It is always annoying to be beaten into print, but it is particularly galling to discover that one was scooped more than half a millennium earlier. The paper by Reichberg that revealed to me the poverty of my understanding of the history of just war theory is "Just War and Regular War: Competing Paradigms," in Rodin and Shue, eds., *Just and Unjust Warriors*, pp. 193–213. For a splendid history of thought about the just war, see Stephen C. Neff, *War and the Law of Nations* (Cambridge: Cambridge University Press, 2005).

27. G. E. M. Anscombe, "War and Murder," in *Ethics, Religion, and Politics*, p. 53. Also see Robert L. Holmes, *On War and Morality* (Princeton: Princeton University Press, 1989). Although Holmes develops an essentially pacifist argument, he anticipates some of the positions I take in this book. One other contemporary work that defends the notion of innocence found in classical just war theory is Nicholas Denyer, "Just War," in Roger Teichman, ed., *Logic, Cause, and Action: Essays in Honour of Elizabeth Anscombe* (Cambridge: Cambridge University Press, 2000), pp. 137–51.

28. Nicholson Baker, *Human Smoke: The Beginnings of World War II, the End of Civilization* (New York: Simon & Schuster, 2008), p. 134.

CHAPTER 2

1. This claim is both an objection to my view that unjust combatants act impermissibly in fighting and a defense of the moral equality of combatants. I am greatly indebted to Uwe Steinhoff for developing and defending it. For a fuller presentation of his argument and a more detailed response to it, see Uwe Steinhoff, "Jeff McMahan on the Moral Equality of Combatants," *Journal of Political Philosophy* 16 (2008): 220–6, and Jeff McMahan, "Justification and Liability in War," *Journal of Political Philosophy* 16 (2008): 227–44. My argument here is a revised and condensed version of this earlier response to Steinhoff.

2. See Jeff McMahan, "War as Self-Defense," *Ethics and International Affairs* 18 (2004): 75–80, pp. 75–6.

3. I am indebted here to Adil Ahmad Haque. See his "Rights and Liabilities at War," in Paul H. Robinson, Kimberly Ferzan, and Stephen Garvey, eds., *Criminal Law Conversations* (New York: Oxford University Press, forthcoming). My analysis of the mistake is slightly different from Haque's.

4. Jules Coleman, *Risks and Wrongs* (Cambridge: Cambridge University Press, 1992), pp. 219–20.
5. Judith Jarvis Thomson, "Self-Defense," *Philosophy and Public Affairs* 20 (1991): 283–310.
6. Exceptions include Yitzhak Benbaji, "A Defense of the Traditional War Convention," *Ethics* 118 (2008): 464–95; Jonathan Quong, "Killing in Self-Defense," *Ethics* (forthcoming); and Haque, "Rights and Liabilities at War."
7. I owe the suggestion discussed in this paragraph to Frances Kamm, who is well aware that its significance in war is limited to situations in which just combatants can be attacked defensively without jeopardizing their mission.
8. I attempted to defend this claim in "The Basis of Moral Liability to Defensive Killing," *Philosophical Issues* 15 (2005): 386–405, esp. pp. 399–402.
9. Walzer, *Just and Unjust Wars*, p. 37.
10. Thomas Hurka, "Liability and Just Cause," *Ethics and International Affairs* 20 (2007): 199–218, p. 210.
11. Ibid., p. 211.
12. Leo Tolstoy, *War and Peace*, translated by Richard Pevear and Larissa Volkhonsky (New York: Alfred A. Knopf, 2007), pp. 774–5.
13. I am indebted to Raymond Martin for suggesting to me a version of this argument.
14. Vitoria, "On the Law of War," p. 308. Emphasis in the original.
15. Ibid., p. 313.
16. David Estlund, "On Following Orders in an Unjust War," *Journal of Political Philosophy* 15 (2007): 213–34, p. 213.
17. Ibid., p. 215.
18. Ibid., p. 228.
19. Ibid., p. 224.
20. Grotius writes that "it is probable that even the executioner, who is going to put a condemned man to death, should know the merits of the case, either through assisting at the inquiry and the trial or from a confession of the crime, in such a degree that it is sufficiently clear to him that the criminal deserves death." As this passage occurs in the context of argument for the permissibility of refusing to obey an order to fight in an unjust war, the reasonable inference is that Grotius holds that the executioner ought to refuse to conduct the execution if it is not sufficiently clear to him that the potential victim is guilty. (Grotius, *De Jure Belli Ac Pacis*, p. 593. Bk. II, ch. 26, §IV, 9.)
21. For a brief account of both groups and the effects of their action, see Guy Grossman and Rami Kaplan, "Refusal in Israel: The Third Wave 2002–2005," *Peace Review* 18 (2006). For an important contribution to the debate in Israel, see David Enoch, "Some Arguments Against Conscientious Objection and Civil Disobedience Refuted," *Israel Law Review* 36 (2004): 227–53.

22. Lizette Alvarez, "Army Giving More Waivers in Recruiting," *New York Times*, February 14, 2007.

23. Thom Shanker, "Young Officers Leaving Army At a High Rate," *New York Times*, April 10, 2006.

24. Some passages in this section draw on arguments first presented in my "Collectivist Defenses of the Moral Equality of Combatants," *Journal of Military Ethics* 6 (2007): 50–9

25. Jean-Jacques Rousseau, *The Social Contract*, translated by Gerard Hopkins, in *Social Contract: Essays by Locke, Hume, and Rousseau* (London: Oxford University Press, 1947), pp. 249–50.

26. Walzer, *Just and Unjust Wars*, p. 58.

27. Ibid.

28. Rousseau, *Social Contract*, p. 251.

29. Noam J. Zohar, "Collective War and Individualistic Ethics: Against the Conscription of 'Self-Defense'," *Political Theory* 21 (1993): 606–22.

30. Christopher Kutz, "The Difference Uniforms Make: Collective Violence in Criminal Law and War," *Philosophy and Public Affairs* 33 (2005): 148–80, p. 173. For a further elaboration of a collectivist approach to the morality and law of war, see George P. Fletcher, *Romantics at War: Glory and Guilt in the Age of Terrorism* (Princeton, NJ: Princeton University Press, 2002).

31. Ibid., p. 156.

32. Ibid., p. 173.

33. Ibid., p. 176.

34. Ibid., pp. 176–8.

35. Augustine, *The City of God*, translated by Marcus Dods (New York: Modern Library, 1950), bk. i, ch. 21, p. 27. The same passage has been differently translated as follows: "The divine authority itself has made certain exceptions to the rule that it is not lawful to kill men. These exceptions, however, include only those whom God commands to be slain, either by a general law, or by an express command applying to a particular person at a particular time. Moreover, he who is commanded to perform this ministry does not himself slay. Rather, he is like a sword which is the instrument of its user. And so those who, by God's authority, have waged wars . . . have in no way acted against that commandment which says, 'Thou shalt not kill.'" *The City of God Against the Pagans*, ed. R. W. Dyson (Cambridge: Cambridge University Press, 1998), p. 33.

36. *Henry v*, iv. i. 128–35.

37. Thomas Hobbes, *De Cive*, ch. 12, para. 11. This book may be found online at <http://www.constitution.org/th/decive.htm>.

38. Ibid., para. 1. Judging from the context, it does not appear that Hobbes here makes any distinction between a King and a Prince.

39. Samuel Pufendorf, *De Jure Naturae et Gentium, Libri Octo* (Oxford: Clarendon Press, 1934), pp. 1141–2. (Bk. viii, ch. i, §6.)

40. Ibid.
41. Stanley Milgram, *Obedience to Authority* (New York: HarperCollins, 1974), p. 160.
42. F. M. Kamm, "Responsibility and Collaboration," in *Intricate Ethics: Rights, Responsibilities, and Permissible Harm* (New York: Oxford University Press, 2007), p. 312.
43. Ibid., p. 315.
44. For articulations of this argument, see Cheyney Ryan, "Moral Equality, Victimhood, and the Sovereignty Symmetry Problem," and Dan Zupan, "A Presumption of the Moral Equality of Combatants: A Citizen-Soldier's Perspective," both in Rodin and Shue, eds., *Just and Unjust Warriors*.
45. Michael Winerip, "Recognizing the Honor of a Son," *New York Times*, November 11, 2007.
46. See, for example, David Malament, "Selective Conscientious Objection and the *Gillette* Decision," in Marshall Cohen et al., eds., *War and Moral Responsibility* (Princeton: Princeton University Press, 1974): 159–82.
47. See <http://money.cnn.com/2008/06/11/news/economy/iraq_war_hearing/index.htm?cnn=yes>.
48. See <http://obf.cancer.gov/financial/historical.htm> and <http://www.cancer.org/downloads/STT/2008CAFFfinalsecured.pdf>.
49. For further discussion, see Jeff McMahan, "Humanitarian Intervention, Consent, and Proportionality," in N. Ann Davis, Richard Keshen, and Jeff McMahan, eds., *Ethics and Humanity: Themes from the Philosophy of Jonathan Glover* (New York: Oxford University Press, 2009).
50. Milgram, *Obedience to Authority*, p. 187.
51. Hannah Arendt, *Eichmann in Jerusalem: A Report on the Banality of Evil* (New York: Penguin, 1977), p. 247.
52. Gitta Sereny, *Into That Darkness* (New York: Vintage, 1974), p. 260.
53. Arendt, *Eichmann in Jerusalem*, p. 231.
54. Vasily Grossman, *Life and Fate* (New York: Harper & Row, 1985), pp. 304–5.

CHAPTER 3

1. Vitoria, "On the Law of War," p. 307.
2. Ibid., p. 313. (Italics in the original.)
3. Walzer, *Just and Unjust Wars*, p. 36.
4. Ibid., p. 136.
5. Ibid., p. 38.
6. Ibid., pp. 28–9.
7. For a dissenting view, at least about the status of excuses in the criminal law, see Peter Westen and James Mangiafico, "The Criminal Defense of Duress: A Justification, Not an Excuse—And Why It Matters," *Buffalo Criminal Law Review* 6 (2003): 833–950.

8. Michael Massing, "The Volunteer Army: Who Fights and Why?," *New York Review of Books* 55 (3 April 2008): 34–6.

9. Tim O'Brien, *The Things They Carried* (Boston: Houghton Mifflin, 1990), pp. 21 and 61–2.

10. Ibid., pp. 61–2.

11. See Michael Holroyd, *Lytton Strachey: The New Biography* (New York: Farrar, Straus, and Giroux, 1994), esp. pp. 337–51.

12. Milgram, *Obedience to Authority*.

13. Noam Zohar, "Innocence and Complex Threats: Upholding the War Convention and the Condemnation of Terrorism," *Ethics* 114 (2004): 734–51, pp. 750–1. Zohar argues that if we accept the permissibility of killing those who threaten us but are nonetheless morally innocent, we will be unable consistently to maintain the prohibition of the killing of civilians.

14. Zohar, "Collective War and Individualistic Ethics, 615.

15. Gerhard Øverland, "Killing Soldiers," *Ethics and International Affairs* 20 (2006): 455–75, pp. 462 and 455. While Øverland explicitly contrasts moral innocence with moral *responsibility*, surrounding passages suggest that he may here be identifying responsibility with *culpability*.

16. I discussed this problem earlier, when I was more sympathetic than I am now to the view that moral culpability is a necessary condition of liability to defensive attack. See Jeff McMahan, "Innocence, Self-Defense, and Killing in War," *Journal of Political Philosophy* 2 (1994): 193–221, esp. pp. 209–11.

17. Walzer, *Just and Unjust Wars*, p. 39.

18. I have been influenced here by Lionel McPherson, who contends that "if soldiers can bear moral responsibility for their conduct in war, I see no morally consistent basis for denying that they also can bear moral responsibility for fighting for an unjust cause. Their situation with respect to knowledge, authority, and viable options is not so much better regarding justice in war than justice of war." (McPherson, "Innocence and Responsibility in War," *Canadian Journal of Philosophy* 34 (2004): 485–506, p. 497.) After writing these passages I discovered that Igor Primoratz earlier made systematic use of this same point in a critique of Walzer's reasons for exempting unjust combatants from responsibility for fighting in an unjust war. See his "Michael Walzer's Just War Theory: Some Issues of Responsibility," *Ethical Theory and Moral Practice* 5 (2002): 221–43.

19. Carolyn Marshall, "Corpsman Sentenced to Prison in Case of Iraqi Civilian Who Was Killed," *New York Times*, 7 October 2006.

20. Compare McPherson, "Innocence and Responsibility in War," p. 496.

21. <http://www.cfo.doe.gov/me70/manhattan/hiroshima.htm> (viewed on 6 June 2008).

22. See, for example, the 1923 Hague Rules of Aerial Warfare, Articles 22 and 24, reproduced in Roberts and Guelff, eds., *Documents on the Laws of War*, pp. 126–7.
23. Richard Goldstein, "Paul W. Tibbets Jr., 92, Dies; Dropped Atomic Bomb on Hiroshima," *New York Times*, 2 November 2007; Bob Greene, "Life After Wartime," *New York Times*, 12 November 2007.
24. Quoted in Goldstein, "Tibbets Jr. Dies."
25. S. L. A. Marshall, *Men Against Fire* (Gloucester, MA: Peter Smith, 1978). For discussion, see Lt. Col. Dave Grossman, *On Killing* (Boston: Little, Brown, & Co., 1996).
26. Gordon C. Zahn, *In Solitary Witness: The Life and Death of Franz Jägerstätter* (Springfield, IL: Templegate Publishers, 1986). On the advice and counsel he received from the Church, see esp. pp. 58, 76, 105, and 106.
27. Ibid., p. 105.
28. Ibid., pp. 106–7.
29. This claim has some affinities with the view known as "epistemic contextualism," but even more with the view defended by Jason Stanley in his excellent book, *Knowledge and Practical Interests* (Oxford: Oxford University Press, 2005), according to which the conditions for knowledge may vary with the importance of the practical interests that are at stake.
30. For an illuminating discussion of some of the issues that are relevant here, see Alexander A. Guerrero, "Don't Know, Don't Kill: Moral Ignorance, Culpability, and Caution," *Philosophical Studies* 136 (2007): 59–97. For general discussion, see Ted Lockhart, *Moral Uncertainty and Its Consequences* (New York: Oxford University Press, 2000), Jacob Ross, "Rejecting Ethical Deflationism," *Ethics* 116 (2006): 742–68, and Dan Moller, "Abortion and Moral Risk" (unpublished manuscript).
31. Anscombe, "War and Murder," p. 52.
32. Compare McMahan, "Innocence, Self-Defense, and Killing in War," pp. 206–7.
33. For another example, see McMahan, "The Basis of Moral Liability to Defensive Killing," pp. 399–402. Also see the discussion in Chapter 4 of "symmetrical defense cases."
34. Vitoria, "On the Law of War," pp. 311–12.
35. Grotius, *De Jure Belli Ac Pacis*, p. 592 (bk. ii, ch. 26, §4).
36. Pufendorf, *De Jure Naturae et Gentium*, p. 1141 (bk. viii, ch. 1, §6).
37. Emmerich de Vattel, *The Law of Nations* (Philadelphia: T. & J.W. Johnson, 1863), p. 304.
38. Primo Levi, *The Drowned and the Saved* (New York: Vintage, 1989), pp. 28–9.
39. For a dissenting view, though one that is articulated through a selective presentation of historical material rather than through moral argument, see Baker, *Human Smoke*.

CHAPTER 4

1. Anscombe, "War and Murder," p. 53.
2. For a defense of this assumption, see McMahan, "The Ethics of Killing in War," esp. sections VI and VII.
3. Robert Nozick, *Anarchy, State, and Utopia* (Oxford: Blackwell, 1974), pp. 34–5, and Thomson, "Self-Defense," p. 287.
4. Warren S. Quinn, "Actions, Intentions, and Consequences: The Doctrine of Double Effect," *Philosophy and Public Affairs* 18 (1989): 334–51, p. 344.
5. Zohar, "Collective War and Individualistic Ethics," pp. 612–13.
6. For a related but different argument for the claim that Nonresponsible Threats are not liable to defensive action, see Jeff McMahan, *The Ethics of Killing: Problems at the Margins of Life* (New York: Oxford University Press, 2002), pp. 405–7.
7. For a fuller discussion, see McMahan, "The Ethics of Killing in War," pp. 709–14.
8. Here I agree with Michael Otsuka, who writes that "a morally responsible agent may be held accountable for engaging in such activity that puts the life of a potentially innocent person at risk even if she acts from the justifiable (but false) belief that this person is a villain. When one is in possession of rational control over such a dangerous activity as the shooting of a gun at somebody, it is not unfair that if the person one endangers happens to be innocent, one is by virtue of engaging in such dangerous activity stripped of one's moral immunity from being killed." (Michael Otsuka, "Killing the Innocent in Self-Defense," *Philosophy and Public Affairs* 23 (1994): 74–94, p. 91.)
9. McMahan, "The Basis of Moral Liability to Defensive Killing," pp. 399–401.
10. For further discussion of what I call symmetrical defense cases, see Benbaji, "A Defense of the Traditional War Convention," pp. 464–95. And for an excellent general discussion of cases in which the moral difference between the Threat and the potential victim is minimal, see Seth Lazar, *War and Associative Duties* (D.Phil. thesis, Department of Politics and International Relations, Oxford, 2009).
11. Øverland, "Killing Soldiers."
12. For further discussion, see Jeff McMahan, "Commentary," in Michael Doyle, *Striking First: Preemption and Prevention in International Conflict* (Princeton: Princeton University Press, 2008).
13. Vitoria, "On the American Indians," in Pagden and Lawrance, eds., *Political Writings*, pp. 282–3.
14. Michael Walzer, "Response to McMahan's Paper," *Philosophia* 34 (2006): 43–5, p. 44.
15. Walzer, *Just and Unjust Wars*, pp. 155 and 156.

16. *The U.S. Army/Marine Corps Counterinsurgency Field Manual* (Chicago: University of Chicago Press, 2007), p. 244.
17. Ibid., p. 245.
18. Levi, *The Drowned and the Saved*, p. 43.
19. For a detailed discussion of the processes of recruiting and training child soldiers, see P. W. Singer, *Children at War* (New York: Pantheon Books, 2005), esp. chs. 4 and 5.

CHAPTER 5

1. Graham Greene, *The Quiet American* (New York: Viking, 1956), p. 63.
2. Jeff McMahan, "Self-Defense and the Problem of the Innocent Attacker," *Ethics* 104 (1994): 252–290, p. 258; and McMahan, "Innocence, Self-Defense, and Killing in War," p. 200.
3. Levi, *The Drowned and the Saved*, p. 174.
4. Samantha Power, *"A Problem From Hell": America and the Age of Genocide* (New York: HarperCollins, 2002), p. 36.
5. George Orwell, *The Collected Essays, Journalism and Letters of George Orwell, vol. III: As I Please, 1943–1945*, Sonia Orwell and Ian Angus, eds. (London: Secker and Warburg, 1968), pp. 151–2.
6. Ibid., p. 151.
7. Ibid., p. 183.
8. Michael Walzer, "Terrorism and Just War," *Philosophia* 34 (2006): 3–12, p. 4.
9. I am indebted here to the unpublished work of Saba Bazargan.
10. Locke, *Two Treatises of Government*, section 179, p. 388.
11. See <http://www.cnn.com/SPECIALS/cold.war/episodes/18/interviews/hunt/>. For a general history of the invasion and its aftermath, see Stephen Kinzer and Stephen Schlesinger, *Bitter Fruit: The Story of the American Coup in Guatemala* (Cambridge, MA: Harvard University David Rockefeller Center for Latin American Studies, 2005).
12. The full text of bin Laden's letter can be found at <http://www.guardian.co.uk/world/2002/nov/24/theobserver>. The translation is attributed to "Islamists in Britain" and is ungrammatical in potentially misleading ways in various places. For example, where the translation says, roughly, that "you may dispute that these accusations do not justify aggression against civilians," what is meant is that "you may dispute whether these accusations justify aggression against civilians."
13. For further discussion, see Jeff McMahan, "The Morality of War and the Law of War," in Rodin and Shue, eds., *Just and Unjust Warriors*: 19–43; and Jeff McMahan, *The Morality and Law of War* (forthcoming).

Index

Index